Palgrave Insights into Apocalypse Economics

Series Editor
Richard Westra, Institute of Political Science, University of Opole, Opole, Poland

The series offers a non-sectarian outlet for Marxist and critical heterodox economics scholarship on the tsunami of apocalyptic tendencies enveloping the global economy and society. Its guiding premise is that neoliberal policies from the 1980s not only failed to rejuvenate capitalist prosperity lost with the demise of the post-Second World War 'golden age' economy, but in fact have generated a widening spectrum of pathologies that threaten humanity itself. The series cultivates cutting-edge political economic analysis of the processes euphemised as 'globalization' and 'financialization', examining the impact of crises, austerity and inequality in the context of the recessionary, deflationary, inflationary, and stagflationary conditions that have beset the world economy in recent decades and into the 21st century. It covers themes such as the impact of monopolization and oligopolization in the new economy of information technologies, and the low wage production outsourcing and global social marginalization which accompanies that, as well as climate change, global environmental despoliation, disease pandemics, corrupted food systems and land-grabbing, rampant militarism, cybercrime and terrorism – all issues which defy mainstream economics and conventional political policy solutions.

The series invites work that is hard-hitting, inter/trans-disciplinary and multi-perspectival. It welcomes both theoretical and empirical writing with foci upon advanced and developing economies and encourages future-directed thinking on possibilities for another, better world. In particular, new and up-and-coming scholars are invited to submit their critical ideas and analysis. The series readership draws in academics, researchers, students, progressive governmental and non-governmental actors and the academically-informed public.

William Jefferies

War and the World Economy

Trade, Tech and Military Conflicts in a De-globalising World

palgrave
macmillan

William Jefferies
Ravensbourne University and SOAS
University of London
London, UK

ISSN 2523-8108 ISSN 2523-8116 (electronic)
Palgrave Insights into Apocalypse Economics
ISBN 978-3-031-85235-0 ISBN 978-3-031-85236-7 (eBook)
https://doi.org/10.1007/978-3-031-85236-7

Cover illustration: Dina Belenko/Alamy Stock Photo

This Palgrave Macmillan imprint is published by the registered company Springer Nature Switzerland AG
The registered company address is: Gewerbestrasse 11, 6330 Cham, Switzerland

A fierce competition is underway to define a new age in international affairs. A small number of countries—principally Russia, with the partnership of Iran and North Korea, as well as China… seek to erode the foundations of the United States' strength: its military and technological superiority, its dominant currency, and its unmatched network of alliances and partnerships[1].

Antony J. Blinken U.S. Secretary of State 2024.

[1] Blinken Antony J. 2024. *America's Strategy of Renewal Rebuilding Leadership for a New World*. Foreign Affairs. https://www.foreignaffairs.com/united-states/antony-blinken-americas-strategy-renewal-leadership-new-world.

Introduction

The about-to-be President Donald Trump commented on Ukraine in September 2024 that "if I win, as president-elect, I'll have a deal made, guaranteed"[1]. Trump's American First foreign policy aims to win the "fierce competition in international affairs" by refocussing U.S. foreign policy towards China. Trump's immediate priorities are; to end the war in Ukraine with some sort of ceasefire along the current front line, retreating from talk of Ukrainian NATO membership, while demanding that Europe provides the troops to police the deal. To continue the Israeli expansion in Gaza with the U.S. likely confirming Israeli plans to ethnically cleanse it and incorporate large parts of Palestine into a Greater Israel, (with the collapse of Assad's Syrian regime at the hands of a loose rebel coalition originating in Al-Qaeda which followed the Israeli-Hezbollah truce and Russia's focus on the Ukraine further strengthening his hand) while maintaining Iran a s a key enemy to be isolated and pressured. The focus of the Trump regime will be distinctively U.S. interests, not the alliance it leads, so his actions drive his friends away. European allies may face 20% tariffs exports to the U.S. combined with demands that they pay 2% of GDP towards defence. Tariffs on China will be ramped up to 60% or and will include those countries that have served as an entrepot to the U.S. like

[1] Schwartz Felicia 2024. 'I'll have a deal made': how Donald Trump will handle US foreign policy. Financial Times. https://www.ft.com/content/b446937d-6ab8-4264-b818-aa30633ca189.

Vietnam and Mexico, which have thus far enabled China to sidestep the impact of the U.S. trade war, "if I'm going to be president of this country, I'm going to put a 100, 200, 2,000% tariff" on cars from Mexico, Trump warned. Tariff is "the most beautiful word in the dictionary"[2].

For all the bluster Trump's foreign policy is nothing really new. It will continue the bi-partisan direction of the previous Trump then Biden administrations, what Adam Tooze, the Columbia University History Professor, described as the "controlled demolition of the 1990s post-cold war order"[3]. The extent of the difference between the two U.S. parties is largely presentational insofar as it exists at all. Both U.S. ruling parties support Israel's genocidal war in the Middle East, the defence, albeit conditional, of Ukraine against Russia and the Sino-U.S. trade conflict, both share responsibility for destroying the international rules-based order they purport to uphold.

Even Saudi Arabia has denounced the Israeli slaughter in Gaza and warned Israel against attacking Iran[4]. Trump's expected promotion of U.S. oil and gas exports to bring down prices and sustain his own working-class base threatens to further alienate the Saudis. Antony Blinken, Biden's outgoing Secretary of State formerly promised "not to take any steps that would escalate tensions, that would risk provoking a wider conflict"[5], while being "fully on board with Israel's goal of degrading Hezbollah"[6]. It is not so much hypocrisy as double speak a policy cleft stick. There are only bad choices for the U.S. leaders as they embrace China-U.S. conflict.

[2] FT 2024. From cars to planes: global manufacturers brace for Trump's tariffs. Financial Times. https://www.ft.com/content/716b7c10-1bfd-4927-8789-c65bf70afe69.

[3] Tooze Adam 2024.Facing war in the Middle East and Ukraine, the US looks feeble. But is it just an act? The Guardian. https://www.theguardian.com/commentisfree/2024/oct/10/war-middle-east-ukraine-us-feeble-biden-trump.

[4] Gardner Frank 2024. Saudi crown prince says Israel committing 'genocide' in Gaza. BBC. https://www.bbc.co.uk/news/articles/cp8x5570514o.amp.

[5] Blinken Antony J. 2024. Secretary Antony J. Blinken Remarks to the Press. U.S. Department of State.
https://www.state.gov/secretary-antony-j-blinken-remarks-to-the-press-27.

[6] Jalabi Raya, England Andrew and Zilber Neri 2024. Israel pushes for expanded UN peacekeeping mission in Lebanon. Financial Times. https://www.ft.com/content/2a00fd8e-b1f4-4c04-89bf-b8b096a17565.

War and the World Economy explains the new period of Great Power competition as the necessary and inevitable outcome of the exhaustion of globalisation's dynamism and the retreat towards a multi-polar world. In 1991 the collapse of Communism—the destruction of the Soviet Union and the coincident transition of China to the market—was celebrated as the culmination of liberal democratic dreams in general and of American Exceptionalism in particular of Western values over foreign ones. Free market nirvana would remake the world unimpeded by any social barriers whatsoever. The political expansion of the market into the former Centrally Planned Economies (CPEs)was the greatest one-off growth of the capitalist ever. It doubled the labour force that could be exploited by capital and transferred the stolen means of production of the former CPEs to the capitalists at no cost. It ushered in a new long wave period of capitalist development that ended the crisis phase of the 1970s and 1980s.

From the outset the new period of expansion contained the seeds of its own demise. In 1899 the Marxist Alexander Parvus had described longer phases of capitalist development or *Sturm und Drang* (Storm and Stress) of stormy advance in capitalist accumulation. These phases did not abolish but conditioned the functioning of the business cycle for entire historical periods until their dynamic potential was exhausted. When they inevitability transitioned into a period of *Zusammenbruch* or collapse. Just as the Belle Epoque ended in the chaos of crisis and war so would the period of contemporary globalisation. The combination of newly extended markets, the incorporation of new labour forces, highly skilled and motivated and with low wages, the removal of barriers to trade and technological innovation mean the mass and rate of profit soared as trade grew faster than industrial output and turnover times dramatically fell. The new long wave would consist of three broad phases, a period of preparation, a period of hyper-expansion and a period of slow down, before it was replaced by a period of crisis or decline, expressed today in the slide to war and increase in social tension.

War and the World Economy explains how the 1990s expansion of capitalism across the globe, was systematically mismeasured, and so underestimated or dismissed, by neo-classical statisticians, through two different but related mistakes. Neo-classical economics has no explanation for the origin of value or profit and treats all production as market production, even the hated and despised output of the CPEs. They simultaneously ignore, indeed deny, the difference between modes of production, while despising that difference and seeking to destroy non-market centrally planned production. The incorporation of the Former Soviet Union (FSU) and China into the world market dramatically expanded world market production and therefore, its measure in national income. Although centrally planned economies produced output or use values their economies were not predicated on exchange, there were no markets, no sales, and so no market production or its measure as national income. Rather output was measured by what planning officials labelled the Material Product System (MPS). While neo-classical economists agitated for the immediate and total destruction of the plan in the Soviet Union and China, while they celebrated the collapse of the CPEs, after Yeltsin's 1991 Big Bang, they treated all production as market production, so they measured the collapse of the material output of the plan as a collapse of national income. They measured the expansion of market production, the creation of national income, as its contraction so their figures underestimated the expansion of national income in the 1990s by around half.

The measures of profitability of neo-classical statisticians are similarly irrational and absurd. They aggregate estimates of future earnings to produce fictional "data", tautological guestimates of the discounted aggregate of future "services" generated by the fixed capital stock. Capitalist accountants measure the rate or profit (the amount of profit a capitalist yields relative to their investment) as the ratio of the mass of profit to the value of capitalist advanced, but neo-classical statisticians reject such "accountant valuations" in favour of fictional "economist valuations" labelled Net Present Value (NPV). The value of an investment is the amount of net profit or "services" it is expected to yield multiplied by the "service life" or duration for which services are returned to the investor. As profits are necessarily higher than costs, this procedure overvalues the actual cost of the fixed capital stock by between five and seven times. Most fundamentally as the mass of profit rises the value of the fixed capital stock rises more so a rise in the mass of profit is measured as a fall in the rate of profit. The misuse of these neo-classical statistics underpins the wildly inaccurate estimates of catastrophist economists who describe hyper-globalisation as a period of stagnation and decline or a "Great Depression".

The period of preparation for the upward long wave lasted from 1991 to 2001. Globalisation had freed capitalism and freed capitalism went to work. Commodification spread everywhere, all relations were reduced to a cash nexus, unbridled free trade knew no limits, production was outsourced from the Western imperialist powers to China and the former planned economies of Central and Eastern Europe (CEE). The beneficent hegemon of the United States (U.S.) bestrode the world like a colossus. It had crushed its Cold War opponents and now it remade the world. Dismantling trade barriers, founding the World Trade Organisation (WTO) in 1995, ending national liberation struggles in South Africa, with the release of Mandela and abolition of apartheid, in Palestine with the Palestine Liberation Organisation's (PLO) acceptance of Israel's right to exist, in Ireland with the Anglo-Irish peace treaty and the defeat and murder of Saddam Hussein in Iraq and Gaddafi in Libya. The consolidation of the defeat of trade union struggles demonstrated by a worldwide very sharp fall in strike figures, by the deindustrialisation which was enabled by the hi-tech revolution.

The bursting of the hi-tech bubble in 2000 did not signal the ending of the internet and computer technology revolution, but its beginning. China joined the WTO in 2001 and manufacturing was outsourced. Western powers became above all, financial powers, divesting themselves of their manufacturing base, relying instead on control of finance, key technologies and markets for their super profits, while Western multinationals gave up on production, money created more money, its link to accumulation was apparently severed once and for all. Capitalism is after all a system of private property; the rich are rich because the poor are poor. The powerful are powerful because the weak are weak. The U.S. spread democracy through the barrel of a gun. The apex predator oversaw the international rules-based order, the guarantor of its profits, as financial instruments proliferated, debt and securitisation rocketed and the internet revolution created dense networks of production and sale while the tech firms hoovered up the profits.

The second phase extended from 2001 until 2010. A period of frenzied, apparently unlimited, capitalist hyper-expansion or hyper-globalisation induced a huge residential boom which collapsed into financial meltdown the Great Financial Recession of 2008-2010. It was nonetheless, the fastest growth of capital accumulation ever. There was wealth for all, or if not all, at least a bit of wealth for all, the crumbs from the billionaire oligarchs' table. Income inequality soared as did environmental degradation and climate crisis, and against all expert forecasts, China soared too. The technological revolution cheapened the cost of fixed capital and reduced the cost of the reproduction of labour time, expressed in the deflation of manufactured consumer goods, so the purchasing power of wages grew, even as their value, expressed in the proportion of wages in national income fell. Profits and income inequality soared. These factors, that Marx famously enunciated as offsetting the tendency of the rate of profit to fall, are being exhausted and so their exhaustion defines the new world period today—deepening crisis, war and decay.

The third phase of stagnation stretched from 2010 to 2019 to end with the Covid-19 pandemic; the proximate cause for the end of globalisation, but not the essential one. For all the experts disavowal of the laws of capitalist accumulation, the laws did not disavow them. The untrammelled capitalist expansion of the market to embrace the globe simultaneously undermined that expansion, the barriers to capitalist accumulation arose from within. Crises abound, the degradation of the environment, untrammelled carbon emissions, deforestation and collapse of biodiversity threaten the natural world. The migration of populations in search of a better life, or fleeing war and oppression, challenges the accepted limits of liberal Western toleration. The rise of the populist right undermines the social concessions won by liberal neo-liberalism around women's rights, LGBT equality and multiculturalism. The enrichment of the billionaire oligarchs exposes the crude inequality and rank unfairness of the capitalist system. While financial instability and uncertainty threaten the stability of society—banks are too big to fail and are bailed out—but this socialism saves only the rich. These crises for capitalism are not yet crises of it. They are indirect manifestations of capital's relentless search for profit, sacrificing everything to individual aggrandisement and enrichment irrespective of social upheaval and oppression. These crises pose challenges to the system it must overcome, but they are not in themselves challenges to the continued existence of the system itself, they are not crises of capitalism. The crisis to come is far more fundamental, manifest first of all in global military competition and war.

The fourth phase, the replacement of the period of *Sturm and Drang* by one of crises and eventually collapse *Zusammenbruch* describes the world today. In some respects the world seems to have hardly changed at all, the rich are rich, America is powerful, and the seeds of social content have still not grown, ignoring war, but the sheer number of regional conflicts, the direct and indirect involvement of the major powers in them, and their bitter intensity and unrelenting viciousness, mean war cannot be ignored. War is, in the words of Carl von Clausewitz, (the Prussian philosopher of war much quoted by U.S. military think tanks) the continuation of policy by other means. It is no inexplicable aberration but reflects the political struggles of nations to exert their self-interest against rival competitor nations. But competitors in what? Above all the economic struggle for markets and profits, what Blinken labels Great Power competition. U.S. power rests on the international rules-based order it established after the Second World War and which was revivified by the collapse of its only, albeit non-capitalist rival, the Soviet Union in 1991. That international rules-based order protects U.S. investments abroad the vast revenues repatriated to the U.S. by dollar seigniorage, the monopoly of its tech companies over the internet, and its vast investments abroad. That international rules-based order is threatened by the new Great Power China and conflict between them (around markets, technology, trade and investments) is as inevitable as economic competition itself. China's very presence undermines U.S. power; whatever China's subjective yearning for the "China Dream", equality within the world order, peace and prosperity for all. Equality is forbidden in an international rules-based order designed to protect U.S. interests above all others. The rise of China erodes, and will destroy, a key condition for the long wave of globalisation, the hegemony of a world power, acting as a guarantor of free trade and so it undermines the entire global economy itself.

Chapter 1

Polycrisis and the Thucydides Trap

Polycrisis is a defining term of the moment, reflecting the multiple and overlapping crises for capitalism, environmental degradation and climate change, income inequality, the threat of right-wing populism for democracy, de-globalisation, trade wars and wars. Chapter 1 discusses how these crises evolved from the aftermath of the U.S. victory in the Cold War, what Francis Fukuyama notably described as "the End of History", and how contemporary theorists, albeit from different ends of the neoliberal political spectrum, such as Nouriel Roubini, Adam Tooze and Niall Ferguson disagree about the causes of the crisis while agreeing such causes are unknowable, thus excusing their inability to explain them. Contemporary military think tanks describe the war as a "Thucydides Trap", echoing Thucydides' explanation for the inevitable war between Athens, the established power and Sparta, the upstart threat. While denying that war is inevitable, contemporary theorists of U.S. military and economic supremacy nonetheless concede that political, economic and national conflict is. But what is war other than the violent expression of these conflicts? The U.S. military establishment cannot countenance China's challenge to the international rules-based order which underpins U.S. world power, interest and profits. Wars are a natural outcome of geopolitical conflict as they were for Thucydides. The polycrisis are not yet challenges to the capitalist order but events have an unforgiving logic.

Chapter 2

China's Challenge to the West

China forms what Western analysts and foreign policy officials define as "the Pacing Challenge" to the West in general and the U.S. in particular. Chapter 2 considers how Biden's Democrats and the Western defence officials that advised them built on Trump's American First policy to develop a systematic anti-Chinese policy that presages ever widening and deepening conflict. Western military analysts justify the deepening trade, tech and cold war as a necessary response to China's threats to the international rules-based order it dominates. They combine an external hostility to China's growth through tariffs, military treaties and a renewed arms race with domestic industrial policy in an attempt to on-shore industry, revive particular geo-strategic industries such as chip manufacturing and automobiles, preparing for the forthcoming military conflict while deluding themselves about their readiness for it and its likely outcome.

CHAPTER 3

The Collapse of the Centrally Planned Economies and the Expansion of Capitalism

The collapse or transition of the Centrally Planned Economies (CPE) to capitalism during the 1990s formed the material prerequisite for globalisation. It was the extension of the global market across the whole world for perhaps the first time. Chapter 3 discusses how the transition resulted in the doubling of the world labour force available for capitalist exploitation and transferred massive physical quantities of infrastructure to capital at no cost. This transition underpinned the restoration of profits, trade and industrial production from the crisis years of the 1970s and 1980s, but it was systematically underestimated and mismeasured by official statistical agencies like the World Bank, IMF and the OECD. Fictional estimates for the value of Soviet output were developed by Abram Bergson for the CIA and generalised across the CPEs. These conflated the output of the plan with that of the market, so that when planned output collapsed during the transition to the market, this was measured as a collapse of market production rather than its creation. This similarly effected estimates of world trade. Consequently, the transformative effect of the extension of the world market across a third of the world's surface was on the whole ignored or dismissed by contemporary economic theorists.

CHAPTER 4

The Long Wave of Globalisation

The creation of the world market in the 1990s formed the first phase of a new long wave. U.S. political victory in the Cold War enabled capitalist accumulation to escape stagnation. Chapter 4 describes how the new period of globalisation fulfilled Ernest Mandel's, the Belgian Marxist, criteria for an upward long wave or what Alexander Parvus (Helphand) described as a period of *Sturm und Drang* (Storm and Stress). The incorporation of new populations extended the base of consumption and production, and was consolidated by the defeat of national liberation movements, labour movements—strike figures slumped—the collapse of trade barriers, re-establishment of U.S. global hegemony and the consequent technological revolution. The 1990s established the conditions for the subsequent hyper-globalised expansion of capitalism after 2001, but nothing good lasts forever. Understanding the reasons for the long wave also implies understanding their limits. The wave would inevitably break as the dynamism of the technological advances was exhausted and the growth of new powers, notably China, threatened U.S. global hegemony.

Chapter 5

Hyper-Globalisation and the Laws of Political Economy

The Project for a New American Century (PNAC) advocated a more assertive championing of U.S. democratic values—to be delivered at the point of a gun. The 2001 Al-Qaeda Twin Tower attack provided the excuse and George W. Bush's demonisation of the Axis of Evil, Afghanistan, North Korea and Iraq, none of which were involved in the attack, followed naturally; as did the invasion of Iraq and toppling of Saddam Hussein. Meanwhile, China acceded to the World Trade Organisation (WTO) in 2001 and world growth, trade and profits took off. Chapter 5 describes the period of hyper-globalisation which exploded in the 2008 financial crisis Great Recession. It traces the rise of Factoryless Goods Producers (FGPs) in the West as manufacturing production was relocated to cheaper producers abroad. It shows how Marx's conditions for a recovery of profit rates were fulfilled. It discusses how neo-classical valuations of the fixed capital stock, using methods developed by Hulten and Wykoff to estimate the future profits of investments or their Net Present Value (NPV), transform a rise in the mass of profit into a fall in the rate of profit. This absurd misreading of the period has resulted in some catastrophist Marxists describing hyper-globalisation as a Great Depression.

Chapter 6

Rising Profits and the Great Recession

The period labelled hyper-globalisation from 2001 to 2008 was the strongest period of capitalist growth in history, with industrial production, trade and profitability soaring. Chapter 6 analyses how and why profitability grew and develops some original estimates for the level of profits across the whole U.S. economy and within its various sectors.

It describes how this rise was compounded by the housing bubble that peaked in 2006 and ultimately collapsed in September 2008. It provides an analysis of the financial crisis and shows how, although it arose in the U.S. and UK, it paradoxically reinforced their dominance within financial markets and reminded the City of London of its dependence on the U.S. Federal Reserve. For the EU their lack of a national state bank almost fatally undermined the Euro, with the aftermath of the recession lingering until 2015. While for China it reinforced their turn towards the domestic market as the authorities turned to domestic investment to avoid the short-term collapse of trade over the winter of 2008/9.

Chapter 7

China—The New Great Power

China's growth into a new Great Power fatally undermines the international rules-based order as its equality is incompatible with U.S. hegemony. Chapter 7 traces how China's transition to Great Power status was the inevitable result of its transition to the market completed in the late 1990s and its later pivotal role in global value chains. China's State-Owned Enterprises (SOE) provide it with a key advantage in the competition with the U.S. and their size and role is assessed. The growth of China's patents provides a rough indicator of its technological strength, as are the quantities of its foreign investments including through the Belt and Road Initiative (BRI), and the reduction in its dependence on U.S. Federal Debt.

Chapter 8

Russia's Collapse and Recovery and Iran and the Middle East

Russia's traumatic transition to the market saw its economy collapse by around two-thirds as Russian oligarchs stole its natural resources and Western banks and oil companies sought to dominate its economy. Chapter 8 traces its recovery after Putin's Presidential victory in 2000 as a now capitalist petro-exporter and its alienation from the Western sphere as Russian capitalists reasserted their national and Great Power rights over their near neighbours with a series of wars, that successively reduced

Western influence. It briefly discusses how the Great Power struggle is extended through the Middle East including Syria, Iran and Israel.

Chapter 9

The War Potential of China and the U.S.

National war potential attempts to assess the fighting capacity of a nation. Chapter 9 develops the work of Lord Kaldor, who considers the relative population, industrial capacity and control of key war materials to be the ultimate determinants of war potential and contrasts the U.S. to China. It finds that although the U.S. has a ten-power defensive standard, spending more on arms than the next ten nations combined, it is far inferior to China in terms of population, industrial development and control of key materials. That does not mean war will be avoided, but rather points to a certain unfavourable result—for the U.S.

Chapter 10

The End of Globalisation and the New Period of Crisis

The end of Globalisation, the break-up of the monopolar world and its replacement by Great Power competition was the inevitable result of the capitalist accumulation process, the waning of the dynamic impetus provided to world capitalism with the collapse of the USSR and transition of China to the market. Crises for capitalism, climate change, migration, income inequality, nationalism, tech and trade wars, will be transformed into crises of capitalism, the questioning of the legitimacy of the capitalist system itself and the re-entry of the masses into history.

Contents

About the Author

William Jefferies completed his PhD at Manchester Metropolitan University in 2014, which was subsequently published as *Measuring National Income in the Centrally Planned Economies: Why the West Underestimated the Transition to Capitalism*. He has written widely on issues of value theory and the political economy of globalisation. He is an Associate Professor at Ravensbourne University London, and a Senior Lecturer at SOAS University of London. He would like to thank all his family, Eleanor, Alex, Oli, Lily, Louise and Tom, and friends for their love and support over the years.

List of Figures

List of Tables

CHAPTER 1

Polycrisis and the Thucydides Trap

"Perhaps this very prospect of centuries of boredom at the end of history will serve to get history started once again". Francis Fukuyama 1989.[1]

Francis Fukuyama's classic *End of History* celebrated U.S. victory in the cold war. A RAND (Research and Development) analyst and member of the U.S. military-academic establishment, Fukuyama rejected economic determinist[2] explanations of Great Power struggle in favour of a Hegelian triumph of the idea. Fukuyama mused that so triumphant was the idea of democracy that only centuries of boredom might serve to get history started again. The power of Fukuyama's insight was his prediction of Communist collapse, coinciding with the Tiananmen massacre and fall of the Berlin Wall, while anticipating Yeltsin's 1992 Shock Therapy privatisation of the Soviet economy. As Leon Trotsky, the leader of the 1917 socialist insurrection and founder of the Red Army had contemplated,

[1] Fukuyama Francis 1989. The end of history? *The National Interest,* 16 (Summer), pp. 3–18.

[2] Kennedy Paul 1987. *The Rise and Fall of the Great Powers; Economic Change and Military Conflict.* New York, Random House.

W. Jefferies, *War and the World Economy*, Palgrave Insights into Apocalypse Economics,
https://doi.org/10.1007/978-3-031-85236-7_1

the apparatus had devoured the workers' state.[3] No material or ideological barriers stood in the way of the triumph of the American dream. The collapse of the USSR and transition of Chinese communism to the market was, in one sense, the end of history.

Mark Fisher, a British post-modern sociologist, made the same point, but from the opposite end of the political spectrum, and twenty years later. Fisher pointed to the 2008 financial crisis, climate change and the lack of any coherent social opposition to lament "it's easier to imagine the end of the world than the end of capitalism".[4] Certainly, the ideological and material, subjective and objective, defeat of the legacy of the Russian 1917 revolution and Mao's transformation of China in the 1950s, appeared to change the world almost beyond recognition. There were no more ideals to realise. No longer would liberalism face the challenge of a real social alternative. The collapse of the Centrally Planned Economies (CPEs) meant that the very notion of an alternative society, socialism or communism, as a practical other to capitalism, vanished for an entire historical period. Fukuyama's broadly accurate assessment of the fundamental ideological impact of those events vindicated American exceptionalism, it was American manifest destiny fulfilled. Western democracy had prevailed and would recreate the world in its image.

In 2022 Nouriel Roubini who, in 2008, had earned the nickname Dr Doom for his accurate forecasts of the Great Recession financial crash, identified ten broad Megathreats that faced a world teetering "on a precipice".[5] Roubini described economic, financial, political, geopolitical, trade, technological, health and climate-based challenges of such immense scale and urgency that they threatened to "destroy us". Global debt was 2021 350% of global national income up from 1999 220%, the world capitalist economy was addicted to cheap money, the low interest rate regime that prevailed from 2008 to 2021. The world workforce was ageing. Stagflation had arrived. Bitcoin was a scam. Globalisation was ending. AI would replace human jobs. While climate change could render

[3] Trotsky Leon 1936. *The Revolution Betrayed. What is the Soviet Union and Where is it Going?* Translated by Max Eastman. https://www.marxists.org/archive/trotsky/1936/revbet/revbetray.pdf.

[4] Fisher Mark 2009. *Capitalist Realism*. London, Zero, p. 1.

[5] Roubini Nouriel 2022. Megathreats: Our Ten Biggest Threats, and How to Survive Them. New York, Little Brown and Co., p. 11, 17, 252.

the planet uninhabitable. Roubini wailed can we "survive the coming crises?".

Adam Tooze of Colombia University advocated the term "polycrisis" to describe the overlapping crises of the contemporary world; the Ukraine war, Covid-19, inflation, China, climate collapse, stagflation and the possibility of U.S. Democratic Party electoral failure. These "multiple and compounding risks" were "more dangerous than the sum of its parts". It goes without saying, yet it apparently always needs to be said, that polycrisis was "not inevitable, this is not a prophecy of doom".[6] Tooze produced a matrix, a tangled mess of overlapping and mutually reinforcing parts, which buried his lack of explanation beneath a mass of interrelationships "in the polycrisis the shocks are disparate, but they interact so that the whole is even more overwhelming than the sum of the parts". No single solution to these problems could be imagined "in the 1970s, whether you were a Eurocommunist, an ecologist or an angst-ridden conservative, you could still attribute your worries to a single cause—late capitalism, too much or too little economic growth, or an excess of entitlement. A single cause also meant that one could imagine a sweeping solution, be it social revolution or neoliberalism". The polycrisis, in contrast, was so disorienting that it was no longer plausible to suggest a single problem and a single solution. As if ignorance or rejection of the cause of the crisis meant it was outside of the frame of social laws, beyond explanation. Crisis was a perpetual (but not inevitable so maybe not) condition of the contemporary world. It's root as inexplicable as the lack of Tooze's explanation as to how to avoid it or why.

Niall Ferguson, the Scottish Harvard Professor, and British Empire nostalgist, disagreed with Tooze. He ridiculed the notion of Polycrisis, poo-pooing de-globalisation, while simultaneously arguing the New Cold War with China may well result in a Chinese attack on Taiwan "yes" within two years or less. Following Robert Kaplan[7] and Henry Kissinger[8] (the beloved war criminal of the American ruling class responsible for

[6] Tooze Adam 2022. *Chartbook #130 Defining polycrisis—from crisis pictures to the crisis matrix*. Jun 24, https://adamtooze.substack.com/p/chartbook-130-defining-polycrisis.

[7] Kaplan Robert D. 2018. *A New Cold War Has Begun*. Foreign Policy. https://foreignpolicy.com/2019/01/07/a-new-cold-war-has-begun/.

[8] Ferguson Niall 2023. *Cold War II: Niall Ferguson On The Emerging Conflict With China*. Uncommon Knowledge, interview with Peter Robinson. https://www.hoover.org/research/cold-war-ii-niall-ferguson-emerging-conflict-china.

three or four million deaths)[9] Ferguson claimed that the Cold War had broken out because Xi Jingpin is a "Marxist-Leninist". Although Ferguson wanted to deter China from war, he was not sure Taiwan was defending, it is a lot closer to China than the U.S., but in any respect, this was not crisis anything beyond the normal.[10] Globalisation lives, Ferguson cried, citing Richard Baldwin.[11] Trade in services was rising as a proportion of GDP, while fluctuations in the goods trade largely reflected the ups and downs of the raw material commodities cycle, and by the way, his kids listened to BTS, a Korean K-pop sensation. Although, he added, in a note of caution, the absence of de-globalisation did not exclude Great Power rivalry.

Pol Antràs of Harvard University argued there was no de-globalisation, but rather the end of the hyper-globalisation experienced with the integration of the former planned economies into the world capitalist economy. Antràs provided a detailed breakdown of trends within globalisation, and concluded there was a slowdown, although not de-globalisation.[12] Antràs really only showed that the end of hyper-globalisation and de-globalisation are the same thing. Unless globalisation goes forward it goes backward. Gita Gopinath, Deputy Director of the IMF,[13] addressed Ferguson's argument in similar terms,

> The end of the Cold War also coincided with the hyper-globalization period of the 1990s and 2000s: technological innovations, unilateral and

[9] Ackerman Spencer 2023. *Henry Kissinger, War Criminal Beloved by America's Ruling Class, Finally Dies*. Rolling Stone. https://www.rollingstone.com/politics/politics-news/henry-kissinger-war-criminal-dead-1234804748/amp/.

[10] Ferguson Niall 2023 *Take It From K-Pop's Finest: Globalization Lives!* Bloomberg. https://www.bloomberg.com/opinion/articles/2023-01-29/from-k-pop-to-tiktok-globalization-lives-niall-ferguson.

[11] Baldwin Richard 2022. The peak globalisation myth. Vox. https://rbaldwin.substack.com/p/the-peak-globalisation-myth.

[12] Antràs Pol 2020. *De-Globalisation? Global Value Chains in the Post-COVID-19 Age*. Harvard University, ECB Forum on Central Banking, "Central Banking in a Shifting World," originally scheduled to take place in Sintra, Portugal.

[13] Gopinath Gita 2023. Cold War II? *Preserving Economic Cooperation Amid Geoeconomic Fragmentation*. Plenary Speech by IMF First Managing Deputy Director Gita Gopinath 20th World Congress of the International Economic Association Colombia December 11, 2023. New York International Monetary Fund (IMF).

https://www.imf.org/en/News/Articles/2023/12/11/sp121123-cold-war-ii-preserving-economic-cooperation-amid-geoeconomic-fragmentation1/.

> multilateral trade liberalization, and geopolitical and institutional changes all coalesced to lift economic integration to levels not seen before. Since 2008, however, the pace of globalization has stagnated—the so-called slow-balization—with trade to GDP stabilizing as the forces that helped spur hyper-globalization naturally waned.

It was a coincidence these factors had coalesced, and so presumably, a coincidence now that they naturally waned, implying their coalescence was no coincidence but not their waning? Irrespective, they no longer did so, which was a shame. Gopinath noted that in 2023 around 3,000 trade restrictions were imposed, around six times the level of 2017 and three times that of 2019. The share of global trade in world GDP remained relatively stable, but bilateral trading relations, and global foreign direct investment (FDI) were fragmenting along geopolitical lines so coincidentally no doubt, or perhaps naturally, or maybe both "if fragmentation deepens, we could find ourselves in a new Cold War". In fact, this shift was entirely predictable and was predicted. William Jefferies, a British political economist wrote in 2016,

> China in the coming years will increasingly challenge Western hegemony over the world market...Chinese technology combined with the more rapid product cycle of modern manufacturing means that in coming years China's multinationals will increasingly compete with and replace Western transnational corporations in the highest value-added sectors. As they do so, the dependence on Western finances and services will simultaneously decline. At this point China will challenge the United States and Europe for the leadership of the world economy, though paradoxically, when this does happen a crucial condition for unhindered global trade, the existence of a single power able to guarantee open trade, will disappear.[14]

The explanation for hyper-globalisation and de-globalisation is neither natural nor coincidental, it is social, the law of accumulation that defines the capitalist system. Capitalists relentlessly expand to accumulate profits, to extract surplus labour from the working class and appropriate the profits of their rival capitalists. Capital subordinates everything in the search for these riches, in a ceaseless quest for aggrandisement to, as Marx exclaimed in *Capital,* "Accumulate! Accumulate! That Is Moses and the

[14] Jefferies William 2017. China's Challenge to the West: Possibility and Reality. *International Critical Thought*, 7(1), pp. 32–50, p. 46/47.

Prophets!".[15] The profit motive provides the incentive, the means and the whip for accumulation. Fail to accumulate and the punishment is fatal, succeed and Midas awaits. Moreover, Marx noted in the *Grundrisse*, just as capitalists seeks to appropriate the profits of their rival through competition, so "nations may continually exchange….even…on an ever-expanding scale, without for that reason necessarily gaining in equal degrees" so nations "appropriate…the surplus labour of the other" returning "nothing for it",[16] this same economic competition produces national rivalry.

Capital accumulation creates crises for the world, crises that capitalism must address; climate change, environmental degradation, income inequality, national rivalry and war, but addressing does not mean solving. These are not crises for capital, and a capitalist solution need only resolve them for capital, not the world. These crises do not immediately threaten the continued rule of capital, they destabilise the balance of the world economy, but simultaneously provide new profit accumulating opportunities. The 2020 RAND and U.S. Air Force (USAF) report the *Future of Warfare Report* noted that climate change exacerbated national rivalry through "its second-order impacts on the food supply"[17] and as "the number of extreme weather events increases, so too do the chances of one of these events triggering internal instability or cross-border migration flows".[18] Climate change and environmental degradation are not a problem in and of themselves, except to the extent that they result in social dislocation, upheaval and revolt, and exacerbate therefore, the chances of war.

[15] Marx Karl 1995 [1867]. *Capital; A Critique of Political Economy Volume I.* Moscow, Progress.

[16] Marx Karl 1973. *Grundrisse.* Translated by Martin Nicolaus. London, Penguin.

[17] Cohen Raphael S., Chandler Nathan, Efron Shira, Frederick Bryan, Han Eugeniu, Klein Kurt, Morgan Forrest E. Rhoades Ashley L. Shatz Howard J. and Shokh Yuliya 2020. *The Future of Warfare 2030; Project Overview and Conclusions.* Santa Monica Calif. RAND

www.rand.org/t/RR2849z1, p. 12.

[18] Cohen Raphael S., Chandler Nathan, Efron Shira, Frederick Bryan, Han Eugeniu, Klein Kurt, Morgan Forrest E. Rhoades Ashley L. Shatz Howard J. and Shokh Yuliya 2020. *The Future of Warfare 2030; Project Overview and Conclusions.* Santa Monica Calif. RAND

www.rand.org/t/RR2849z1, p. 67.

The Biden administration that in 2021 rejoined the Paris climate accords with the ostensible purpose of avoiding "catastrophic planetary warming"[19] in 2023 approved 758 new licences for gas and oil drilling, twice the rate of the climate denier Trump, as the U.S. became the largest exporter of oil and Liquid Natural Gas (LNG) in the world, even surpassing Saudi Arabia by around half.[20] The COP 28 climate talks were hosted by the United Arab Emirates (UAE) as a vehicle for the oil trade.[21] Sheikh Ahmed Dalmook al-Maktoum of UAE's oil rich royal oligarchy is the founder and chair of Blue Carbon a private carbon offset company, acquiring management rights to millions of hectares of African land, up to a tenth of Liberia, a fifth of Zimbabwe and swathes of Kenya, Zambia and Tanzania.[22] From 2026 the EU will impose the Carbon Border Adjustment Mechanism (CBAM) on emissions of carbon-intensive imports. The first ever tax of carbon-intensive imports will include cement, iron, aluminium, fertilisers, electricity, hydrogen and steel, incidentally, protecting core, relatively inefficient European industries from Chinese exports. Fu Cong, the Chinese ambassador to the EU called it "another green trade barrier".[23] These crises for capitalism may grow into crises of capitalism, threats to the social power of the system itself, but they are not in and of themselves challenges to capitalist social relations, the rule of private property and commodity production. It is still too early to speak of a crisis of capitalism, even if there are numerous crises for it. Capitalism as a system will only create the opposition capable of overthrowing when it is unable to offer the mass of the population the possibility of social reproduction and advance.

[19] Blinken Anthony 2021. *The United States Officially Rejoins the Paris Agreement.* U.S. Department of State. www.state.gov/the-united-states-officially-rejoins-the-paris-agreement.

[20] Milman Oliver 2024. *This used to be a beautiful place': how the US became the world's biggest fossil fuel state.* The Guardian. https://www.theguardian.com/environment/article/2024/jul/24/fossil-fuel-liquified-natural-gas-louisiana?

[21] Rowlatt Justin 2023. *UAE planned to use COP28 climate talks to make oil deals.* London, BBC. www.bbc.co.uk/news/science-environment-67508331.

[22] Bryan Kenza 2023. *The looming land grab in Africa for carbon credits.* London, Financial Times.https://www.ft.com/content/f9bead69-7401-44fe-8db9-1c4063ae958c.

[23] Hancock Alice and Pfeifer Sylvia 2024. How global trade could fragment after the EU's tax on 'dirty' imports. London, Financial Times. https://www.ft.com/content/ca51ebf5-fbb8-4c88-a93d-ded3d6d3bcdd?.

Ferguson denies the existence of crisis, Tooze and Roubini describe the inevitability of crisis, but deny the inevitability of the crises they describe. Roubini, unlike Ferguson, felt unable to comment on the likelihood of the Great Power conflict, or war, between China and the U.S., even while observing that "the Western consensus—that China's joining the global trading and financial system will cause it to slowly, slowly, embrace a market economy and become less authoritarian—has been flat-out wrong".[24] In 2017 Graham Allison, a Harvard professor and part of the U.S. academic-military-intelligence establishment labelled the emerging China-U.S. conflict a "Thucydides' Trap".[25] Allison's work anticipated the future course of U.S. foreign and domestic policy and is much referenced including by U.S. military strategic think tanks like the RAND institute.[26] Allison explained that when a "rising power threatens to displace a ruling power" conflict emerges or as Thucydides put it in his classic *History of the Peloponnesian War*[27] it was "the rise of Athens and the fear that this instilled in Sparta that made war inevitable".[28]

In 2018 Robert D. Kaplan[29] of the Foreign Policy Research Institute announced that the U.S./China conflict had resulted in a New Cold War. This may not lead to a bloody war, although it might; war was possible rather than probable. The threat was more than the "famous Thucydidean paradigm of fear, honor, and interest" due to China's emotional connection to Taiwan, and because the fear of nuclear holocaust had receded. The risk of war would further increase should the Chinese economy slow, and the leadership turn to nationalism. The U.S. would win by waiting China out, the collapse of the Chinese autocracy would resolve the Great

[24] Roubini Nouriel 2022. *Megathreats: Our Ten Biggest Threats, and How to Survive Them*. New York, Little Brown and Co., p. 186.

[25] Graham, Allison 2017. Destined for War; Can America and China Escape Thucydides Trap. New York, Houghton, Mifflin, Harcourt, p. 12.

[26] Heath Timothy R., Grossman Derek and Clark Asha 2021. *China's Quest for Global Primacy An Analysis of Chinese International and Defense Strategies to Outcompete the United States*. RAND Institute www.rand.org/t/RRA447-1.

[27] Thucydides 1974. *The History of the Peloponnesian War*. M. I. Finley (Introduction), Rex Warner (Translator), London, Penguin.

[28] Graham, Allison 2017. *Destined for War; Can America and China Escape Thucydides Trap*. New York, Houghton, Mifflin, Harcourt, p. 12.

[29] Kaplan Robert D. 2018. *A New Cold War Has Begun*. Foreign Policy. https://foreignpolicy.com/2019/01/07/a-new-cold-war-has-begun/.

Power struggle. Thucydides would disagree, China's emergent power will rival the U.S., just as Sparta did Athens, irrespective of its governmental system. In 2021 Barry Naughton, a veteran U.S. China expert exclaimed "Conflict Among Technological Powers is NOT Inevitable". It was not some "Thucydides trap". Things were more complex than that; a new set of rules needed to be hammered out. What rules? China needed to turn away from "industrial policy" which had "played no role" in its "explosive growth".[30] Paradoxically one of the "global economic trends" that increased the "chances of future conflict" was "the rise in protectionism" which originated in the U.S. but was naturally not their fault. When is anything ever their fault?

For Thucydides the inevitable nature of the war was an expression of the inner laws of history, the operation of which necessitated their violent resolution. War was not some inexplicable disaster, but the necessary expression of the historical conditions that created it. War was, as later defined by Carl von Clausewitz, a Prussian General of the Napoleonic wars in the 1830s, and Hegelian in *On War*, "not merely an act of policy but a true political instrument, a continuation of political intercourse, carried on with other means".[31] Michael Mazarr a senior RAND analyst considered that an assessment of Chinese competition demands,

> a sober, objective assessment of the nature of any competition. Scholars of warfare are fond of quoting Carl von Clausewitz to the effect that 'the first, the supreme, the most far-reaching act of judgment that the statesman and commander have to make is to establish by that test the kind of war on which they are embarking; neither mistaking it for, nor trying to turn it into, something that is alien to its nature.' The same could be said about this topic: The first and most essential task for any nation is to understand the character of the rivalry in which it is participating—not mistaking the rivalry for a competition that may be very different in kind, scope, or intensity.[32]

[30] Naughton Barry 2021. *The Rise of China's Industrial Policy 1978 to 2020. Universidad* Nacional Autónoma de México, p. 17, 137.

[31] Clausewitz Carl Von 1976. *On War*. Edited and translated by Michael Howard and Peter Paret. New Jersey, Princeton University Press, p. 86.

[32] Mazarr, Michael J. 2022. *Understanding Competition; Great Power Rivalry in a Changing International Order—Concepts and Theories*. Santa Monica, Calif. RAND. https://doi.org/10.7249/PEA1404-1.

Mazarr could not explain the inevitability of such conflict but nonetheless explained at length the sober steps necessary for the U.S. to win it. Allison did not view such a Chinese American war as "inevitable", claiming that Thucydides' use of the term was not a theory of the world but a literary device, "hyperbole, exaggeration for the purpose of emphasis".[33] Rather, Allison abjured, war was simply "more likely than not". It could be avoided on condition that the U.S. military-academic establishment of which he, as a Harvard professor and geo-strategic adviser to the army, had intimate personal knowledge, could learn to Do Strategy, Understand China and Clarify its Vital Interests. But what if, after understanding China and clarifying its vital interests, the U.S. determined a strategy set on escalating confrontation towards war? To fulfil its manifest destiny to impose world peace by disarming China, rendering it helpless before its will?

The Future of Warfare 2030 espoused a "Clausewitzian definition of *warfare* as 'an act of force to compel our enemy to do our will'".[34] It considered "that war be a deliberate, coercive act applied against an adversary". Competition between states was expressed in policy and resolved through violent means, the violence was a necessary consequence of the competition, itself inevitable. Violent, military means were as much a method for achieving policy as peaceful ones.

Clausewitz noted that the aim of war was to "disarm the enemy",[35] to compel your enemy to obey your will, to defeat them and enforce their surrender to you through force of arms. If two rival powers seek to impose their desire for peace on their rival, then war is certain. A 2016 RAND report, for the U.S. Army, *The Power to Coerce*,[36] explained that "we look especially at alternatives to force that can *coerce* unfriendly

[33] Graham, Allison 2017. *Destined for War; Can America and China Escape Thucydides Trap*. New York, Houghton, Mifflin, Harcourt, p. 7, 15.

[34] Cohen Raphael S., Chandler Nathan, Efron Shira, Frederick Bryan, Han Eugeniu, Klein Kurt, Morgan Forrest E. Rhoades Ashley L. Shatz Howard J. and Shokh Yuliya 2020. *The Future of Warfare 2030; Project Overview and Conclusions*. Santa Monica Calif. RAND
www.rand.org/t/RR2849z1, p. 14.

[35] Clausewitz Carl Von 1976. *On War*. Edited and Translated by Michael Howard and Peter Paret. New Jersey, Princeton University Press, p. 77.

[36] Gompert David C., Binnendijk Hans 2016. *The Power to Coerce; Countering Adversaries Without Going to War*.
Santa Monica, Calif. RAND HQD156919. Emphasis in the original, pp. 1–2.

states to comply with U.S. wishes. In it, we advance and develop two propositions: First, alternatives to military force are increasingly *important* in U.S. strategy. Second, at least some such alternatives are increasingly *promising*". Peace is simply another coercive policy, forcing an actor to comply with U.S. interests, *peacefully*. The report continued "Chinese authorities frankly acknowledge the inevitability of competition but also reject the notion that conflict is inevitable",[37] but war is the continuation of policy by other military means, as much as peace is.

William R. Thompson, Professor of International Relations at Indiana University, asserted that "inherently, conflicts are about relative scarcity and overlapping interests and goals.... Someone's gain means somebody else's loss. We cannot attain all of our goals because to do so would interfere with somebody else's maximal goal attainment. Hence, conflicts are about real incompatibilities in attaining material and nonmaterial goals".[38] The inevitability of war flows from conflicting economic interests of nation states, notwithstanding Thompson observed a lack of consensus amongst international relations academics as to the causes of conflict or their nature. His empirical approach contrasted historical pairs of conflicts, but his method was far from a universal theory and in fact counterposed to it.

G.W. Hegel the dialectical idealist philosopher and provider of Clausewitz's method, observed that,

> Those sciences, which thus got the name of philosophy, we call empirical sciences, for the reason that they take their departure from experience. Still the essential results which they aim at and provide are laws, general propositions, a theory — the thoughts of what is found existing.[39]

Hegel, the idealist, sought to know God by discovering the laws that governed the universe. God, the idea, created the universe, so the way to know God was to know the universe, the objective, necessarily lawful and

[37] Heath Timothy R., Grossman Derek and Clark Asha 2021. *China's Quest for Global Primacy An Analysis of Chinese International and Defense Strategies to Outcompete the United States*. Santa Monica, Calif, RAND www.rand.org/t/RRA447-1, p. ixi.

[38] Thompson William R. 2001. Identifying Rivals and Rivalries in World Politics. *International Studies Quarterly*, 45(4), pp. 557–586, p. 559.

[39] Hegel G.W. 1989 [1830]. *Hegel's Logic, Being Part One of the Encyclopaedia of Philosophical Sciences*. Translated by William Wallace with Foreword by J.N Findlay. Oxford, Oxford University Press, p. 11.

logical expression of HIS thought. Hegel concluded, all that is rational is real, all that is real is rational, the contradictions or imperfections of the world, as an expression of a logical God, were also logical and so knowable. The imperfect was perfect, and the perfect imperfect, including mathematical imperfections, which was logical if real, i.e. if they corresponded to the world or true, but illogical if perfect but unreal or untrue. Marx, the materialist, took Hegel's method but inverted it, the world created thought, hence the world created the laws of thought or logic, so to know the laws of thought it was necessary to know the necessarily lawful world. If a thought is real, i.e. in accord with the world, it is logical including if mathematically imperfect. Experience, or empirical science, was the highest criterion of human reason. The purpose of empirical study is to reveal the laws, the general propositions or theory, necessary to explain a phenomenon. Clausewitz's theory of war was simply one very effective application of this method.

In 1986 Senator Biden, of the U.S. Senate's Foreign Relations Committee, explained the U.S.' unflinching support for Israel was an expression of "naked self-interest of the U.S.". U.S. Israel policy was and remains, entirely of a piece with the U.S.' wider geopolitical strategy. In 2018, Robert P. Haffa Jr. a retired Air Force colonel and adjunct professor at Johns Hopkins University in Washington, DC, explained that with the return of Great Power struggles, in order to "strengthen credibility, the use of force may be necessary in some cases for deterrence to hold in other crises" as "potential aggressors may not be persuaded that the United States will readily respond with force when its interests are threatened" due to "past declaratory policy and practice of preferring diplomatic or economic instruments to the use of military force, or, even worse, backing away from a declared redline".[40] RAND concluded that proxy wars fought by client states would be a defining feature of contemporary major state rivalry. Israel's proxy war on the Palestinian population of Gaza in 2023/4, expresses the interests of the U.S. global order. Biden's administration bypassed Congress to approve an emergency arms package of nearly 14,000 tank cartridges and other items for an estimated

[40] Haffa Robert P. Jr. 2018. The Future of Conventional Deterrence: Strategies for Great Power Competition. *Strategic Studies Quarterly*, 12(4), pp. 94–115, pp. 102–103.

cost of $106.5 mn to support Israel's offensive[41] with a further $20bn in August 2024. By July 2024 overwhelmingly U.S. supplied bombs had damaged an estimated 215,137 housing units,[42] and killed an estimated 40,000 people including at least 10,000 children, the Lancet[43] observed that including indirect deaths and the unaccounted for could raise the total to around "186,000 or even more deaths".

A 2021 RAND *Stabilizing Great-Power Rivalries* report published in conjunction with the U.S. Department of Defense (DoD) concluded,

> The consensus of official U.S. government policy and most analysis outside government is that the international system is headed for a renewed era of intense and sometimes bitter competition among leading states, particularly between the United States and both Russia and China.[44]

Strategic state rivalry was the key driver of international conflict, beyond "a localized bilateral dispute" to include contestation over regional or global issues. Such rivalry required certain conditions; roughly comparable amounts of national power and influence, a perception of mutual hostility, the expectation of future competition and possibly conflict, contended national interests and some history of conflict. The report coyly noted "these characteristics clearly apply to the U.S.-Russia and U.S.-China relationships in 2019". It concluded that, as of 2019, the U.S./China rivalry was "trending toward instability and volatility" and that "the two countries are unavoidably locked in a deepening competition at the regional and global levels" while ritually observing that although "competition might be inevitable, but conflict need not be" unavoidably but not inevitably. *The Future of Warfare 2030* considered that the backdrop to the change of period were "the geopolitical trends shaping the strategic environment starting with those within the world's

[41] Palma Stefania 2023. *U.S. bypasses Congress to approve sale of tank shells to Israel.* London, Financial Times. https://www.ft.com/content/e7780881-8cde-4262-8a27-50433cc18114.

[42] UNitar 2024. UNOSAT Gaza Strip 8th Comprehensive Damage Assessment–July 2024. https://unosat.org/products/3904.

[43] Khatiba Rasha, McKee Martin and Yusuf Salim 2024. Counting the dead in Gaza: difficult but essential. *The Lancet*, 404(10,449), pp. 237–238.

[44] Mazarr Michael J., Charap Samuel, Casey Abigail, Chindea Irina A. and Curriden Christian Demus 2021. *Stabilizing Great-Power Rivalries. Santa Monica, Calif.* RAND. www.rand.org/t/RRA456-1.

remaining superpower, the United States".[45] To understand war, it is necessary to understand the social and political environment shaping the world.

Allison observed that in Thucydides account "the catastrophic outcome of their competition necessitated a new category of violent conflict: world war".[46] Allison rejected, as is typical of the contemporary American academic-military commentary, the inevitability of war, of social laws in general and of historical and military laws in particular. He substituted real theoretical understanding with a combination of empirical analysis of former conflicts and American exceptionalism or Manifest Destiny. John O'Sullivan's 1839 law of American *Manifest Destiny*[47] expresses the rationale of American foreign policy theorists if not their, largely absent, theories. O'Sullivan saw in the Westward March of the American people the God-Given advance of the America nation, capitalism and civilisation, proclaiming, "the far-reaching, the boundless future will be the era of American greatness". America,

> must onward to the fulfilment of our mission -- to the entire development of the principle of our organization -- freedom of conscience, freedom of person, freedom of trade and business pursuits, universality of freedom and equality. This is our high destiny, and in nature's eternal, inevitable decree of cause and effect we must accomplish it... Who, then, can doubt that our country is destined be the great nation of futurity?

As William J Bennett a contributor to the Project for a New American Century put it at the turn of the millennium,

> It has become something of a cliché to talk of American "exceptionalism," but there is no ignoring the fact that the American nation itself was founded in exceptional circumstances and on an exceptional statement

[45] Cohen Raphael S., Chandler Nathan, Efron Shira, Frederick Bryan, Han Eugeniu, Klein Kurt, Morgan Forrest E. Rhoades Ashley L. Shatz Howard J. and Shokh Yuliya 2020. *The Future of Warfare 2030; Project Overview and Conclusions.* Santa Monica California, RAND.
www.rand.org/t/RR2849z1, p. 17.

[46] Graham, Allison 2017. *Destined for War; Can America and China Escape Thucydides Trap.* New York, Houghton, Mifflin, Harcourt, p. 6.

[47] O'Sullivan John L. 1839. *A Divine Destiny for America.* Civics Online. http://www.civicsonline.org/library/formatted/texts/manifest_destiny.html.

of timeless principles. Put simply, the United States was the first nation ever to base its very sense of nationhood on a set of universal principles derived from natural rights, as enunciated in its Declaration of Independence.

Bennett elaborated,

> Behind our attempt to advance American ideals abroad has been the belief that basic rights are unalienable, universal, God given and therefore all people wherever, they may be, are deserving of them.[48]

Nadège Rolland for the National Bureau of Asian Research considered that,

> The Chinese leadership's critique of the existing international order reveals its unswerving objection to the values on which this order has been built. At stake is not only the predominant position of the U.S. in the current system but more importantly the potential erosion of fundamental human rights, freedom of thought and expression, and self-government around the world.[49]

While RAND explained,

> China wishes to enjoy the same exceptionalism that the United States applies to itself. When China's interests are best served by violating rules, it has acted unilaterally against the will of international organizations and other countries.[50]

Contemporary China and Russia threaten the Destiny of that now Great Nation. China's 2015 *Military Strategy* explained that "China's destiny is vitally interrelated with that of the world as a whole.... China will...pursue an independent foreign policy of peace and a national defense policy that is defensive in nature, oppose hegemonism and power politics in all forms,

[48] Bennett William J 2000. Morality, Character and American Foreign Policy. In: *Present Dangers; Crisis and Opportunity in American Foreign and Defense Policy*, pp. 269–273 Edited by Robert Kagan and William Kristol, New York, Encounter Books.

[49] Rolland Nadège 2020. *China's Vision for a New World Order*. Special Report (83), Washington DC, National Bureau of Asian Research (NBAR).

[50] Mazarr Michael J., Heath Timothy R. and Cevallos Astrid Stuth 2018. *China and the International Order*. Santa Monia, Calif, RAND. www.rand.org/t/RR2423, p. 30.

and will never seek hegemony or expansion…realizing the Chinese Dream of achieving the great rejuvenation of the Chinese nation".[51] President Trump's 2017 National Security Strategy (NSS) shrieked they "challenge American power, influence, and interests, attempting to erode American security and prosperity. They are determined to make economies less free and less fair, to grow their militaries, and to control information and to repress their societies and expand their influence".[52] The RAND report *China's Quest for Global Primacy* asserted that China intends to surpass the U.S. to become the "paramount regional power and the leading global power". It pursues "national rejuvenation" or the "China Dream" which while "typically infused with an often-abstruse political terminology … bear little resemblance to the orthodox Marxist doctrines of proletarian revolution". Even so this Dream cannot be countenanced,

> The consequences of Chinese success in strategic competition could be severe for the United States. Sitting astride the heart of the global economy, Beijing would be well situated to privilege its needs and those of its clients over those of the United States and its allies. This situation would likely entail a deleterious downgrading in the prospects for the United States. Poorly positioned to unseat China or easily reverse its own flagging fortunes, the United States could face dwindling economic prospects, international marginalization, and a diminishing ability to shape global affairs.[53]

It is Chinese Destiny no less than that of the U.S., to oppose the hegemony, expansion and power of any other rival nation, as Clausewitz observed, war seeks to disarm the enemy.

U.S. exceptionalism precludes equality in the international rules-based framework established to serve U.S. exceptionalism. Hence, Congress

[51] The State Council Information Office of the People's Republic of China 2015. *China's Military Strategy,* Beijing, Xinhua, https://english.www.gov.cn/archive/white_paper/2015/05/27/content_281475115610833.htm.

[52] White House 2017. *National Security Strategy of the United States*, Washington, D.C. White House, p. 25.

[53] Heath Timothy R., Grossman Derek and Clark Asha, 2021. *China's Quest for Global Primacy An Analysis of Chinese International and Defense Strategies to Outcompete the United States*. RAND Institute www.rand.org/t/RRA447-1, p. xvi.

complained of "China's continued disregard for the rules-based international order".[54] In 2018 Timothy Heath from RAND pondered the possibilities for competition or cooperation with China, emphasising China's modest ambitions.[55] This report was an outlier however, the *Strategic Futures Group of* the Direct of National Intelligence Council observed that the world faced increasing challenges to "International Economic Governance" the rules-based order of international institutions and conventions dominated by the U.S. Large developing economies led by China "could increasingly demand more influence over the direction of economically focused international organizations, altering standards and norms to reflect their economic interests, some of which may be incompatible with the interest of advanced economies".[56] The growth of China poses a challenge to the very definition of U.S. national interest. The rules-based order that it created, and which remains the source of its enormous wealth, the right to the private property that the U.S. nation, or state, or the owners of the U.S. state, demand. Trump's 2017 NSS concluded,

> Today, they are fielding military capabilities designed to deny America access in times of crisis and to contest our ability to operate freely in critical commercial zones during peacetime. In short, they are contesting our geopolitical advantages and trying to change the international order in their favor.[57]

The international rules-based is unequal. It serves U.S. interests and excludes China even while China engages "in proxy or other more-limited

[54] U.S.-China Economic and Security Review Commission 2023. *Report to Congress of the U.S.-China Economic and Security Review Commission*. One Hundred Eighteenth Congress, First Session, Washington, U.S. Government Publishing Office. www.USCC.gov, p. 20.

[55] Heath Timothy R. 2018. *China's Pursuit of Overseas Security*. Santa Monica, RAND. www.rand.org/t/RR2271.

[56] NIA (National Intelligence Council) 2021. *Global Trends; A More Contested World 2040*. The Strategic Futures Group National Intelligence Council, Washington DC, Office of the Director of National Intelligence.

[57] White House 2017. *National Security Strategy of the United States*, Washington, D.C., White House, p. 27.

conflicts to protect the interests of client states and demonstrate the superiority of Chinese power".[58] *The Future of Warfare 2030* identified a "Trend; China's rise. Who will Fight? China and its immediate neighbors. Where will the U.S. fight? Taiwan, South China Sea, Senkakus. When will the U.S. fight? If China's economy slows; potentially as Xi's tenure comes to a close. Why the U.S. will fight? Domestic pressure; expanding strategic periphery". It delineated other threats "upheaval in Europe" due to a "Revanchist Russia". The impact of China on its near neighbours, or as one interviewee explained, a Chinese takeover of Taiwan would be "game over for Japan",[59] provoking an "Asian reassessment" and finally "Islamic turmoil" in the Middle East. The Chinese (and to a lesser extent Russian) threat was exacerbated as "U.S. conventional overmatch is declining", the absolute superiority of American arms was becoming relative. The U.S. now lacked "the technological superiority it enjoyed during the immediate aftermath of the Persian Gulf War" meanwhile "the Chinese and (to a lesser extent) Russian militaries are becoming increasingly capable, space and cyber warfare". The 2022 RAND report *Designing a Shared U.S. China Future* acknowledged the absence of a vision of how the two rival powers could design a shared future,[60] rather the *Future of Warfare* observed that China's Belt and Road Initiative (BRI) would significantly expand Chinese economy and "control of natural resources and access to them have long been considered a potential cause of war"[61] although

[58] Heath Timothy R., Grossman Derek and Clark Asha, 2021. *China's Quest for Global Primacy An Analysis of Chinese International and Defense Strategies to Outcompete the United States*. RAND Institute www.rand.org/t/RRA447-1, p. xvi.

[59] Cohen Raphael S., Chandler Nathan, Efron Shira, Frederick Bryan, Han Eugeniu, Klein Kurt, Morgan Forrest E. Rhoades Ashley L. Shatz Howard J. and Shokh Yuliya 2020. *The Future of Warfare 2030; Project Overview and Conclusions*. RAND Santa Monica California.
www.rand.org/t/RR2849z1, p. 67, 18, 29.

[60] Kerrigan Amanda, Grek Lydia and Mazarrr Michael J. 2023. *The United States and China—Designing a Shared Future*. Santa Monica, RAND. www.rand.org/t/RRA2850-1.

[61] Cohen Raphael S., Chandler Nathan, Efron Shira, Frederick Bryan, Han Eugeniu, Klein Kurt, Morgan Forrest E. Rhoades Ashley L. Shatz Howard J. and Shokh Yuliya 2020. *The Future of Warfare 2030; Project Overview and Conclusions*. Santa Monica Calif. RAND.
www.rand.org/t/RR2849z1, p. 29, 53.

the possibility of war in the "2020s" existed the "chances of high-end conflict, although still not likely, will probably increase by 2030".

The 2022 RAND report *Understanding a New Era in State Competition* summarised earlier analysis, China represented a challenge to the U.S.'s geopolitical status and vital interests through its very existence, irrespective of its intentions or otherwise. Four key factors shaped this challenge; the overall environment, national power and competitiveness, the international position and finally; the shape of bilateral competition.[62] This was little more than a list, which when elaborated produced a longer list. The *New Era of Competition* developed a "general analysis of the nature of competition grounded in historical and theoretical analyses that aimed to identify consistent patterns within the larger complexity", to describe how periods of "zero-sum competition and warfare" alternated with periods when "states reined in their ambitions and cooperated to achieve a degree of collective security". The outcome of Great Power struggle was determined by another list, this time, five factors, overall productive capacity, domination of frontier technologies, discretionary spending power and resources, quality of national institutions and military resources and capabilities listed. The model sounds like the programme of the Biden administration but it contained an unresolved tension between the institutional framework of a given period and the economic foundation of that framework. The multitude of factors delineated to explain competition and cooperation are ruthlessly partisan, not a theory but a bullet point manifesto for sustained American domination, hence the relationship between the factors was not established, and could not be given the partisan nature of the U.S. academic-military establishment. There was no explanation for the more fundamental point, why Great Powers struggle at all. It is enough that in the Great Power struggle the U.S. must win.

This is still a crisis for capitalism, not a crisis of it. Crises of capitalism are social challenges to the system, the maintenance of the capitalist system itself. As Fukuyama shrewdly assessed with the collapse of the Soviet Union and transition of China to the market in the late 1980s,

[62] Mazarr Michael J. Frederick Bryan, Crane Yvonne K. 2022. *Understanding A New Era of Strategic Competition.*
Santa Monica California, RAND National Defense Research Institute, p. 1, 5.

would not confront, and still do not confront, the capitalists for the foreseeable future. Crises for capitalism, on the other hand, abound, crises for the world, the inhabitants of the earth and the non-capitalist population, are everywhere. Both crises are as inevitable as competition. And so is war, the continuation of capitalist competition by other violent means.

CHAPTER 2

China's Challenge to the West

> The bourgeoisie, by the rapid improvement of all instruments of production, by the immensely facilitated means of communication, draws all, even the most barbarian, nations into civilisation. The cheap prices of commodities are the heavy artillery with which it batters down all Chinese walls, with which it forces the barbarians' intensely obstinate hatred of foreigners to capitulate. It compels all nations, on pain of extinction, to adopt the bourgeois mode of production; it compels them to introduce what it calls civilisation into their midst, i.e. to become bourgeois themselves. In one word, it creates a world after its own image. Karl Marx *Communist Manifesto* 1848.[1]

Now cheap Chinese commodities batter down the walls of what America calls civilisation. In 2023 the Chinese car maker BYD overtook Tesla as the largest EV manufacturer in the world, while China overtook Japan as the largest car exporter in the world.[2] In 2018 Takero Kato, Toyota's

[1] Marx Karl and Engels Friedrich 1969 [1848]. *Selected Works Volume One.* Progress Publishers, Moscow, pp. 98–137.

[2] White Edward, Jung-a Song, Lewis Leo and Lin Andy 2023. *China set to overtake Japan as world's biggest car exporter.* London, Financial Times. https://www.ft.com/content/cdcb0d7e-3ec2-42bc-bfcc-9489290aa9ae.

W. Jefferies, *War and the World Economy*, Palgrave Insights into Apocalypse Economics,
https://doi.org/10.1007/978-3-031-85236-7_2

electric vehicle Head wrote of a visit to Chinese auto factories "laying eyes on equipment that I had never seen in Japan and their state-of-the-art manufacturing, I was struck by a sense of crisis" he recalled "we're in trouble!". Michael Dunne, CEO of Dunne Insights, said "no one can match BYD on price. Period... Boardrooms in America, Europe, Korea and Japan are in a state of shock". In the U.S. the Alliance for American Manufacturing considered "a flood of Chinese imports has devastated several of America's domestic industries in the past, notably undercutting American solar and steel manufacturers...It's the same formula for disaster that we're seeing play out with EV batteries". Dunne noted that the average price of a new car in the U.S. this year is about $48,000, "imagine [Chinese automakers] come in with a $20,000 product. The current tariff of 25% knocks it up to $25,000 or $26,000. They are still in a very good position".[3] Elon Musk warned investors that Chinese competitors " 'will pretty much demolish most other car companies in the world' unless trade barriers are put in place".[4]

In October 2023 the European Commission (EC) investigated alleged subsidies to Chinese Electric Vehicles (EV) imports. Europe's car industry accounts for between 7% to 8.5% of GDP and even though it is heavily reliant on imports of Chinese parts from European owned (but China based) subsidiaries and that in 2022 European investment in China's auto sector rose to €6.2bn,[5] in June 2024 the EC imposed tariffs of up to 48% on imports of Chinese EV.[6] EU imports of Chinese EV had risen from 2020 €1.6bn to 2023 €11.5 bn or a 19% market share. BYD makes around €14,300 in profit on each SEAL U model sold in the EU, compared to €1,300 on units sold in China. Only duties of between 45 and 55% could "render exports to the European market

[3] White Edward and Campbell Peter 2024. *China's electric vehicle dominance presents a challenge to the West.*
London, Financial Times. https://www.ft.com/content/de696ddb-2201-4830-848b-6301b64ad0e5.

[4] Hoskins Peter 2024. *Tesla: Electric carmaker's shares slide after Musk warns of slowdown.* BBC. https://www.bbc.co.uk/news/business-68102516.

[5] White Edward European carmakers play catch-up in China with record investment. Financial Times. https://www.ft.com/content/aa3472f2-c8d5-4a80-8a24-5b6b7c2fd7bc.

[6] Bounds Andy, Hancock Alice and Li Gloria 2024. *EU to hit Chinese electric cars with tariffs of up to 48%.* Financial Times. https://www.ft.com/content/0545ed62-c4b9-4e8a-80fa-c9f808e18385.

unappealing on commercial grounds".[7] The rapid shift of the world economy towards sustainable green energy, the prerequisite for avoiding catastrophic climate change,[8] is a problem for the West.

Jake Sullivan, Foreign Policy Advisor to President Biden, confirmed that while "nothing in world politics is inevitable", some things are nonetheless, definitively certain. The "post-Cold War era" from the collapse of the Soviet Union and the U.S. victory over Communism was "now definitively over". The shift of manufacturing abroad had lowered costs and raised profits while simultaneously weakening the U.S. and strengthening China. Consequently, geopolitical and security competition, with important economic aspects, now defined international relations. The climate crisis was an immediate reality, and income inequality had damaged U.S. democracy, but Sullivan was clear that the U.S. needed to "pick its battles" to end the war with Afghanistan; not to end war but to better support the war of Ukraine against Russia, of Israel against Hamas and to crucially prepare to fight for democracy against the authoritarianism of China. Public investment to support private initiative was to be the watchword of the Biden administration and should define the direction of U.S. strategic development from hereon in. Biden's presidency would restore the U.S. middle class, develop the industrial base, and create a secure and sustainable economy to confront China's military challenge. Above all the U.S. needed to develop its domestic material strength through onshoring, the creation of domestic resources to guarantee domestic stability, mitigating extremes of wealth and poverty to develop the social basis for a national struggle through the support of middle-class layers in well paid jobs, while offsetting the potential social dislocation of climate change to fend off Chinese competition. Sullivan explained that the "United States now finds itself at the start of the third era: one in which it is adjusting for a new period of competition in an age of interdependence and transnational challenges".[9]

[7] Sebastian Gregor, Barkin Noah and Kratz Agatha 2024. *Ain't No Duty High Enough*. Rhodium Group. https://rhg.com/research/aint-no-duty-high-enough/.

[8] Nijsse Femke J. M. M, Mercure Jean-Francois, Ameli Nadia, Larosa Francesca, Kothari Sumit, Rickman Jamie, Vercoulen Pim and Pollitt Hector 2023. The momentum of the solar energy transition. *Nature Communications*, 14(1), pp. 1–10.

[9] Sullivan Jake 2023 The Sources of American Power; A Foreign Policy for a Changed World. *Foreign Affairs*. November/December 2023, p. 20.

Sullivan described the trade tariffs begun by Trump but broadened and deepened by Biden as "protecting our foundational technologies with a small yard and high fence".[10] Yet the yard keeps extending and the fence rising. The Bank of England reported that between 1994 and 2017 the average global tariff rate fell from 8½% to 2½%, yet since mid-2018 that trend has reversed, as bilateral tariffs between the U.S. and China "have risen substantially".[11] The U.S.-China governments have enacted 15,000 trade limitations so that, Congress confirmed, five years after U.S. imposed tariffs targeting Chinese imports "the composition of bilateral trade has changed dramatically".[12] In 2023 Chinese exports to the U.S. in 2023 fell by 13.1% a greater decline than during the global financial crisis of 2008–09 or the start of the U.S.-China trade war in 2018–19.[13] Although the impact is mitigated as Chinese exports are re-rooted through countries like Vietnam[14] and Mexico,[15] the trade war had already lengthened "the distance between suppliers in China and customers in the United States".[16]

[10] Sullivan Jake 2023. *Remarks by National Security Advisor Jake Sullivan on Renewing American Economic Leadership at the Brookings Institute.* April 27, 2023. https://www.whitehouse.gov/briefing-room/speeches-remarks/2023/04/27/remarks-by-national-security-advisor-jake-sullivan-on-renewing-american-economic-leadership-at-the-brookings-institution/.

[11] Bank of England 2019. *In focus—Trade protectionism and the global outlook, Sect. 3 of the Monetary Policy Report.* London. Bank of England.
https://www.bankofengland.co.uk/monetary-policy-report/2019/november-2019/in-focus-trade-protectionism-and-the-global-outlook.

[12] USCC 2023. *Report to Congress of the U.S.-China Economic and Security Review Commission.* Washington DC, U.S. Government Publishing Office, p. 5.

[13] Siqi Ji 2024. *China's exports to U.S. endure steepest plunge in nearly 30 years.* South China Morning Post. https://www.scmp.com/news/china/article/3248292/chinas-exports-us-endure-steepest-plunge-nearly-30-years.

[14] U.S.-China Economic and Security Review Commission 2023. *Report to Congress of the U.S.-China Economic and Security Review Commission.* One Hundred Eighteenth Congress, First Session, Washington, U.S. Government Publishing Office. www.USCC.gov, p. 6.

[15] Jones Claire, Murray Christine, and Fray Keith 2024. *China circumvents U.S. tariffs by shipping more goods* via *Mexico.* London, Financial Times. https://www.ft.com/content/2ca4da83-f858-4215-88e7-544adf0aa18e.

[16] Qiu Han, Shin Hyun Song and Zhang Leanne Si Ying 2023. *Mapping the realignment of global value chains.* Bulletin 78 Bank of International Settlements (BIS), p. 5.

Trade barriers increase costs, slow turnover times and so the International Monetary Fund (IMF) worried "inequality could increase. Greater trade barriers lead to higher prices, which mean lower real wages".[17] It consoled itself that aggregates of trade to GDP had not yet fallen,[18] but a contrary effect of trade tariffs is to raise the price of traded goods, so trade aggregates may rise relative to the value added or GDP, even as the trade war deepens. As integrated production networks are disrupted and more expensive, re-shored domestic or alternative foreign production, replaces cheap Chinese imports, so rising inflation becomes an index of Western success in isolating China even as it lowers living standards and workers struggle to raise wages, will de-globalisation re-launch the class struggle?

The integration of China into the world economy has hollowed out America's industrial base so that the social partnership necessary to wage Great Power conflict had been eroded. The American Federation of Labour—Congress of Industrial Unions (AFL-CIO) reported President Biden's claim "I meant what I said when I said I'm going to be...the most pro-union president in American history. And I make no apologies for it".[19] Biden's love of the unions did not extend to rail workers he banned from striking over sick pay,[20] but the establishment of a revived middle class was at least part of the rhetoric that underpinned the 2022 Inflation Reduction Act (IRA) and CHIPS and Science Act. The IRA disbursed around $370bn to tackle dependence on carbon energy sources, to this extent environmental concerns dovetailing nicely with the need to combat Chinese sectoral dominance. It subsidised clean energy,

[17] IMF 2023, *Trade Disrupted. Finance and Development*, June 2023. New York, IMF. https://www.imf.org/-/media/Files/Publications/Fandd/Article/2023/June/FD0623.ashx, p. 9.

[18] IMF 2023, *Trade Disrupted. Finance and Development*, June 2023. New York, IMF. https://www.imf.org/-/media/Files/Publications/Fandd/Article/2023/June/FD0623.ashx.

[19] AFL-CIO 2023. President Biden: I'm 'the Most Pro-Union President In American History. And I Make No Apologies for It'. AFL-CIO.

https://aflcio.org/statements/icymi-president-biden-im-most-pro-union-president-american-history-and-i-make-no.

[20] Shepardson David and Bose Nandita 2022. Biden signs bill to block U.S. railroad strike. Reuters. https://www.reuters.com/world/us/biden-signs-bill-block-us-railroad-strike-2022-12-02/.

wind, solar, battery and electric vehicles (EV).[21] While the CHIPS and Science Act provided $52.7bn for semiconductor research, development, manufacturing and workforce development to bolster U.S. "leadership in semiconductors". It included $39bn in manufacturing incentives, $13.2bn in R&D and workforce development and $174bn for broader STEM research.[22] This doubled real manufacturing construction 2021–2023 and quadrupled investment in new chipmaking facilities, with over 50 new semiconductor ecosystem projects announced.[23] Meanwhile the European Commission announced €43bn of subsidies for semiconductor production.[24] Whether it is capable of a more widespread revival of U.S. industry remains to be seen. The narrow focus of the CHIPS Act falls far short of an industrial strategy, as industry groups lobbied for their own private interest, to grab subsidies, retain the option of producing in China and prevent the creation of a wider manufacturing revival.[25] That being said, the run up to both Great Wars saw rival powers reviving their domestic manufacturing to guarantee war production. In the last analysis economic interest determines both the necessity of war and the willingness of the competitors to wage it.

Marx considered that the economic base constitutes "the real foundation, on which arises a legal and political superstructure and to which correspond definite forms of social consciousness. The mode of production of material life conditions the general process of social, political and

[21] (IEA) International Energy Agency 2023. *Inflation Reduction Act of 2022*. Paris, IEA. https://www.iea.org/policies/16156-inflation-reduction-act-of-2022.

[22] White House, 2022, *Fact Sheet: CHIPS and Science Act Will Lower Costs, Create Jobs, Strengthen Supply Chains, and Counter China*. Washington DC, White House. https://www.whitehouse.gov/briefing-room/statements-releases/2022/08/09/fact-sheet-chips-and-science-act-will-lower-costs-create-jobs-strengthen-supply-chains-and-counter-china/.

[23] U.S. Department of the Treasury (DoT) 2023. *Unpacking the Boom in U.S. Construction of Manufacturing Facilities*. Washington DC, (DoT). https://home.treasury.gov/news/featured-stories/unpacking-the-boom-in-us-construction-of-manufacturing-facilities.

[24] European Commission 2022. *Digital sovereignty: Commission proposes Chips Act to confront semiconductor shortages and strengthen Europe's technological leadership*. Brussels, European Commission.

[25] Krein Julius 2022. *Where the Chips Fell*. Foreign Affairs. https://americanaffairsjournal.org/2022/08/where-the-chips-fell/.

intellectual life existence".[26] The economic foundation of society provides the key to explaining its anatomy and, as RAND noted, the means for conducting war "without a dominant economic base to support further military investments, it will become much more difficult for the United States to check the already existing trends of declining U.S. conventional military forces to counteract the military modernization and professionalization of near peers". Jeffrey Sachs, a Harvard and Columbia University Professor, who advised Communist governments on the transition to capitalism, and who now advises the United Nations on sustainability, complained that U.S. foreign policy is determined by a "a small, secretive and tight-knit coterie" of elected officials, secret services, the military and defence industries such that "the public interest plays little role". It is a "scam".[27] Sachs should know. The American people are no more asked to determine the foreign policy of the U.S. government, than the Soviet people were asked whether their economy should be destroyed by the small, secret tight-knit coterie of Western economists who devised the destruction of the plan. American foreign policy is only a scam when measured against the interest of the people, not the interest of the state, the national interest.

In the *Communist Manifesto* Marx noted that "the bourgeoisie has at last, since the establishment of Modern Industry and of the world market, conquered for itself, in the modern representative State, exclusive political sway. The executive of the modern state is but a committee for managing the common affairs of the whole bourgeoisie".[28] The national interest is the interest of the governing class. Frederich Engels, the German Communist philosopher, observed in the 1880s, that the will of the state is no independent factor but, in the last analysis, is determined "by the changing needs of civil society, by the supremacy of this or that class.... by the development of the productive forces and the relations

[26] Marx Karl 1977. *A Contribution to the Critique of Political Economy*, Moscow, Progress Publishers.

[27] Sachs Jeffrey D. 2023 U.S. Foreign Policy Is a Scam Built on Corruption. The Commons. www.commondreams.org/opinion/corruption-of-us-foreign-policy.

[28] Marx Karl and Engels Friedrich 1969 [1848]. *Selected Works Volume One*. Progress Publishers, Moscow, pp. 98–137.

of exchange".[29] The insights of the American academic-military establishment and the clique on behalf of which they strategise about U.S. foreign policy, are defined by their roles as actors for the U.S. state whose supremacy they seek to ensure.

That state is easily the richest nation on earth. In 2022 the U.S. had 22.7 mn millionaires or roughly 7% of its population or 38.2% of the world total of millionaires. U.S. income inequality is nonetheless profound, the bottom 50% of the population held 3% of wealth, the top 1% owned 34.2% and the top 0.1 owned 18.5%.[30] The richest 0.1% account for 19.8% of shares owned by households, the richest 1% own 44.6% while the poorest 50% own just 1%.[31] African Americans owned just 12.8% of white wealth and their poverty is exacerbated by cruel and active racist repression. Imprisonment rates are five times higher amongst African American men than whites, such that one third of the African American adult male population have a felony conviction.[32] The U.S. is a society for the rich and of the rich, if not by the rich. The U.S. "enters the contest" with China burdened by "domestic fiscal strains, domestic political polarization, and competing international and domestic priorities". These matter as "the most-critical factors that will determine the outcome of U.S.-China competition are fundamentally domestic. Which side can build the more technologically innovative and prosperous economy, flourishing and well-governed society, and durable and responsive politics will likely be the side to gain a decisive advantage in competition". In the last two decades China achieved the fastest median wealth growth of any region, with median wealth rising more than eight-fold from USD 3,155

[29] Engels Frederich, 1976 [1886]. *Ludwig Feuerbach and the End of Classical German Philosophy*. Peking, Foreign Languages Press, p. 51.

[30] UBS 2023. *Global Wealth Report, Leading perspectives to navigate the future*. Credit Suisse SG.

[31] Oxfam 2024. *Inequality Inc. How corporate power divides our world and the need for a new era of public action*. Oxford, Oxfam GB. https://www.oxfam.org/en/research/inequality-inc, p. 23.

[32] Shannon Sarah K. S., Uggen Christopher, Schnittker Jason, Thompson Melissa, Wakefield Sara and Massoglia Michael 2017. *The Growth, Scope, and Spatial Distribution of People With Felony Records in the United States, 1948–2010*. Demography, 54(5), pp. 1795–1818.

in 2000 to USD 30,696 in 2022, compared to Europe 4.3 and more than five in Africa, in the Asia-Pacific region and in the world as a whole.[33]

President Biden's 2022 *National Security Strategy* (NSS)[34] summarised the argument "the United States is strong abroad because we are strong at home. Our economy is dynamic. Our people are resilient and creative. Our military remains unmatched—and we will keep it that way". The People's Republic of China (PRC) "is the only competitor with both the intent to reshape the international order and, increasingly, the economic, diplomatic, military, and technological power to advance that objective".[35] The U.S. would invest in its democracy, its industrial strength and innovation, to develop its alliances and "modernize and strengthen its military". The publication of the 2022 U.S. NSS and National Defense Strategy (NDS)[36] which identified China as the "pacing challenge" facing the U.S., confirmed "the existence of a new era in defense planning". The U.S. focus on non-state extremist groups has been replaced by "an overriding emphasis on threats posed by near-peer major powers" this shift had been anticipated by the 2018 iterations of these documents but "it is now clear, especially in the wake of Russia's invasion of Ukraine, that the emphasis will persist".[37]

In 2022 RAND complained that the 2002 U.S. *National Security Strategy* of George W. Bush and Dick Cheney NSS had essentially declared "large-scale national rivalries to be a thing of the past". It claimed that the 2002 NSS had argued in the triumphalist vein that "we have our best chance since the rise of the nation-state in the seventeenth century to build a world where the great powers compete in peace

[33] UBS 2023. *Global Wealth Report, Leading perspectives to navigate the future.* Credit Suisse SG.

[34] CRS 2024. Great Power Competition: Implications for Defense—Issues for Congress R43838.Congressional Research Service. https://crsreports.congress.gov.

[35] Biden Joe 2022. *National Security Strategy.* The White House, Washington D.C., p. 8, 11.

[36] Department of Defense 2022. *National Defense Strategy of the USA.* Washington DC, Department of Defense.

[37] Mazarr Michael J. Frederick Bryan, Crane Yvonne K. 2022. *Understanding A New Era of Strategic Competition.*

Santa Monica California, RAND National Defense Research Institute.

instead of prepare for war".[38] The 2022 RAND text uses the royal "we" replacing the U.S. with "the International Community",[39] in the sense that the U.S. is the international community,[40] but the accusation of peace mongering is overdone. The 2002 NSS was published the year before the second Iraq war. U.S. dominance would be unchallenged and perpetual with democracy imposed at the point of a gun against the Axis of Evil.

Subsequent RAND reports traced the rise of China and its threat to the U.S. In 2012 RAND cautioned the U.S. Army that over the next 20 years, China's GDP and defence budget could exceed those of the U.S., making it a "true peer competitor". However, it consoled itself, China's focus on its "immediate periphery" and lack of interest "in matching U.S. military expenditures, achieving a comparable global reach, or assuming defense commitments beyond its immediate sphere" meant that although the direct defence of Taiwan has already become a challenge and was "likely to become increasingly difficult in coming years"[41] nonetheless "armed conflict between the United States and China is unlikely". Assuming of course that "the United States will retain the capacity to deter behavior that could lead to such a clash throughout this period". By 2017 the RAND still considered that naked large-scale Chinese aggression was "not indicated" however, there were "a range of potential flash points"[42] but "the United States will likely find itself forced to shift from deterrence by denial, based on direct defense of its interests and allies in the Western Pacific, to deterrence by punishment, based on the threat of escalation, using longer-range weapons and more survivable platforms". In 2018

[38] Bush, George 2002. *National Security Strategy (NSS)*. Washington D.C. The White House. https://georgewbush-whitehouse.archives.gov/nsc/nss/2002/nss8.html.

[39] Mazarr Michael J. Frederick Bryan, Crane Yvonne K. 2022. *Understanding A New Era of Strategic Competition.*

Santa Monica California, RAND National Defense Research Institute, p. 4.

[40] The use of 'we' instead of 'I' by a single person, as traditionally used by a sovereign. "I'm using the royal 'we' here as I actually did all of this myself".

[41] Gompert David C., Dobbins James, Shlapak David A.and Scobell Andrew 2012. *Conflict with China, Prospects, Consequences, and Strategies for Deterrence?* RAND W74V8H-06-C-0001; Santa Monica, California. Emphasis in the original, p. 3, 1.

[42] Dobbins James, Scobell Andrew, Burke Edmund J., Gompert David C., Grossman Derek, Heginbotham Eric and Shatz Howard J. 2017. *Conflict with China Revisited; Prospects, Consequences, and Strategies for Deterrence.* RAND Santa Monica, California.www.rand.org/t/PE248, p. 13, 10.

RAND remarked "China's expanding influence is not, however, dependent principally on its growing military prowess. Militarily, China can be contained for a while longer; economically, it has already broken free of any regional constraints". By 2020 the challenge of "near-peer competition" to confer "geopolitical advantage" meant the U.S. and allies must "run faster" and seek to ensure its competitors must "run more slowly" including rejecting "hypocritical disarmament proposals, policies, and agreements that threaten the current rules-based international order".[43]

China's accession to the WTO in 2001 was the completion of its transition to the market. The boom that ensued, the hyper-globalisation of 2001–2008, enabled China's rise outside of the domination of Western finance and this explains the shift in contemporary world geopolitics. U.S. power no longer rests on competitive advantage, manufacturing and trade dominance, but on the rules-based framework it imposed on the world after the Second World War, and which was revived in the 1990s. From around 2020 the growth of China has re-established a multi-polar world whether it intended to or not. It is an objective, not a subjective, factor. It cannot be wished away.

However, that did not stop the Western commentariat from trying. In 2017 *Foreign Affairs*, a journal of the U.S. international establishment, held a poll of experts asking Will Globalisation End?[44] Of the thirty assorted economists, business leaders, and international relations experts only two agreed, only one strongly. Martin Wolf, the *Financial Times* economics commentator, disagreed too. By 2023 he had changed his tune, albeit he consoled himself that in its economic rivalry with China the U.S. retained its advantage. He summarised a report from Capital Economics on the fragmentation of the world economy into rival trade blocks. The U.S. and its allies Canada, Europe (except Hungary), Japan, Australia and New Zealand were contrasted with China, Russia, Iran and Pakistan. The China bloc accounted for half of the world's (non-Antarctic) land mass and 46% of its people, against the U.S. bloc's 35% and 43%. The China bloc produced 27% of world GDP, 38% of industrial

[43] Ford Christopher A. 2020. *Arms Control and International Security vis-a-vis China and Russia: A View from the "T Suite"*. Competitive Strategy Papers. I(61) Washington D.C., Department of State.

[44] Foreign Affairs 2017. *Will Economic Globalization End? Foreign Affairs Asks the Experts.* https://www.foreignaffairs.com/ask-the-experts/2017-06-12/will-economic-globalization-end.

output and 49% of agricultural production against the U.S. bloc's GDP 67%, industrial output 55% and agricultural production 38%.

In 2022 144 countries traded more goods with China than with the U.S. The U.S. was the bigger trading partner for only 60 countries, even while half of global goods trade was amongst the U.S. bloc. The U.S. bloc dominated financial activities and capital flows with 84% total FDI stock by investor country and 87% by recipient in 2022 and 86% of global portfolio investment compared to only 2% within the China bloc.[45] Derek Scissors for the American Enterprise Institute (AEI) summarised the hopes of these denialist commentators for a slow down or collapse of the Chinese economy. An event which is, paradoxically, considered to increase the war threat.[46] Scissors considered the ageing of the Chinese population, debt levels, land nationalisation and its export dependence, as explanations for the decline in China's rate of growth. Certainly, China will slow from the early globalisation peaks, but this is largely a statistical function of growth.

The Global Power Index (GPI) of the Jonathan Moyer and Alanna Markle of the University of Denver is an algorithmic assessment of material power categories such as GDP, military spending, population, trade, and research and development (R&D) spending they concluded "history and theory offer a clear and consistent message that a country's basic economic productive output is the essential basis of its competitive strength—and the most common measure of such output is GDP".[47] More precisely, the national economic power is based on industrial production in general and manufacturing in particular. In 2021 China manufactured 35% of gross world manufactures and 29% of manufacturing value added more than the next 10 highest nations combined.[48] This understates the value of China's manufactures, when they are landed

[45] Wolf Martin 2023. *The U.S. retains the economic advantage in its rivalry with China*. Financial Times https://www.ft.com/content/28f0f57a-df50-442c-9f8e-75672d012742.

[46] Brands Hal and Beckley Michael 2021. *China Is a Declining Power—and that's the Problem*. Foreign Affairs. https://foreignpolicy.com/2021/09/24/china-great-power-united-states/.

[47] Moyer Jonathan D. and Markle Alanna, 2018. *Relative National Power (Power) Codebook*, Frederick Pardee Center for International Futures, University of Denver, p. 14.

[48] Baldwin Richard 2024. *China is the world's sole manufacturing superpower: A line sketch of the rise*. https://cepr.org/voxeu/columns/china-worlds-sole-manufacturing-superpower-line-sketch-rise.

at U.S. ports they have one price, but when they are sold, they have a much higher retail price, with the difference attributed to U.S. GDP.

The brazenly pro-American Hamilton Index provided a measure of the relative strength of national production in selected key hi-tech industries. These range from information technology and services, to machinery, and processed and basic metals. In 2020 China dominated the index producing a quarter of world output, a larger amount than the total of all producers outside the top 10. China's output of these strategically advanced industries "skyrocketed" after its accession to the World Trade Organisation (WTO) in 2001, increasing from 6 to 25%. China's growth mirrored the decline of the G7 nations which dropped by 27.9% while China increased by 21.9%. In 2020 China was the leading producer in seven of the ten strategically important industries. The Index authors warned,

> for the United States, losing this race, either because policymakers are indifferent to the country's industrial structure or because they choose to focus on other economic or societal goals, would be catastrophic, as it would turn the United States into a deindustrialized, United Kingdom-like economy. Time is short.[49]

According to Nicolas Chaillan, the Pentagon's first chief software officer, it is already too late. Chillian explained in his resignation letter to the Department of Defense, "we have no competing fighting chance against China in 15 to 20 years. Right now, it's already a done deal; it is already over in my opinion", adding that there was "good reason to be angry".[50] The Department of Defense (DoD) DoD's *Industrial Capabilities Report* 2021, after describing at length how U.S. firms are uncompetitive against their Chinese rivals disagreed concluding that American industry still leads the world in innovation and production. Supply chain challenges will be best met with a "market-based approach" that will "outpace adversaries' reliance on state-directed command-and-control for their

[49] Atkinson Robert D. and Tufts Ian 2023. *The Hamilton Index, 2023: China Is Running Away With Strategic Industries.* Hamilton Center on Industrial Strategy, Information Technology and Innovation Foundation (ITIF) itif.org, p. 4.

[50] Mason, Katrina 2021. "U.S. Has Already Lost AI Fight to China," Financial Times, https://www.ft.com/content/f939db9a-40af-4bd1-b67d-10492535f8e0.

innovation and production capacity over the long run".[51] Recent history suggests otherwise.

In GDP Purchasing Power Parity (PPP) terms China surpassed the U.S. in 2012, but at Market Exchange Rates (MER) it has somewhat further to go, as the U.S. $ has increased since Covid-19 due to the expansion of its oil and gas exports. Accordingly, China it is claimed, will not surpass the U.S. for "some time, if ever".[52] The figures mask the trend. The U.S. is a shadow of its former self. Like the United Kingdom at the end of the long nineteenth century, its empire no longer corresponds to the economic power which created it. U.S. wealth rests not on its competitive advantage, the efficiency and dynamism of its industry, but its empire, its ability to extract profits from across the world, to feed its billionaires. Between 2020–2023 the richest five men doubled their fortunes, while 60% of humanity grew poorer.[53] That order was originally created after the Second World War as the U.S. emerged its winner, with Germany crushed, Japan nuked, the British Empire on its knees, and the USSR and satellites, a military, but not economic, rival to it. The end of the Cold War and collapse of the centrally planned economies in the late 1980s combined with the transition of China to the market meant U.S. dominance was re-established in the 1990s. A truly global market was created perhaps for the first time. The boundless character of capitalist expansion since then, oblivious to all social or natural barriers, apparently without an alternative, explains contemporary environmental and social crises. The exhaustion and degradation of the natural world, the threat of irreversible climate change rendering the world uninhabitable, social oppression and racism, extreme income inequality, tech and trade wars, and the recreation of military rivalry, the daily conflicts of Great Power proxies and their agents, as well as the growing potential for a direct clash between them, define the world today. The crises of the contemporary world are as inevitable as the gruesome end they prepare.

[51] Department of Defense (DoD) 2023. *Fiscal Year 2021 Industrial Capabilities Report to Congress*. OASD Industrial Base Policy, Washington D. C., DoD., p. 80.

[52] Mazarr Michael J. Frederick Bryan, Crane Yvonne K. 2022. *Understanding A New Era of Strategic Competition*. Santa Monica California, RAND National Defense Research Institute, p. 5.

[53] Oxfam 2024. *Inequality Inc. How corporate power divides our world and the need for a new era of public action*. Oxford, Oxfam GB. https://www.oxfam.org/en/research/inequality-inc, p. 8.

CHAPTER 3

The Collapse of the Centrally Planned Economies and the Expansion of Capitalism

> "The system of centralist planning that in essentials has now been in effect in the USSR over six decades. There is no indication now of its prospective demise". Abram Bergson, the leading U.S. Sovietologist, 1983.[1]

In 1980 a team of CIA Sovietologists, under the direction of Abram Bergson, met at Airlie House Virginia to assess the prospects for the Soviet economy until the new millennium. Bergson was the CIA's foremost Soviet Union (USSR) economics expert.[2] The Sovietologists sagely concluded that unless the USSR was involved in a major war there were no existential threats to its economic progress and that even their worst-case scenario "does not portray a Soviet economy verging on collapse".[3]

[1] Bond Daniel L. and Levine Herbert S. 1983. An Overview, pp. 34–79 in *The Soviet Economy: Toward the Year 2000*, edited by Bergson Abram and Levine Herbert S., London, George Allen and Unwin, p. 21.

[2] Bergson Abram 1961. *The Real National Income of Russia since 1928*. Cambridge, MA: Harvard University Press.

[3] Bergson Abram 1983. Technological Progress, pp. 34–79 in *The Soviet Economy: Toward the Year 2000*, edited by Bergson Abram and Levine Herbert S., London, George Allen and Unwin, p. 65.

W. Jefferies, *War and the World Economy*, Palgrave Insights into Apocalypse Economics,
https://doi.org/10.1007/978-3-031-85236-7_3

In 2000, nine years after Boris Yeltsin the President of the Russian Federation criminalised Soviet Union Communist Party membership, the Soviet economy had utterly collapsed. Yeltsin's 1992 Big Bang shock therapy, the complete and immediate introduction of totally unregulated market prices everywhere, destroyed the centrally planned economy. Output fell by around two-thirds, around twice as deep as in the U.S. after the 1929 Wall Street Crash and subsequent 1930s Great Depression. Working-class living standards fell even faster than output. In 1998 the World Health Organization commented,

> There has been a dramatic rise in mortality, which is both unprecedented in a twentieth century industrial nation and exceptionally costly in human terms. Since 1990 Russian male life expectancy at birth has declined by seven years and in 1994 was 57.3, on a par with Pakistan.[4]

By the end of 1991 all of the planned economies of Central and Eastern Europe (CEE) and the Former Soviet Union (FSU) had adopted a price liberalisation and privatisation or "stabilisation" programmes to varying degrees. Yugoslavia broke up after the 1988 "stabilisation programme" saw inflation reach 1200%. In 1987 in Eastern Europe and the USSR 2.2 mn people lived on less than US$1 a day by 1993 that had risen to 14.5 mn. Excess deaths across the restoration period were in the region of 12 million.[5] Not for the first time did capitalism come into the world dripping in blood.

The tiny coterie of free market economists who advised the governments of the Former Soviet Union (FSU) and Central and Eastern Europe (CEE) on the restoration of the free market, estimated the welfare benefits that would accrue to an expectant people with the introduction of capitalism. They insisted that "price liberalization and the dismantling of central coordination can be accomplished overnight".[6] The IMF drily commented "ideally, a path of gradual reform could be laid out which

[4] World Health Organization. 1998. *Health Care Systems in Transition: Russian Federation*. Copenhagen: WHO Regional Office for Europe.

[5] Cockshott Paul 2020. *How the World Works: The Story of Human Labor from Prehistory to the Modern Day*. New York: Monthly Review Press.

[6] Dhanji Farid 1991. Transformation programs: Content and sequencing source. Papers and proceedings of the Hundred and Third Annual Meeting of the American Economic Association. *American Economic Review* 81 (2): 323–28, p. 323.

would minimize economic disturbance and lead to an early harvesting of the fruits of increased economic efficiency. But we know of no such path".[7] David Lipton of the IMF and Jeffrey Sachs from Harvard University were the architects of Poland's big-bang transition to the market. Stanley Fischer was the World Bank chief economist, while János Kornai was a Hungarian economist who worked at Harvard from the late 1980s. They insisted that the collapse of communist rule was the "sine qua non for an effective transition to a market economy".[8] Excess demand, excess popular consumption, should be ended at a stroke. The welfare of the people would be increased through a reduction in their consumption to that consistent with free market provision, combined with an austerity programme to rid them of the burden of state funded nurseries, health care, educational establishments and state investment in infrastructure and research and development. The people would be better off by being poorer. The promotion of market competition, the deregulation of prices, free trade, full liberalisation of the private sector and the demonopolisation of the public sector would cure the people of their dependence on the state.

Sweder van Winbergen on behalf of the World Bank insisted that microeconomic and macroeconomic case against price controls was "unassailable",[9] so "decontrol immediately", the total abandonment of the central plan, was "necessary and desirable". The Nobel Laureate Ronald Coase and his Nobel winning theorem, that public goods should never be provided by the state in a system of perfect competition, required that all traces of one-party communist rule would be "wiped out first". As a market economy could be constructed "only if the traces of socialism were thoroughly erased".[10] In 1994 Anders Åslund, who collaborated with Lipton and Sachs as an adviser to the Yeltsin government, argued that government should not deliver public goods, but enable the market

[7] IMF. 1990. *The Economy of the USSR: Summary and Recommendations*. New York: International Monetary Fund, p. 2.

[8] Lipton David, Sachs Jeffery, Fischer Stanley and Kornai Janos 1990. Creating a Market Economy in Eastern Europe: The Case of Poland. *Brookings Papers on Economic Activity* 1, pp. 75–147, p. 100.

[9] Wijnbergen Sweder van. 1991. Should price reform proceed gradually or in a "big bang"? *World Bank Working Paper Series* no. 0702, p. 1, 27.

[10] Coase Ronald and Wang Ning 2012. *How China Became Capitalist*. New York: Palgrave Macmillan, p. 154/155.

to do so, and as soon as possible.[11] In 1999 Åslund commented on the failure of the programme of immediate privatisation and concluded "the financial collapse made it obvious that Russia's problems were actually caused by reforms that were too slow and partial".[12] The immediate introduction of a universal and unlimited free market was too slow and partial. Nothing was enough for this clique. The promised welfare benefits were a scam.

This collapse of the central plan was the creation of a market economy, the production of commodities for sale. As national income is a measure of market prices so the collapse of the plan was the creation of national income an absolute addition to it. The clique of academic, IMF and World Bank economists who advised the former Communist governments understood the distinction between the despised planned production and market production, but no such distinction existed in the theory of neoclassical economics. Their subjective prejudice was an objective reflection of the subjective basis of marginal economics as propounded by William Stanley Jevons[13] and co. Hence, the collapse of planned production was measured as the collapse of value production. The expansion of the market was measured as its contraction.

United Germany increased capitalist Germany's population by 29% or 18.4 mn to 81.1 mn and its land mass by 44%. After unification there were significant subventions from the German government totalling around €2,000bn by 2007 or around €100bn/year,[14] but this was nothing compared with the assets gained. The United Germany inherited whole cities, Leipzig, Halle, Dresden and Berlin without cost. The United German government established the Treuhand to oversee the privatisation of East Germany, 95% of East German production units were given away.[15] Mass closures reduced East German industrial employment from 1988 3.5 mn to 1992 1.6 mn but, after restructuring, by 2022 its capital

[11] Åslund Anders 1994. The case for radical reform. *Journal of Democracy* 5(4), pp. 63–74.

[12] Åslund Anders 1999. Russia's Collapse. *Foreign Affairs*, 78(5), pp. 64–77.

[13] Jevons William 1871. *The Theory of Political Economy*. London, Macmillan.

[14] Boyes R 2007. *Germany Starts Recovery from €2,000bn Union*. Times Online. www.timesonline.co.uk/tol/news/world/europe/article2317382.

[15] Dornbusch R., and Wolf H., 1994. East German Economic Reconstruction. In O.J. Blanchard, K.A. Froot, & J.D. Sachs, eds. *The Transition in Eastern Europe*. Chicago, University of Chicago Press, pp. 155–90.

stock per worker exceeded that of the West.[16] The influx of skilled East German workers drove down wage costs, allowed German manufacturing to take advantage of cheap centrally planned infrastructure, and the East Germany's links to Central and Eastern Europe (CEE) provided a conduit for its expansion there.[17] The integration of East Germany into the united Germany meant a one-off increase in West German GDP of around 16%, an expansion of German national income by any definition except the official national income statistics. They measured the creation of the market as its collapse. As East German planned production collapsed, this was measured as a decline of national income. The statistics inverted the actual process of the creation of capitalist production.[18]

Angus Maddison, the noted neo-classical economic historian and custodian of the Groningen Growth and Development Centre (GGDC), drew up estimates of world national income covering the last 2000 years. Maddison attributed market values to physical quantities of output produced, irrespective of whether this output had a market price, was exchanged or sold. It was a fictional, albeit counter-factual method, so as with the Ancient Egyptians, Greek slavery and feudalism, so with the central plan. Maddison followed Abram Bergson "the founder of the CIA's building block method for estimating Soviet national income to... create a counter factual estimate of what Soviet prices would have been if the economy were run on capitalist lines, removing the 'distortions' created by the command economy, and getting a better picture of the real cost of production".[19] From the point of view of neo-classical economics

[16] Enenkel Kathrin and Rösel Felix 2022. *German Reunification Lessons from the German approach to closing regional economic divides*. Resolution Foundation. https://economy2030.resolutionfoundation.org/wp-content/uploads/2022/12/German-reunification.pdf.

[17] Jovanovic Branimir and Hanzl-Weiss Doris 2022. *Economic and Social Impacts of FDI in Central,*

East and Southeast Europe. The Vienna Institute for International Economic Studies, Research Report 464. https://wiiw.ac.at/economic-and-social-impacts-of-fdi-in-central-east-and-southeast-europe-dlp-6407.pdf.

[18] Jefferies William 2015. On the Alleged Stagnation of Capitalism. *Review of Radical Political Economics*, 47(4), pp. 588–607.

[19] Maddison Angus 1998. Measuring the performance of a communist command economy. An assessment of the CIA estimates for the USSR. *Review of Income and Wealth* (March), pp. 327–323, p. 311.

the entire period of central planning was a distortion from market prices, as was the entire history of humanity prior to the market economy.

The World Bank's Historically Planned Economies (HPEs) noted that, "HPEs have no economy wide 'markets' for most goods or services", but nonetheless "...the equivalent of 'market prices' in the SNA is 'established prices' in the MPS, which include net indirect taxes by sector".[20] The equivalence of market and non-market prices was established by ignoring their non-equivalence. The OECD in partnership with the CIS Statistical Committee[21] developed production, distribution, use of income, and capital accounts for the USSR for the last three years of the centrally planned economy 1988, 1989, 1990. They redefined the categories of the Soviet Material Product System (MPS) as if they were the categories of a market economy and so failed to measure the actual growth of market production within the plan. They concealed the process they sought to reveal.

The World Bank and Goskomstat[22] used the change in physical non-market indicators to construct an index of GDP at market prices for the central plan in 1990, that is, before there were any market prices. Their revised estimates for GDP at constant prices for 1991–1994 used either physical volume indicators or production or employment data for each economic activity to extrapolate the base year. According to their estimates GDP in constant prices declined by about 35% between 1990 and 1994, less than the former official estimate of about 47%. These estimates conflated non-capitalist and capitalist production, physical output with national income and so confused the decline of the physical output of the plan with the creation of the market. There was no national income in the USSR. It could not decline if it did not exist.

This new period of capitalist development, aptly named globalisation, was the creation of a global market for perhaps the first time. Whole cities, Moscow, St Petersburg, Prague, Berlin, Warsaw, Budapest and Bucharest,

[20] Marer Paul, Arvay Janos, O'Connor John, Schrenk Martin and Swanson Daniel 1992. *Historically Planned Economies: A Guide to the Data (English)*. Washington DC, World Bank Group. http://documents.worldbank.org/curated/en/754031468765028613/Historically-planned-economies-a-guide-to-the-data, p. 14.

[21] OECD 1993. *National Accounts for the Former Soviet Union*. Paris, OECD.

[22] World Bank ECA Country Department III and Goskomstat of the RFSSC 1995. *Russian Federation: Report on the National Accounts*. Washington, DC. World Bank, p. 92.

whole countries indeed, were privatised, handed over to capital, for nothing or next to nothing. The USSR had 147,400 km of railways with; 53,900 km electrified, not including industrial lines, 1,757,000 km of highways, 1,310,600 km hard-surfaced (asphalt, concrete, stone block, asphalt treated, gravel, crushed stone); 446,400 km earth, 123,700 km inland waterways navigable, exclusive of the Caspian Sea, 82,000 km of pipelines for crude oil and refined products; 206,500 km pipelines for natural gas, and major ports in; St. Petersburg (formerly Leningrad), Riga, Tallinn, Kaliningrad, Liepaja, Ventspils, Murmansk, Arkhangel'sk, Odessa, Novorossiysk, Il'ichevsk, Nikolayev, Sevastopol', Vladivostok, Nakhodka; inland ports are Astrakhan', Baku, Nizhniy Novgorod (Gor'kiy), Kazan', Khabarovsk, Krasnoyarsk, Kuybyshev, Moscow, Rostov, Volgograd, Kiev.[23] The countries of Central and Eastern Europe had around 150,000 km of railways in 1991 (capitalism had destroyed around half by 1998).[24]

World capitalist aluminium production increased by 60.3%; hydraulic cement, 96%; steel, 56%; electricity, 61%; automobiles, 27%. By 2001, when the process of capitalist restoration was complete, the transition economies accounted for 37% of world capitalist employment, 31% of its aluminium, 44% of its hydraulic cement, 24% of steel, 16% of electricity, 8.5% of cars and passenger vehicles and 17% of GDP (PPP). The official agencies underestimated the growth of the Chinese economy during the transition from central planning to capitalism by 20%. They underestimated the growth of the market economies in CEE and the CIS by more than $2.1 trillion (GDP PPP). They underestimated world growth in the 1990s by half.

The U.S. System of National Accounts (SNA) developed by Kuznets in 1931 were eventually generalised by Richard Stone on behalf of the League of Nations and United Nations in 1948. They were used to measure the value of capitalist production, but originated in the early Soviet application of Marx's schemes of reproduction in *Capital II* to post-revolutionary Russia. In the 1920s, during the New Economic Policy (NEP) period of a state managed commodity economy, Soviet economists

[23] CIA 1991. *Soviet Union Communications—1991.* Central Intelligence Agency. https://theodora.com/wfb1991/soviet_union/soviet_union_communications.html. SOURCE: 1991 CIA WORLD FACTBOOK.

[24] ECM 2001. What Role For the Railways in Eastern Europe? European Conference of Ministers. Round table 120. OECD.

addressed, and in large part invented, measures of commodity production. In 1923/4 P. I. Popov and L. N. Litoshenko produced the first state commissioned *Balance* of national income.[25] Wassily Leontief, a graduate of Leningrad University, who worked on the *Balance* before his exile to the U.S. in 1931,[26] explained that the *Balance* "provides a possibility of comparing the economic weight of all the areas of production with one another" for the "total amount of goods" in "a commodity economy".[27]

Simon Kuznets, the founder of the SNA, was a Soviet exile and former member, like Plekhanov, Lenin and Trotsky, of the Russian Social and Democratic Labour Party (RSDLP). Kuznets never shook off, by his own admission, the influence of Georgi Plekhanov, the founder of Russian Marxism, even years later. Kuznets' intimate knowledge of Marx's political economy, including no doubt the Legal Marxist S.N. Prokopovich's[28] original 1913 estimate of Russian national income, meant he was uniquely placed to apply Marxism without Marx to the measurement of U.S. national income. Upon his arrival in the U.S., in the early 1920s, Kuznets was employed by the U.S. National Bureau for Economic Research (NBER) to translate Soviet economic texts into English. These texts would have presumably included the Soviet Balance of 1923/24, as well as the original versions of input–output matrices developed in the USSR. Wassily Leontief was exiled to the U.S. in 1931, after completing his PhD on the circulation of commodities in Germany where he developed the original input–output measures of the U.S.[29] Kuznets recommended Leontief be employed at the NBER on his arrival in the U.S. in 1931 and worked on his national income monograph during Leontief's visit

[25] Spulber Nicolas 1965. *Foundations of Soviet strategy for economic growth: Selected Soviet essays, 1924–1930*. Bloomington: Indiana University Press.

[26] Hagemann H 2022. Wassily Leontief and his German period. In *Russian and Western Economic Thought: Mutual Influences and Transfer of Ideas*, pp. 363–388. Cham, Springer International Publishing.

[27] Leontief Wassily 1964. The Balance of the Economy of the USSR: A methodological analysis of the work of the central statistical administration. *Foundations of Soviet Strategy for Economic Growth: Selected Soviet Essays, 1924–1930*, pp. 88–94. Bloomington: Indiana University Press, pp. 91–92.

[28] Falkus M. E. 1968. Russia's National Income, 1913: A Revaluation. *Economica*, 35(137), pp. 52–73.

[29] Leontief Wassily 1951. Str*ucture of American economy, 1919–1939, second ed.* New York, Oxford University Press.

to the NBER in 1932.[30] Leontief neglected to mention his own role in developing the *Balance* from Marx's *Capital II*, but rather attributed the development of the circular flow of commodities to Marx's inspiration, François Quesnay's Physiocratic *Tableau Économique*.[31] Kuznets' definition of national income would have similarly been familiar to Marx,

> If all the commodities produced and all the direct services rendered during the year are added at their market value, and from the resulting total we subtract the value of that part of the nation's stock of goods that was expended (both as raw materials and as capital equipment) in producing this total, then the remainder constitutes the net product of the national economy during the year. It is referred to as national income produced, and may be defined briefly as that part of the economy's end product that results from the efforts of the individuals who comprise a nation.[32]

Kuznets followed Marx's *Capital* and the Soviet *Balance* in defining newly produced value added in income terms as the sum of wages, profits and rent; in product terms as the sum of consumer goods and net investment goods; and as gross value added the sum of wages, profits, rent and capital replacement. Paul Studenski's classic history of the national accounts explained "national income is an expression, in monetary terms of the current achievements of the national economy"; it is strictly separated by the market boundary from non-economic production that "does not possess economic value".[33] Marx noted that replacement of capital is never a part of income, but always flows back into the economic system in the form of capital.[34] The "value of the product" was equivalent to the "Gross National Product" (GNP), which included duplicated values of raw materials and supplies and the replacement of used up capital; while net value, what Marx called the "gross income of society",

[30] Bjerkholt Olav 2016. Wassily Leontief and the discovery of the input–output approach. *University of Oslo, Department of Economics* Memorandum, 18/2016.

[31] Schachter Gustav 1991. Francois Quesnay: Interpreters and Critics Revisited. *The American Journal of Economics and Sociology*, 50(3), pp. 313–322.

[32] Kuznets Simon 1934. *National Income, 1929–1932*. New York. NBER. http://www.nber.org/books/kuzn34-1.

[33] Studenski P. 1958. *The income of nations: Theory, measurement, and analysis: Past and present*. New York, New York University Press, p. 163.

[34] Studenski P. 1958. *The income of nations: Theory, measurement, and analysis: Past and present*. New York, New York University Press, p. 23.

consisted of "wages, profit (including interest), and rent" or "net national income".[35,36]

In the USSR the NEP period of a state supervised commodity economy, ended with the introduction of the five-year plans in 1928. N. Osinskii, in the 1931 *Materialy,* developed a measure of the material output of the centrally planned economy in its first phase from 1928 to 1930.[37] The application of value measures to a non-commodity economy was controversial but (after Stalin physically liquidated (murdered) the Idealists around II Rubin) from the late 1920s on, the category of national income was extended to the physical output of use values in the now centrally planned economy. The *Materialy* explained that the "crucial distinguishing feature of our expanded reproduction in comparison with capitalist reproduction is that it is not the reproduction of capital but the reproduction of use-values". There was no exchange, so no commodity production and no market prices, nonetheless the *Materialy* asserted that "national income may be taken to be the sum of labor expended by society in production in the given year".[38] Planners developed a *post factum* measure of "national income" to distinguish the contribution of living labour to annual physical production.[39] They could not match physical transactions with a financial equivalent,[40] but by aggregating concrete labour hours a subjective estimate of "national income" could be produced. This was national income without national incomes. It

[35] Marx Karl 1981. *Capital a Critique of Political Economy Volume III.* London, Penguin Classics.

[36] Studenski P. 1958. *The income of nations: Theory, measurement, and analysis: Past and present.* New York, New York University Press.

[37] Davies R., Wheatcroft S. and Harrison M. 1994. The crooked mirror of Soviet statistics. In *The economic transformation of the Soviet Union 1913–45*, ed. Wheatcroft S. G., Davies R. W. Cambridge: Cambridge University Press, p. 28.

[38] Pervukhin A. 1985. Methodological questions concerning the Balance of the National Economy. In *Materials for a Balance of the Soviet national economy 1928–30*, ed. Wheatcroft S. G., Davies R. W., 100–124. Cambridge: Cambridge University Press, p. 106.

[39] Wheatcroft, S. G., Davies, R. W. and Stone, Richard 1985. *Materials for a Balance of the Soviet National Economy 1928–30*, ed. Wheatcroft S. G., Davies R. W. Cambridge: Cambridge University Press, p. 44.

[40] Gregory P. R. 2004. *The political economy of Stalinism: Evidence from the Soviet archives.* Cambridge: Cambridge University Press, p. 241.

prefigured the Western subjective measurements of the centrally planned economy, ironically based on the same subjective figures.

During the Second World War U.S. military and diplomatic authorities required independent estimates of Soviet output, to determine the USSR's military capacity, ability to resist the Nazi invasion and entitlement to reparations at the wars end. Leontief drew up the first official U.S. estimate of Soviet output in 1943, under the aegis of the Office of Strategic Services (OSS), the wartime forerunner to the CIA.[41] The OSS Soviet Department was headed by the young Abram Bergson, who as a student of Leontief and Kuznets, had written an early study of the Soviet wage system in 1937.[42] The Soviet Department of the OSS was transformed into the United States Navy Project Research and Development (RAND) Project after the war[43] while Bergson oversaw the extension of the U.S. SNA to the USSR.[44]

National Income is a measure of market prices. The aggregate of sales (less the cost of production or the consumption of intermediate goods) determines new value added in each period. The Soviet Union was a centrally planned economy with no market production and so no sales, no profits, no rents and no wage market. It was illegal to privately own the means of production. Bergson was aware that neo-classical marginalist theory did not apply to an economy without consumer sovereignty.[45] But, while bemoaning the fact, he argued that some theory—even if inapplicable—was better than no theory, so the consumer preference of welfare economics was transmuted into planners' preference. Planners were subject to the laws of neo-classical economics, Bergson asserted, even if the price signals necessary to influence their behaviour did not exist, could not be known and did not influence their behaviour.

[41] Leontief Wassily 1943. *Russian National Income and Defense expenditures*. Washington DC, R and A 1004.

[42] Bergson Abram 1944. *The structure of Soviet wages: A study in socialist economics*. Cambridge, MA, Harvard University Press.

[43] Engerman D. C. 2009. The rise and fall of America's Soviet experts. Oxford: Oxford University Press.

[44] Bergson Abram 1950. Soviet National Income and Product in 1937. *The Quarterly Journal of Economics*, 64(2), pp. 208–241.

[45] Bergson Abram 1964. *The Economics of Soviet planning, first ed*. New Haven, CT, Yale University Press.

Bergson's 1930s study of Soviet wages had argued that as there were wage differentials based on skills and output, a form of capitalist wage market existed[46] in the USSR, even though this market did not exist, or was not a market and so did not determine the price of labour, the supply of labour or the quantities of consumer goods supplied. Bergson's Adjusted Factor Cost (AFC) re-priced Soviet output by redistributing official estimates of Soviet "value" or amounts of physical production, according to the categories of the market economy. This formed the basis for his AFC standard; it assumed the existence of a capitalist economy in the national accounts, even though no such economy existed. Bergson's AFC imagined that (i) All commodity prices resolve fully into charges for primary factors, particularly capital, land and labour. (ii) For capital, there is a net charge, corresponding to the average internal return on this factor in the economy generally, and an allowance for depreciation of a conventional sort. (iii) The charge for land, "rent", corresponds on the average to the differential return to superior land. (iv) "Wages" are at a uniform rate for any occupation and as between occupations differ on the average in accord with differences in productivity and disutility. (v) Similar principles apply in the case of the relation of wages to farm labour income. vi) Commodity prices are uniform in any given market area.[47] Never mind the absence of profits, rent, interest, real wage labour and the differential pricing of identical outputs. Bergson assumed "a hypothetical charge of 25 billion roubles for agricultural rent and a hypothetical interest charge of 10% per annum on Soviet fixed capital". He went on, "In all cases, the cited figures supposedly represent both direct and indirect incidence, that is, charges not only on final goods but on immediate articles used in production".[48] These estimates were "supposed", not real. This was a statistical exercise only. Ironically, precisely because Bergson's estimates were a reworking of official data. As the Soviet authorities similarly misused national income measures to measure the planned economy without commodity production or exchange, Bergson's

[46] Bergson Abram 1944. *The Structure of Soviet wages: A Study in Socialist Economics*. Cambridge, MA, Harvard University Press.

[47] Bergson Abram 1953. *Soviet National Income and Product in 1937*. Columbia: Greenwood Press, pp. 42–43.

[48] Bergson Abram 1961. *The Real National Income of Soviet Russia since 1928, first ed*. New York: Harvard University Press, p. 140.

measures were only marginally different from the figures of the Soviet authorities themselves.

Bergson's AFC became the standard applied to all centrally planned economies in Central and Eastern Europe (CEE), China, and Vietnam. Abraham Becker applied Bergson's AFC to an estimate of the USSR's national income for 1958–64.[49] A CIA team based in Washington DC did the same for China. Thad P. Alton in New York estimated national income for Bulgaria, Czechoslovakia, East Germany, Poland, Romania and Yugoslavia (Alton et al. 1991). In 1961 Alexander Eckstein, with the support of Simon Kuznets and Abram Bergson, published national income estimates for China in 1952,[50] the final pre-plan year. Ta-Chung Liu and Kung-China Yeh, part of the U.S. Air Force Project RAND, worked with Simon Kuznets on an early Western attempt to then reconstruct Chinese national income measurements to conform to Bergson's standard Western definitions corrected for "obvious biases".[51] They noted that Communist policy in 1955 was "designed to wipe out whatever free market activity was left in rural areas" and that by the end of the First Five Year Plan in 1958 private enterprise's share of industry and retail trade had declined to zero.

Inasmuch as these estimates had any relationship to reality, they were based on the reported physical output of the central planning authorities and so reflected the growth of physical use values through the various phases of the plan after the Second World War. This theoretically incoherent treatment of the central plan as a market economy while explicitly accepting it was not, effortlessly evoked George Orwell's doublethink "to know and not to know, to be conscious of complete truthfulness while telling carefully constructed lies, to hold simultaneously two opinions which cancelled out, knowing them to be contradictory and believing in both of them, to use logic against logic".[52] Stephen Rosefielde, a rival Sovietologist to Bergson who criticised some of the assumptions of his

[49] Becker A. S. 1969. *Soviet National Income, 1958–1964*. Berkeley, University of California Press.

[50] Eckstein Alexander 1961. *The National Income of Communist China*. Glencoe, Illinois, Free Press.

[51] Liu Ta-Chung and Yeh Kung-Chia 1965. *Economy of the Chinese Mainland*. Princeton, Princeton University Press, p. 125, 14, 15.

[52] Orwell George. 1949. *Nineteen Eighty-Four*. London: Martin Secker & Warburg Ltd., p. 32.

model while working in broadly the same framework, later concluded that,

> The bottom line after half a century of analysis therefore is that both Bergson's 1953 and 1963 axioms were wrong. Soviet economic performance cannot be . . . transformed to a Western accounting basis, revalued at adjusted ruble factor cost and discounted by replacing value subseries with indices of physical growth at each analyst's discretion . . . Bergson's axiology could always generate 'reasonable' results by bending rules while disregarding reality, but it could not scientifically determine Soviet performance or potential.[53]

The transition of the centrally planned economies to the market greatest expansion of capitalism in history. And yet, according to the national income measurements of the CIA, OECD, World Bank IMF, etc., this gigantic enlargement of market production and so of national income, the measure of market production, led to a decline in market production, and national income, in the very countries where it was introduced.[54] This misestimation had three serious consequences for assessing the impact of the transition to the market from the central plan. Firstly, Bergson and the CIA analysts were unable to model the dissolving effect of commodity production on the plan due to Gorbachev's pro-market reforms in the late 1980s. How could the market dissolve the plan if it was already assumed to exist? Hence, they underestimated the fragility of the centrally planned economy to capitalist restoration from within. Secondly, as the plan was collapsing in the 1990s the various schemes presented for the immediate restoration of the market, failed to account for the impact (the immediate wholesale collapse of production) of the sudden withdrawal of the central planning mechanism, thirdly and finally, they failed to measure the growth of the market with the restoration of capitalism in these economies. They collapsed the collapse of planned use value production into a collapse of the market. As William Jefferies observed in 2006 "the brutal transition from the planned production…destroyed vast swathes

[53] Rosefielde Stephen 2004. Post-war Russian economic growth: Not a Riddle—A Reply. Europe Asia Studies, 56(3), pp. 463–466.

[54] Jefferies William 2014. *Measuring National Income in the Centrally Planned Economies; Why the West Underestimated the Transition to Capitalism*. London, Routledge.

Table 3.1 Private sector % total output, selected countries and years

Country	*1989*	*1991*	*1995*	*1999*	*2000*
Czech Republic	11.2	17.3	70	80	80
Hungary	14.9	33	60	80	80
Poland	28.6	45.3	60	65	70
Russia	5.3	10.1	40	75	70

By the turn of the millennium the transition to a capitalist economy was effectively complete

of the economy…but this collapse in output was a collapse not of capitalist production but of planned production, it was not a decline in the capitalist economy, but the creation of it".[55]

The European Bank of Reconstruction and Development[56] (EBRD) Transition Reports developed estimates of the growth of the "private sector shares" of output inside the CEE and CIS based on available statistics from both official (government) sources and unofficial sources[57] shown here in Table 3.1.

In China pro-market price reforms began in 1978. Over the next three decades this process created a market economy, but with the control of the Chinese Communist Party (CCP) intact. At the outset of the process, the proportion of centrally planned output was fixed and a surplus above that minimum target was sold at market prices. This led to a rapid growth in the proportion of market output from total output, although this was not initially reflected in a change of ownership of the state sector. As national income is a measure of output within the market boundary,

[55] Jefferies Bill 2006. Globalisation; Capitalism's Long Upturn Since the Collapse of Stalinism. London, *Permanent Revolution Magazine 1*, pp. 36–46, p. 43.

[56] EBRD 1995. *Transition report 1995: Investment and Enterprise Report*. London, EBRD.

EBRD 1996. *Transition report 1996: Infrastructure and Savings*. London, EBRD.

EBRD 1997. *Transition report 1997: Enterprise Performance and Growth. London*: EBRD.

EBRD 1998. *Transition report 1998: Financial Sector in Transition*. Brussels, EBRD.

EBRD 1999. *Transition report 1999: Ten Years of Transition*. London, EBRD.

EBRD 2000. *Transition report 2000: Employment, Skills and Transition*. London, EBRD.

EBRD 2001. *Transition report 2001: Energy in Transition*. London, EBRD.

[57] Jefferies William 2015. On the Alleged Stagnation of Capitalism. *Review of Radical Political Economics*, 47(4), pp. 588–607, p. 596.

Table 3.2 Chinese output at market prices proportion %[60]

	1978	*1985*	*1991*	*1995*	*1999*
Producer	0	13	46	78	86
Retail	3	34	69	89	99
Farm	6	40	58	79	79
Total	3	30	59	81	88

By the mid-1990s the transition to a market economy was complete in China

the growth of market production was the creation of national income. Except in China's case the transition to the market did not destroy but rather eventually supplanted and transformed centrally planned production into market production. In 1997 CCP General Secretary Jiang Zemin announced China would develop a socialist market economy. This presaged the dismantling of the iron rice bowl, the system of state guaranteed incomes and employment rights and widespread privatisation. The share of state-controlled enterprises in total employment fell from 62% in 1998 to 38% in 2003 while millions of state employees were made redundant. The opening of China's labour market with industrial workers earning around $1/hour to foreign multinationals drastically reduced their labour costs.[58] State housing was privatised. By the end of the 1990s what remained of the state sector was subordinated to market prices irrespective of state ownership. The price series in Table 3.2 are based on an empirical survey undertaken by the OECD,[59] using the Chinese National Bureau of Statistics (NBS) industrial survey.

The trade measurements of various international agencies the UN, World Bank, IMF, WTO, etc., similarly underestimate the growth of trade with the extension of the market across a third of the world's surface and half its population. They too fail to differentiate between capitalist trade, the only real trade, commodities bought and sold on a market, and the

[58] Hart-Landsberg Martin and Burkett Paul 006. 2China and the Dynamics of Transnational Accumulation: Causes and Consequences of Global Restructuring. *Historical Materialism,* 4(3), pp. 3–43.

[59] Dougherty S. and Herd R. 2005. The Fast-Falling Barriers and Growing concentration: The Emergence of the Private Economy in China. *OECD Economics Department Working Papers,* No. 471. Paris, OECD.

[60] Jefferies William 2015. On the Alleged Stagnation of Capitalism. *Review of Radical Political Economics,* 47(4), pp. 588–607, p. 598.

transfer of centrally planned inputs and outputs across national boundaries. Trade between centrally planned economies was not the exchange of commodities, it did not occur at market prices as there was often no equivalent for goods received, it was not really trade at all, rather it was the political transfer of resources between non-market economies.

Despite this underestimation WTO statistics show that between 1990–2007 trade grew 362%.[61] The World Bank estimated world trade as a proportion of world GDP grew from 1991 38%, 2001 49%, 2011 60%, 2021 57%.[62] The CPB trade monitor estimated global trade grew 0.3% a month during the 2000s, before slowing to 0.2% a month subsequently.[63] Trade is measured in sales not value added, it fails to account for inflation, so the deflation of manufactured goods which accelerated from the end of the 1990s until 2021 meant the volume of trade increased even faster than the increase in sales.

A material expression of the extension of the world market was the growth of the merchant fleet as shown in Fig. 3.1. World merchant fleet growth, 1980–2023.[64]

During the 1980s the fleet had declined by 9% as trade, production and profits stagnated, during the 1990s the fleet expanded by 26%, not including the one-off addition, around 10% of 1990 tonnage, of the ships inherited for free by the capitalists from the former centrally planned economies. The actual growth rate of the capitalist merchant fleet was around half higher than the growth of the total fleet, it accelerated further after the turn of the millennium.

The transformation of the means of production of the former central plan into fixed capital required it be restructured, destroyed and reconfigured, but it was inherited from the plan for nothing. The collapse of planned production obscured the eventual impact of globalisation on world capitalism. It was not immediately obvious through the 1990s, that the ground was being laid for the hyper-globalisation that followed.

61 UNCTAD 2012. *Statistical Database*. United Nations Conference on Trade and Development. http://unctadstat.unctad.org.

62 World Bank 2024. *Trade (% GDP) World*. World Bank. https://data.worldbank.org/indicator/NE.TRD.GNFS.ZS?locations=1W.

63 CPB Netherlands Bureau for Economic Policy Analysis 2024. *World Trade Monitor December 2023*. https://www.cpb.nl/en/world-trade-monitor-december-2023.

64 UNCTAD 2024. *Datacentre*. Geneva, United Nations Conference on Trade and Development. https://unctadstat.unctad.org/datacentre/.

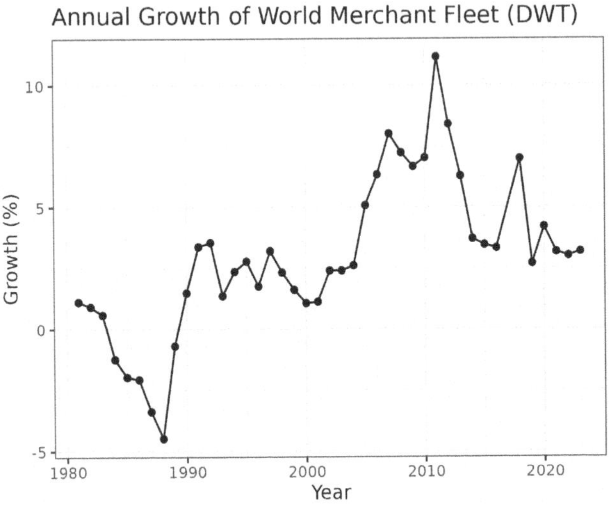

Fig. 3.1 World total merchant fleet growth 1980–2023

Nonetheless, the quality of the basic infrastructure, roads, railways, electrical transmission facilities, engineering works, ports, buildings, bridges, roads and so on, inherited from the planned economies, was high. While the workforce was more highly educated, skilled and healthy, with a higher proportion of industrial employment than in the capitalist West,[65] with excellent housing, education and medical facilities, and so a low cost of reproduction of labour power, or wages. Globalisation fulfilled this first condition to powerfully revive world capitalism, others would follow.

[65] UN 2004. *Development and Globalization: Facts and Figures*. *New* York and Geneva, United Nations.

CHAPTER 4

The Long Wave of Globalisation

> "The entire capitalist economy—in technology, the money market, trade and the colonies—has matured to such an extent that an extraordinary extension of the world market must occur, placing the whole of world production on a new, much more comprehensive basis. This is when a *Sturm und Drang* period begins for capital". Alexander Parvus (Helphand) 1895.

In 1895 Alexander Parvus (Helphand) described periods of stormy advance *Sturm und Drang*[1] (Storm and Stress) in the capitalist economy. These were later popularised by Kondratieff and Mandel under the label 'long waves' of capitalist development.[2] Parvus described how these periods defined capital accumulation as a whole including the business cycle. In 1901 during a "full blown commercial crisis" he predicted that the crisis would not persist but rather presaged a period of rapid world-wide capital accumulation. Parvus highlighted how the combination of factors including the extension or opening of new markets, new sectors

[1] Parvus Alexander (Helphand) 1901 [2024]. *Die Handelskrisis und die Gewerkschaften, nebst Anhang: Gestzentwurf über den achtstündigen Normalarbeitstag*, München: Druck von M. Ernst, translated by Daniel Gaido. Parvus' emphasis.

[2] Kondratieff 1926.

W. Jefferies, *War and the World Economy*, Palgrave Insights into Apocalypse Economics,
https://doi.org/10.1007/978-3-031-85236-7_4

of capital accumulation, reduction in turnover times and new technological advances, were together greater than the sum of their parts. He emphasised how the growth of trade with Russia provided new markets for German industry, the urbanisation of the U.S. alongside the pre-eminence industry had transformed the American economy, the growth in gold mining reduced the price of money, the opening of China provided new markets and trade routes, the expansion of railways gave impetus to the steel industry while reducing the cost and trade, and electrical engineering created new consumer goods and raised productivity. Together they produced a moment when,

> the entire capitalist economy—in technology, the money market, trade and the colonies—has matured to such an extent that an extraordinary extension of the world market must occur, placing the whole of world production on a new, much more comprehensive basis. This is when a *Sturm und Drang* period begins for capital. This does not abolish the periodical alternation of upswing and crisis, but the upswing develops in a stronger progression, while the crisis sharpens but its duration is shortened. This continues until the forces of development have unfolded to their full potential. Then a sharp commercial crisis takes place, which finally turns into an *economic depression*.

This description was widely accepted amongst the orthodox Kautskyite centre of German Social Democracy and on its left wing by Trotsky, Pannekoek and Luxemburg. It provided a key theoretical reference point in the debate around collapse. The perspective of the left and centre was that the crisis of 1900 would be followed by a boom, crisis, boom, war and depression or collapse. In 1913 the Dutch Marxist Jacob van Gelderen's article *Springtide: Reflections on Industrial Development and Price Movements*[3] provided a detailed empirical assessment of Parvus' idea focussing on inflation/deflation, the extension of the market and technological advance. Kondratieff reiterated it after the 1917 Russian Revolution and Trotsky commented in Kondratieff's mechanical alternation of these longer periods, albeit in passing, after the war and during the collapse, in 1920.

The notion of longer waves is also referenced more widely. Jeremy Green, a British economist, considers that there have been two long waves

[3] Van Gelderen 1996 [1913].

of globalisation, from 1870 to 1914 and 1945 to today.[4] This is too broad to be useful. The period from 1848 to 1870, which started with the revolutions of 1848 established the world market with railway mania and the transatlantic trade stimulated by the replacement of sail by steam and the introduction of the propellor. The Californian gold rush cheapened the price of money, while the abolition of slavery in the U.S. civil war, saw the extension of the American system of standard mechanical parts. It was a period of great expansion of capital accumulation. In contrast the period from 1870 to 1890 was popularly described as the Great Depression in Britain, the pre-eminent industrial power in the world at the time. It was followed by the period of *Sturm und Drang* analysed by Parvus, which included the colonisation of the world, creation of monopolies and finance capital from roughly the 1890s until the outbreak of the world war in 1914. Green only excludes the interwar years of world war, crisis and turmoil from his periodisation. Thereby viewing globalisation as practically a natural state of the world capitalist economy. Hence, while noting the recent trend to de-globalisation he cannot really imagine it going too far, even if market excesses need correcting.

Mandel's version of the theory asserted that long periods of downswing, or downward long waves, such as the crisis of the interwar years, or the 1970s and 1980s, arose inevitably through the endogenous functioning of the capitalist economy, including most fundamentally the over accumulation of capital. These long waves appeared to follow a pattern of similar periods of expansion, 1848 to 1870, 1890 to 1914, 1945 to 1971 and by extension it might be added 1991 to 2019. The upward phase would last around 25–30 years or three cycles of around 8–10 years; the first cycle a period of restructuring; the second cycle the period of peak expansion and the third cycle, a period of relative slowdown preparing for a new downward long wave. In contrast to periods of upswing there was no endogenous mechanism that ensured periods of downswing would end, although they could do so. However, this was contingent on the outcome of major events, wars or counter revolutions, of a wide enough scope to enable a decisive restructuring of the world capitalist economy, such as occurred after the Second World War or with the end of the Cold War in 1989.

[4] Green Jeremy 2019. *Is Globalization Over?* London, Polity.

The period of interregnum between 1914 and 45 ended with the Second World War the defeat of Germany and Japan and dismantling of the British Empire. The 1944 Bretton Woods Treaty combined with Dean Acheson's, Truman's Secretary of State, "crescent policy" provided the geopolitical basis for the post-war international rules-based order. Acheson considered it was necessary to surround the Communist states with a crescent of sympathetic powers. He observed that "the reconstruction of those two great workshops of Europe and Asia-Germany and Japan-upon which the ultimate recovery of the two continents so largely depends"[5] would provide a bulwark against Communist expansion into Asia and Europe. The crescent's poles, Japan and West Germany, were granted Most Favoured Nation (MFN) access to markets within the GATT framework, while being allowed domestic protection of industries and provided with military supply contracts. The collapse of Bretton Woods in 1971 instituted a period of crisis which was only resolved by the collapse of the USSR and transition of China to the market after 1991.

The re-establishment of American global might in 1991, also explains Germany and Japan's relative decline. The dismantling of tariff barriers and trade restrictions in the 1990s conferred MFN status to the world. The completion of the GATT Uruguay round of trade talks, and foundation of the WTO in 1995 meant between 1990 and 2010, the number of Preferential Trade Agreements increased from 70 to 300 while Most Favoured Nation (MFN) tariffs declined by around two-thirds from 25 to 8%, and even less in the OECD to less than 4%.[6] Restrictions on trade tumbled to their lowest ever level.[7] Germany and Japan's trade advantage vanished. Germany coped better than Japan, through its role in leading the European Union into the Euro single currency, but Japan stagnated for three decades. Unlike West Germany and Japan, China's development during globalisation was not dependent on U.S. largesse.

In 1995, the year before his death, Mandel identified the preconditions for an end to the long depression of the 1970s/80s,

[5] Schaller Michael 1982 Securing the Great Crescent: Occupied Japan and the Origins of Containment in Southeast Asia. *The Journal of American History*, 69(2), pp. 392–414.

[6] Subramanian Arvind and Kessler Martin 2013. The Hyperglobalization of Trade and Its Future. *Working Paper Series WP*, pp. 13–16.
Washington DC, Peterson Institute.

[7] Federico G. and A. Tena-Junguito 2017. A tale of two globalizations: Gains from trade and openness 1800–2010. *Review of World Economics* 153 (3), pp. 601–26.

> A massive "system shock" which combines a sharp rise in the rate of profit (induced by an even steeper rise in the rate of surplus value) and a considerable broadening of the market. The latter could only occur, in the present world situation, through total integration of the former USSR and the People's Republic of China into the capitalist world market.[8]

This expansion if combined with major defeats of the working class and third world national liberation movements, could enable a new period of upswing. Although Mandel thought this combination of events unlikely, by 1995 these defeats had already occurred. The new period was defined by a series of epochal events. Gorbachev's Glasnost pro-market reforms rapidly dissolved the coherence of the central plan. The abolition of the monopoly of foreign trade in 1988 was probably the fatal blow. What was jokingly referred to as The Sinatra doctrine "My Way" guaranteed the USSR would not intervene into its immediate neighbours, the Berlin Wall duly fell in November 1989. The USSR unravelled. The Warsaw Pact was abolished in March 1991. The ill-feted hardline Soviet coup of August 1991 was incompetently organised and lacked clear goals. The apparatus arrested their man Gorbachev, the General Secretary of the Communist Party Soviet Union (CPSU), while seeking to ally with Yeltsin, the President of the Russian Federation, their most determined enemy. The coup failed after just two days and accelerated the already rapid pace of capitalist restoration. Yeltsin banned the CPSU in November 1991, dissolved the USSR in December and introduced "shock therapy", total price liberalisation, in January 1992.[9]

The collapse of Soviet Communism permitted a managed transition from South African apartheid. Negotiations with the African National Congress (ANC) saw Nelson Mandela released in February 1990, as the U.S. State Department explained "defenders of the Apartheid regime, both inside and outside South Africa, had promoted it as a bulwark against communism. However, the end of the Cold War rendered this argument obsolete".[10]

[8] Mandel Ernest 1995. *Long Waves of Capitalist Development; a Marxist Interpretation Second Revised Edition*. London, Verso, p. 114, 83, 113.

[9] McFaul Michael 2000. Yeltsin's Legacy. *The Wilson Quarterly* 24(2), pp. 42–47, 50–58.

[10] U.S. Department of State 2009. *Archive; The End of Apartheid*. https://2001-2009.state.gov/r/pa/ho/time/pcw/98678.htm.

Saddam Hussein the President of Iraq from 1979, had been an anti-communist bulwark and U.S. ally, launching the 1980 war on Iran after the Iranian revolution of 1979. In August 1990, in a fatal miscalculation, Hussein invaded Kuwait. Elliott Abrams a PNAC contributor explained later that "the Soviet collapse ended Soviet support for client states, like Syria, for the PLO and for Arab nationalism in general".[11] Condemned by the UN a U.S. lead invasion, Operation Desert Shield, crushed his forces in a brutal 100-hour war in February 1991,[12] although the decision to halt the attack for fear of the military occupation that would follow,[13] left Hussein in power for another ten years.

In 1993 the Israel-Palestine Oslo Accords overseen by the new U.S. President Clinton at Camp David, saw the Palestine Liberation Organisation (PLO) recognise Israel's right to exist, but this was not reciprocated. Shortly afterwards in Northern Ireland, the former U.S. senator George Mitchell, brokered the 1998 Good Friday Agreement, where Sein Fein the political wing of the Irish Republican Army (IRA) entered the administration of the Northern Irish six county statelet.

In 1995 the U.S. and (North Atlantic Treaty Organization) NATO bombed Bosnian Serbs and again in 1999, this time without UN approval, citing the ethnic cleansing of Kosovo Albanians. In the new rules-based order the U.S. made the rules. In 1999 Poland, Hungary and the Czech Republic joined NATO.

Clinton supported Boris Yeltsin with IMF loans and brought Russia into the G8, but relations with Russia became frostier with Putin's presidential election in 2000. Putin represented the nationalist wing of the Russian rulers, originating from the security services, he oversaw Russia's war in Chechnya, and moved to limit the power of Western oil companies, financial institutions and the oligarchs in hoc to them. This was the reassertion of Russian Great Power against the West and was ultimately intolerable to them.

[11] Abrams Elliott 2000. Israel and the Peace Process. In: *Present Dangers; Crisis and Opportunity in American Foreign and Defense Policy*. Edited by Robert Kagan and William Kristol, New York, Encounter Books, p. 212.

[12] U.S. Department of State. T*he First Gulf War*. https://history.state.gov/departmenthistory/short-history/firstgulf#.

[13] Baker III James A. 1996. Why the U.S. Didn't March to Baghdad. Los Angeles Times.
https://www.latimes.com/archives/la-xpm-1996-09-08-op-41778-story.html#.

Table 4.1 Manufactured goods tariff effectively applied rate, simple average[15]

	1991	*2001*	*2011*
Argentina	14.8	13.5	10.0
Australia	13.9	5.8	3.1
Brazil	28.8	15.2	14.1
Canada	10.7	5.1	3.2
China	40.8	15.3	7.9
India	79.9	30.7	8.6
Japan	2.8	2.4	2.1
Poland	11.4	2.4	.
Russia	9.5	10.9	7.5
U.S	5.6	3.7	2.9
Vietnam	13.7	19.0	6.9
EU	4.3	3.2	1.4

The 1992 North American Free Trade Agreement (NAFTA), which established a free trade zone with Mexico and Canada, was consolidated by the conclusion of the 1986–94 Uruguay round of the General Agreement on Tariffs and Trade (GATT), which became the largest ever multilateral trade deal, establishing the more domineering WTO in 1995.[14] Tariff rates were slashed as evident in Table 4.1.

The relocation of production to cheaper skilled workforces abroad created integrated production networks without reference to national borders, not least along China's Southeast coast, the Special Economic Zones (SEZs), where Western corporations relocated their production, ensuring that for the next decade China's exports were dominated by the re-exports of these firms back to the West. In 1996 foreign owned firms exported 40% of China's exports peaking at around 58% in 2006.[16] The 2000 UNCTAD World Investment Report observed,

[14] DTI 1994. *The Uruguay Round of Multilateral Trade Negotiations*. London, Department of Trade and Industry UK Government. https://assets.publishing.service.gov.uk/media/5a7b7fb3ed915d131105fa24/2579.pdf.

[15] UNCTAD 2012. *Statistical Database*. United Nations Conference on Trade and Development. http://unctadstat.unctad.org.

[16] Romei Valentina and Minto Rob 2012. *Chart of the week: who makes China's exports—local companies or foreign?* London, Financial Times. https://www.ft.com/content/f4fbea53-6fe4-3e19-8ca1-55ccca4e4596.

> The expansion of international production has been facilitated by virtually all countries through changes in their regulatory environments. Over the period 1991-1999, 94% of the 1,035 changes worldwide in the laws governing foreign direct investment (FDI) created a more favourable framework for FDI. Complementing the more welcoming national FDI regimes, the number of bilateral investment treaties — concluded increasingly also between developing countries — has risen from 181 at the end of 1980 to 1,856 at the end of 1999. Double taxation treaties have also increased, from 719 in 1980 to 1,982 at the end of 1999.[17]

Mandel considered that,

> From a technical point of view, a new expansionist wave that would significantly increase the rate of economic growth above the average levels of the 1970s, 1980s, and 1990s would require an explosive increase in the rate of accumulation and therefore in the average rate of profit and a no less remarkable expansion in the market for capitalist commodities.

Mandel commented that "normally, the capitalist way of securing the first condition conflicts with the capitalist way of assuring the second" but there was nothing normal about the collapse of the USSR and the transition of China to the market. Rudolph Hilferding in *Finance Capital* (1910) observed,

> The larger and more populous the economic territory, the larger the individual plant can be, the lower the costs of production, and the greater the degree of specialization within the plant, which also reduces costs of production. The larger the economic territory, the more easily can industry be located where the natural conditions are most favourable and the productivity of labour is highest.... at an advanced stage of capitalist production free trade, which would amalgamate the whole world market into a single economic territory, would ensure the highest possible labour productivity and the most rational international division of labour.[18]

[17] UNCTAD 2000. *World Investment Report 2000; Cross-border Mergers and Acquisitions and Development.* New York and Geneva, United Nations Conference on Trade and Development (UNCTAD), p. xv.

[18] Hilferding Rudolph 1983 [1910]. *Finance Capital.* Translated by Tom Bottomore. London, RKP.

The creation of a truly global capitalist economy in the 1990s created the largest possible economic territory, the entire world. The transition from the stagnation of the 1970s and 1980s to a new period of expansion was not a result of the endogenous functioning of the capitalist accumulation process itself, but the political victories of the U.S. over its cold war enemies.

Richard Freeman, a U.S. economic professor, famously estimated that after the restoration of capitalism in the former planned economies, the global labour pool, the labour capable of being exploited by the market, rose from approximately 1.46bn workers to 2.93bn. Freeman labelled this the Great Doubling,[19] based on an extrapolation from the Penn World Tables (PWT). Freeman estimated that this doubling lowered the labour/capital ratio by around 61% as "the new entrants to the global economy did not bring much capital with them", and so raised profit rates. The PWT valuations of the Fixed Capital Stock (FCS) apply the neo-classical Hulten and Wykoff method developed in the UN System of National Accounts[20] (SNA). This Net Present Value (NPV) method aggregates estimates of future "services", i.e. profits,[21] such that the value of the fixed capital stock is equal to the discounted total of estimated future earnings, this annual amount of discounted services multiplied by the service life. It is a measure of opportunity costs, imaginary future profits, not costs (or advances) of the actual past expenditures on inputs necessary to produce output. How then did Freeman develop his assertion (albeit inadvertently correct) of the lack of capital in these economies?

If planned (i.e. non-market by definition) production is assumed to be market production (*pace* Bergson, some theory is better than no theory even if the theory is inapplicable) then the physical surplus of the centrally planned economies, the difference between the physical quantity of output and the physical quantity of input, or social surplus, maybe falsely labelled profit. Then, as income inequality was lower and public services higher, so popular consumption was higher, and so surplus/

[19] Freeman Richard 2005. The Great Doubling: America in the New Global Economy Usery Lecture, April 8, 2005. Georgia State University, What Really Ails Europe (and America): The Doubling of the Global Workforce, *The Globalist*. http://www.theglobalist.com/StoryId.aspx?StoryId=4542.

[20] UN 2008. *System of National Accounts*. New York, United Nations.

[21] OECD 2009. *Measuring Capital OECD Manual Second Edition*. Paris, OECD, p. 30.

profits were lower, in centrally planned rather than capitalist economies of a similar level of development, so the net present value, discounted aggregates of future surplus that formed the "capital" valuations, were very low. Freeman's circuitous method achieved the right result albeit accidentally.

More precisely, as profits are the difference between sales and costs, then as centrally planned economies had no sales, so they had no profits, which is a social relationship distinct to market economies in which capitalists extra surplus value from the producers in the form of private property that they own. As it was illegal to accumulate capital, and as the state owned all means of production, which were allocated according to the material priorities of the central plan, not to maximise surplus, so there was no capital in the sense that it exists in a market economy, so the value of their means of production, mislabelled "capital", was nil.

Alternatively, and more prosaically, but nonetheless correctly, as the new capitalists of the former planned economies appropriated, or stole, the means of production so the cost of capital advanced was nil. Thieves do not pay for their booty.

Following the one-off addition of the remnants of centrally planned production, now functioning under the aegis of market prices, the rate of growth of key sectors of physical production and GDP value series sharply accelerated through the first decade of the twenty-first century, even including the Great Crash of 2008–2010. The collapse in class struggle increased productivity, lowering the proportion of wages in national income, while cheapening the cost of reproduction of labour power, workers felt better off even while the value of their wages fell. A prolonged period of the deflation of manufacturing output began, with the quality, range and price of consumer goods falling for a protracted period, wages could buy more goods, even though with the shift to services in the basket of household goods measured for official inflation statistics, its impact was masked. The price of imported consumer goods (excluding automobiles) to the U.S. fell by 8% between 1996 and 2004,[22] while capital goods fell by 32% in the same period. As a result, the price of

[22] U.S. Bureau of Labor Statistics 2024. Import Price Index (End Use): Consumer Goods, Excluding Automotives [IR4], FRED, Federal Reserve Bank of St. Louis; https://fred.stlouisfed.org/series/IR4.

durable consumer goods fell every year between 1994 and 2020.[23] The removal of barriers to trade, and the ICT revolution shortened reproduction times and so increased turnover, while the growth of services with a higher turnover and lower organic composition of capital increased the rate of surplus value, reinforcing the decline in working-class labour movement organisations. Living standards rose even as income inequality soared, the reduction of wasteful arms expenditures, U.S. defence expenditure as a proportion of GDP fell to 1999 3.1% down from 1967 9.4% at the height of the Vietnam war and Reagan's 1982 6.8%[24] the reduction in public spending combined with the masses of profits looted from the former planned economies, reduced the price of money and interest rates fell. Cheap money lead to a housing boom, with prices doubling between 1990 and 2006,[25] which enriched millions, not just enabling the embourgeoisification of whole layers of the working and middle classes, but even the bourgeoisification, as the ownership of property and financial assets became widespread in Western society.[26,27] The shift from industrial employment to services in the G7 economies was consolidated, as shown in Table 4.2, but for a different reason.

During the 1970s/80s the crisis of profitability in Western manufacturing industry lead to a general attack on the terms and conditions of often unionised industrial workers there, this accelerated after 1979/80 with the accession of avowedly neo-liberal governments to power represented by Thatcher and Reagan. After 1991 however, the shift

[23] U.S. Bureau of Economic Analysis 2024. Personal consumption expenditures: Durable goods (implicit price deflator) [DDURRD3Q086SBEA], retrieved from FRED, Federal Reserve Bank of St. Louis; https://fred.stlouisfed.org/series/DDURRD3Q086SBEA.

[24] Stockholm International Peace Research Institute (SIPRI), Yearbook: Armaments, Disarmament and International Security.

[25] U.S. Census Bureau and U.S. Department of Housing and Urban Development 2024. *Average Sales Price of Houses Sold for the United States [ASPUS]*, FRED, Federal Reserve Bank of St. Louis; https://fred.stlouisfed.org/series/ASPUS.

[26] ONS 2023. *English Housing Survey 2021 to 2022: second homes—fact sheet*. Gov.uk https://www.gov.uk/government/statistics/english-housing-survey-2021-to-2022-second-homes-fact-sheet/english-housing-survey-2021-to-2022-second-homes-fact-sheet#.

Department for Levelling Up, Housing and Communities.

[27] Wind Barend, Dewilde Caroline and Doling John 2020, Secondary property ownership in Europe: contributing to asset-based welfare strategies and the 'really big trade-off'. *International Journal of Housing Policy*, 20:1, pp. 25–52.

Table 4.2 G7 percentage of employment in industry and services[28]

		1971	*1981*	*1991*	*2001*	*2011*
France	Industry	39	36	29	25	21
	Services	45	54	64	71	76
Canada	Industry	29	27	22	22	19
	Services	63	68	74	76	79
Italy	Industry	39	37	31	30	27
	Services	41	50	60	65	69
Japan	Industry	36	35	34	30	25
	Services	49	55	59	65	71
UK	Industry	42	34	31	22	18
	Services	59	63	66	77	81
U.S	Industry	32	29	23	21	17
	Services	64	65	74	77	81

towards services was no longer a sign of declining profitability but of increasing profitability—but originating abroad, through the relocation of industry to former centrally planned economies. The various assertions of the stagnation of capitalism through the period of globalisation ignored this distinction. They included various Marxian economists like Guglielmo Carchedi, who wrote that capitalism "lacks an inherent (tendency towards) growth and equilibrium",[29] or Alan Freeman and Boris Kagarlitsky, who concluded globalisation was a period of "absolute stagnation",[30] or Andrew Kliman who applied Maddison's data to conclude that after 1973 the world's real gross domestic product (GDP) per capita growth rate fell by one half,[31] or Robert Brenner who wrote in 2009 "the crisis currently unfolding in the world economy is, without close comparison, the most devastating since the Great Depression, and

[28] Bureau of Labor Statistics 2012. International Labor Comparisons. *International Comparisons of Annual Labor Force Statistics, Adjusted to U.S. Concepts, 16 Countries, 1970–2011*. www.bls.gov/ilc/flscomparelf.htm.

[29] Carchedi Guglielmo 2012. *Behind the Crisis: Marx's Dialectics of Value and Knowledge*. Chicago: Haymarket, p. 100.

[30] Freeman Alan and Kagarlitsky Boris 2004. *The Politics of Empire: Globalisation in Crisis*. Edited by Alan Freeman and Boris Kagarlitsky, London, Pluto, p. 49.

[31] Kliman Andrew 2012. *The Failure of Capitalist Production: Underlying Causes of the Great Recession*. New York, Pluto.

could conceivably come to approach it in severity"[32] and were basically misconceived not to say wrong and wholly unfounded empirically.

The catastrophists' mistakes are bolstered by the use of the use of neo-classical measurements of the fixed capital stock based on their net present value or discounted aggregates of future profits. These are falsely elided with capital advanced measures of capitalist costs but are in fact conceptually incoherent and irrational valuations akin to the securitisation of ground rent. If used in estimates of the profit rate then profit is in the numerator and denominator of the calculation, but as the denominator aggregates the mass of profit for the duration of the assets service life, as the mass of profits rises, so the value of the fixed capital stock will rise more so the rate of profit will fall. The combination of these two neo-classical mis-estimates, the growth of the world market with capitalist restoration and the inversion of the estimate of profit rates, has wrought havoc with Marxian political economy over the last three decades, with perpetual predictions of capitalist collapse, a triumph of wishful thinking over reality.

Mandel had observed "a sharp increase in the rate of surplus value, a sharp slowdown in the rate of increase of the organic composition of capital, a sudden quickening in the turnover of capital, or a combination of several or all of these factors can explain a sudden upturn in the average rate of profit".[33] The subjective defeat of Communist collapse, was compounded by the objective defeat, rebooted capitalist accumulation far surpassed any of its previous achievements. Globalisation was a veritable "belle époque" capable of withstanding the credit crunch of 2008–the Great Recession–possibly the deepest financial crisis in its history, virtually unscathed. In 2008 world output fell an estimated 0.6%, a trivially inconsequential figure in comparison to the increase of capitalist production with the transformation of the centrally planned economies to the market.

[32] Brenner Robert 2009. *What is Good for Goldman Sachs is Good for America: The Origins of the Present Crisis*. London, Verso.

[33] Mandel Ernest 1995. *Long Waves of Capitalist Development; a Marxist Interpretation Second Revised Edition*. London, Verso, p. 10.

The 1992 Defense Planning Guidance,[34] written by Zalmay Khalilzad, on behalf of President George Bush's Secretary of Defense Paul Wolfowitz addressed,

> the fundamentally new situation which has been created by the collapse of the Soviet Union -- the disintegration of the internal as well as the external empire, and the discrediting of Communism as an ideology with global pretensions and influence.

This and the victory of the U.S. coalition over Iraq in 1991 had shaped the "new international environment" these "two great successes" were combined with "a less visible one" the "integration of the leading democracies into a U.S.-led system of collective security and the creation of a democratic 'zone of peace'". As a result "America's strategic position is stronger than it has been for decades. Today, there is no global challenger to a peaceful democratic order. There are no significant hostile alliances". China was only mentioned alongside Cuba and North Korea as potentially entering a period of intense crisis. But Wolfowitz would have to wait his moment. George Bush may have won the Cold War and Desert Storm but, he lost the U.S. presidential election.

Clinton's election promised to focus with a "laser like beam on the economy" while "foreign policy "will come, into play in part as it affects the economy".[35] Clinton's economic policy promoted the hollowing out of U.S. industry as production was transferred abroad, mainly to China, reductions in tariffs and the loosening of financial regulations on the export of capital. The remaining domestic agenda under the umbrella of the war on drugs, built on the Reagan Era 1984 Sentencing Reform Act, to introduce the 1994 Violent Crime Control and Law Enforcement Act or Three Strikes and You're Out laws. This racist policy increased the prison population to 2 million, disproportionately criminalising young black men by 1999 9% of them were in goal,[36] with on average one in

[34] NSC (National Security Council) 1992. *Defense planning: Guidance*. FY 1994–1999. 4/23, Doc#2, 07-M-1928-A1. https://www.archives.gov/files/declassification/iscap/pdf/2008-003-docs1-12.pdf.

[35] Mufson Steven 1992. Clinton to Send Message with Economic Choices Appointments. *Washington Post*. https://www.washingtonpost.com/archive/politics/1992/11/08/clinton-to-send-message-with-economic-choices/.

[36] U.S. Department of Justice 2000. Prisoners in 1999. *Bureau of Justice, Statistics Bulletin*. www.ojp.usdog.gove/bjs/.

every thousand black men killed by the police.[37] This when combined with the privatisation of the U.S. criminal justice system presaged the creation of a Prison Industrial Complex.[38] It established a framework for the social control of the poor and racially excluded, a tolerated but formally criminal distribution of drugs, vicious police repression of young black men, and a very high death rate from opioid addition, which subsequently soared from 20,000 in 1999 to 106,000 in 2021.[39] As William Kristol and Robert Kagan put it in their 1996 *Toward a Neo-Reaganite Foreign Policy,* "somehow most Americans have failed to notice that they have never had it so good".[40]

Kristol and Kagan's famous article initiated what was to become the Project for a New American Century (PNAC),[41] which went on to define U.S. foreign policy from the turn of the millennium. Kristol and Kagan's polemic bemoaned the absence of substantive difference between the Democrats and Republicans. They presented themselves as Reaganites struggling, as Reagan did, against the moral vacuum of Kissinger's Real Politik détente. The new role of the America should be one of "benevolent global hegemony" like Reagan they championed "American exceptionalism" and concluded the "appropriate goal of American foreign policy, therefore, is to preserve that hegemony as far into the future as possible" with a "understanding that its moral goals and its fundamental national interests are almost always in harmony" by "actively promoting American principles of governance abroad, democracy, free markets, respect for liberty". The PNAC's Statement of Principles (SP) followed in 1997 signed by 25 leading Republican thinkers including Cheney, Rumsfeld, Wolfowitz, Khalilzad and Fukyama.

[37] The Lancet 2021. Fatal police violence by race and state in the USA, 1980–2019: a network meta-regression, *The Lancet*.

398 (10,307), pp. 1239–1255.

[38] Davis A.Y. and Shaylor C., 2001. Race, gender, and the prison industrial complex: California and beyond. *Meridians*, 2(1), pp. 1–25.

[39] National Institute of Drug Abuse 2023. *Drug Overdose Death Rates*. https://nida.nih.gov/research-topics/trends-statistics/overdose-death-rates#.

[40] Kristol William and Kagan Robert 1996. Toward a Neo-Reaganite Foreign Policy. *Foreign Affairs, Council on Foreign Relations,* 75(4), pp. 18–32.

[41] PNAC 1997. *Statement of Principles*. http://www.newamericancentury.org/statementofprinciples.htm.

The PNAC's SP is traditionally understood in the terms framed by Kristol and Kagan themselves, the neo-conservative right against the liberal, invariably morally vacuous, Democrats or vice versa. This is to misunderstand the issues at stake. None of the participants disagreed with the objective the neo-cons described—U.S. global hegemony predicated on American Exceptionalism. The U.S. is necessarily benevolent as its interests are moral. Insofar as there is any disagreement between the various wings of the U.S. foreign policy establishment, it is concerned with which knife to best skin the cat, not whether to do so.

Kristol and Kagan called for a bit more arms spending to be ready for future threats including removal of Saddam Hussein,[42] as did Thomas Donnelly who developed the argument in *Rebuilding America's Defences* observing in passing that "coping with the rise of China to great-power status"[43] could become a future defence priority, while calling for a meagre 0.3% rise in defence spending in the here and now.

The March 2000 bursting of the Dot-Com bubble was the largest of a series of 1990s financial crises following the Mexican crisis of 1994–95, the East Asian crisis of 1997–98.[44] The Dotcom bubble began innocuously. Clinton's 1996 Telecommunications Act deregulated the provision of telecommunications and included the internet. The new economy generalised a series of technologies discovered during the 1970s and 1980s, the personal computer, mobile phone and internet. The economies of scale possible with the extension of the world market meant the price of computers fell by 90% between 1990 and 2000[45] and their impact presaged the new economy that was to follow. Alan Greenspan the Chairman of the Federal Reserve spoke of "irrational exuberance" to describe the stock valuations in December 1996.[46] He spoke too soon,

[42] Barry Tom 2006. *IRC Special Report; Rise and Demise of the New American Century*. International Relations Centre. www.irc-online.org.

[43] Donnelly Thomas 2000. *Rebuilding America's Defences; Strategy, Forces and Resources For a New Century*. Washington, D.C. The Project for the New American Century, p. 19.

[44] IMF 1998. The Asian Crisis: Causes and Cures Staff. *Finance & Development* 35(2), New York, IMF. https://www.imf.org/external/pubs/ft/fandd/1998/06/imfstaff.htm.

[45] U.S. Bureau of Labor Statistics 2024. *Import Price Index (End Use): Computers, Peripherals and Semiconductors* [IR213]. FRED, Federal Reserve Bank of St. Louis; https://fred.stlouisfed.org/series/IR213.

[46] Greenspan Alan 1996. *Remarks by the Chairman, at the Annual Dinner and Francis Boyer Lecture of The American Enterprise Institute for Public Policy Research*. Washington

the market became more irrationally exuberant with speculative money flooding into Dot-Com companies, in just five years after the 1996 Act over $500 billion was invested in installing 80 million miles fibre optic cable, switches and wireless networks.[47] Submarine cables forming the backbone of the internet were laid by 2002.[48] Such an enormous amount of new capacity that by 2002 as little as 2% was in use and even by 2005 only around 15%.[49] The Dow Jones Industrial Average (DJIA) rose from 3,600 in 1994 to 11,000 in 1999 passing 11,700 in 2000.[50] The value of the Nasdaq technology index rose five-fold between 1995 and 2000. The Fed had cut interest rates after the brief 1990 recession from 8.25% to 3% by 1993 before increasing them again to around 6% in 1995 and then 7% by 2000.[51] The Nasdaq peaked in March 2000 at 5,048.62 before falling to 1,139.90 by October 2002. In 2002 Bookings complained the internet still awaited its "killer application".[52] Patience is a virtue. The valuations of hi-tech companies could not yet be justified by the profits they created; they would do.

The doubling of the world working class with the integration of the FSU and China into the world market, doubled the only source of surplus value, without any, or only minimal, increase in fixed capital and so raised the rate of profit. This one-off increase was compounded by the extension of the world market, enabling economies of scale to cheapen the

DC, Federal Reserve Board. https://www.federalreserve.gov/boarddocs/speeches/1996/19961205.htm.

[47] Brookings Institution 2002. The Telecommunications Crash: What To Do Now? Policy Brief #112. The Brookings Institution, Washington DC. https://www.brookings.edu/wp-content/uploads/2016/06/pb112.pdf.

[48] Submarine Cable Map 2024. https://www.submarinecablemap.com/multiselect/ready-for-service?ids=2000,2002,2003.

[49] McCullough Brian 2018. *A revealing look at the dot-com bubble of 2000—and how it shapes our lives today*. https://ideas.ted.com/an-eye-opening-look-at-the-dot-com-bubble-of-2000-and-how-it-shapes-our-lives-today/.

[50] Shiller Robert J. 2000. *Irrational Exuberance*. Princeton, Princeton Univ. Press.

[51] Mitra Mallika, Curcio Paul and Tony David 2024. *A history of the federal funds rate*. CNN Underscored Money. https://edition.cnn.com/cnn-underscored/money/federal-funds-rate-history#.

[52] Brookings Institution 2002. The Telecommunications Crash: What To Do Now? Policy Brief #112. The Brookings Institution, Washington DC. https://www.brookings.edu/wp-content/uploads/2016/06/pb112.pdf.

technological revolution which followed. The generalisation of information technology across the economy depreciated fixed capital, the supply of Russian oil and minerals cheapened the price of raw materials, the rush of investment into the new technologies of the internet anticipated the future, and installed the infrastructure for the wireless internet revolution that was to follow shortly, even though this was very slightly the music of the future. By 2001 it was obvious that the worst predictions for the crash would not come to pass. The recession following the bursting of the Hi-Tech bubble was over by January 2002. Hyper-globalisation, a new period of *Sturm und Drang* would follow.

CHAPTER 5

Hyper-Globalisation and the Laws of Political Economy

"I hear people say we have to stop and debate globalisation. You might as well debate whether autumn should follow summer". Tony Blair 2005.[1]

11 September 2001, Osama Bin Laden's Al-Qaeda crashed two commercial planes into the World Trade Centre twin towers, which collapsed. A third into the Pentagon and a fourth into an empty field. Nearly 3,000 people died. It was the worst attack on American soil since Pearl Harbor in 1941. On September 20th, President George W. Bush declared a "war on terrorism".[2] 7 October 2001, Operation Enduring Freedom bombed and then invaded Afghanistan supported by 83% of Americans.[3] In January 2002 Bush's State of the Union Address referred to an "Axis

[1] Blair Tony 2005. *Tony Blair's conference speech 2005*. The Guardian. https://www.theguardian.com/uk/2005/sep/27/labourconference.speeches.

[2] NCTAUS. 2004. *The 9/11 Commission Report*. National Commission on Terrorist Attacks Upon the United States. https://www.9-11commission.gov/report/911Report.pdf.

[3] Hartig Hannah and Doherty Carroll 2021. *Two Decades Later, the Enduring Legacy of 9/11*. Pew Research Centre.
https://www.pewresearch.org/politics/2021/09/02/two-decades-later-the-enduring-legacy-of-9-11/.

W. Jefferies, *War and the World Economy*, Palgrave Insights into Apocalypse Economics,
https://doi.org/10.1007/978-3-031-85236-7_5

of Evil" including Iran, Iraq and North Korea. Through 2001 the U.S. slashed interest rates by 5 percentage points[4] and in December China acceded to the WTO.[5] In January 2002 the European Union (EU) adopted the Euro as a full currency and by the summer the Dot-Com crash had bottomed out.

Bush's accession to the White House was the opportunity for the Project for a New American Century (PNAC) to make their mark. Ten PNAC signatories served in Bush's administration including Dick Cheney, Donald Rumsfeld and Paul Wolfowitz. In the Spring of 2000 Robert Kagan and William Kristol, the think tanks founders, had published *Present Dangers*[6] their analysis of the limitations of Clinton's foreign policy. For all its self-promoting bluster, which included a proposal for the re-invasion of Iraq, in practice it called for a small increase in U.S. defence spending. The twin towers attack stimulated their ambition. September 20th, they wrote to Bush anticipating his declaration of a War on Terrorism and demanding the conquest of Iraq "even if evidence does not link Iraq directly to the attack".[7] In April 2002 another public letter[8] denounced the leader of the Palestinian authority Yasser Arafat as a terrorist and called for Iraq's urgent invasion.[9] This became the bi-partisan policy of the U.S. establishment, with Madeleine Albright Clinton's Secretary of State, Senator Joe Biden, the historian Paul Kennedy, and Will Marshall the Democratic Party grandee and originator of Tony Blair's "Third Way", all signing subsequent PNAC open letters.

[4] Board of Governors of the Federal Reserve System (U.S.) 2024. *Federal Funds Effective Rate [FEDFUNDS]*. FRED, Federal Reserve Bank of St. Louis; https://fred.stlouisfed.org/series/FEDFUNDS.

[5] WTO 2002. *China*. World Trade Organisation. https://www.wto.org/english/thewto_e/acc_e/a1_chine_e.htm.

[6] Kagan Robert and Kristol William 2000. *Present Dangers; Crisis and Opportunity in American Foreign and Defense Policy*. Edited by Robert Kagan and William Kristol, New York, Encounter Books.

[7] PNAC 2001. *Letter to President Bush on the War on Terrorism*. www.militarist-monitor.org.

[8] PNAC 2002. *Letter to President Bush on Israel, Arafat and the War on Terrorism*. www.militarist-monitor.org.

[9] Barry Tom 2006. *IRC Special Report; Rise and Demise of the New American Century*. International Relations Centre. www.irc-online.org.

The Iraq invasion was eventually excused through the search for mythical Weapons of Mass Destruction (WMD). 3 February 2003, Blair's government produced a Dodgy Dossier[10] that pretended to prove Iraq's possession of WMDs. On February 5th Colin Powell U.S. Secretary of State danced the same dance at the UN security council. The necessary resolution for legal war was never passed. Irrespective the invasion decision had already been made. On March 20th war began, three weeks later Hussein's regime collapsed. The Iraq army was disbanded in May. Hussein was arrested in December and executed three years later. In January 2004 the search for WMDs was abandoned.[11] By 2006 *The Lancet* estimated 601,027 Iraqis had met violent post-invasion deaths.[12] In May 2011 Bin Laden was killed, U.S. troops eventually deserted Iraq in December. They gave up on Afghanistan in August 2021.[13] The wars cost the U.S. an estimated $1.79tn.[14]

After the 1998 East Asian crisis Russia reached the limits of economic collapse, the devaluation of the Rouble by around three quarters, combined with a sharp rise in world oil prices after 2001, enabled the economy to begin its post-communist recovery.[15] From 1997 until 2000 the Premier Yevgeny Primakov sought to balance the budget, slashing public expenditures to 14% of GDP, cutting corporation tax from 35 to 24%, but more importantly, applying it to the oligarchs, who during the criminal restoration phase, negotiated their individual tax. Putin's 2000

[10] HM Government 2003. Iraq its Infrastructure of Concealment, Deception and Intimidation). London: Guardian News and Media. https://image.guardian.co.uk/sys-files/Guardian/documents/2003/02/07/uk0103.pdf.

[11] CFR 2024. *The Iraq war 2003–2011*. Council Foreign Relations. https://www.cfr.org/timeline/iraq-war.

[12] Burnham Gilbert, Lafta Riyadh, Doocy Shannon and Roberts Les 2006. Mortality after the 2003 invasion of Iraq: a cross-sectional cluster sample survey. *The Lancet* 368(9545), pp. 1421–1428.

[13] Naval History and Heritage Command 2023. *The 9/11 Terrorist Attacks 11 September 2001*. Naval History and Heritage Command. https://www.history.navy.mil/browse-by-topic/wars-conflicts-and-operations/sept-11-attack.html.

[14] Crawford Neta C. 2023. *Blood and Treasure: United States Budgetary Costs and Human Costs of 20 Years of War in Iraq and Syria, 2003–2023*. https://watson.brown.edu/costsofwar/files/cow/imce/papers/2023/Costs.

[15] Nesterenko Andrei 2000. The Modernization Challenge Facing President Putin. *IMF Finance and Development Magazine*, 37(3). https://www.imf.org/external/pubs/ft/fandd/2000/09/nesteren.htm.

Presidential election continued the "second generation" of Primakov's market reforms, but Putin with the purpose of reconstituting Russian imperial might as a capitalist mineral exporter that dominates neighbouring states of the former Russian imperial empire. A flat income tax of 13% was introduced in 2001. Federal government revenues almost doubled as a share of GDP from 1998 to 2002, even while total state revenues remained close to constant. Putin wanted to see a "strengthening of the role of the state". His government re-established control over foreign exchange, required the registration of foreign trade transactions, took control of Gazprom, renationalised Yukos and Sibneft and legalised the private ownership of agricultural land.[16] Tensions with the close neighbours of the former Soviet Union rumbled on. In 2004 Ukraine's president Kuchma was replaced by Yushchenko an advocate of NATO membership. The conflict in Chechnya continued, not officially ending until 2009, but Putin's presidency meant that Russia would not be reduced to a colony of the West and its recovery posed an increasing irritant to U.S. global hegemony.

Western economists widely predicted that faced with Western competition with China's accession to the WTO in 2001 it would follow Russia into collapse[17] and indeed the terms of China's WTO accession conditions were punitive, designed with this in mind, as Clinton explained,

> by forcing China to slash subsidies and tariffs that protect inefficient industries, which the Communist Party has long used to exercise day-to-day control, by letting our high-tech companies in to bring the Internet and information revolution to China, we will be unleashing forces that no totalitarian operation rooted in last century's industrial society can control.[18]

[16] Åslund Anders 2008. An Assessment of Putin's Economic Policy. (PIIE) *Peterson Institute for International Economics*. https://www.piie.com/commentary/speeches-papers/assessment-putins-economic-policy.

[17] Jefferies William 2021. China's Accession to the WTO and the Collapse That Never Was. *Review of Radical Political Economics*, 53(2), pp. 300–319.

[18] U.S. Congress 2002. *The National Security Implications of the Economic Relationship between the United States and China 2002*. Report to Congress of the U.S.-China Security Review Commission. Accessed at: https://china.usc.edu/us-china-economic-and-security-review-commission-2002-annual-report-congress-july-15-2002, p. 60.

The collapse is yet awaited.[19] The independence of China's financial sector, its domestic banks remained state owned, and the nationalisation of land conferred huge advantages on it. The leasing of land provided rents for local government bodies to fund infrastructure development. The large proportion of China's savings more accurately profits, reinvested into domestic development, facilitated the 1990s increase of 157 mn in the urban population, and consequent growth of the domestic market. But still not fast enough to absorb China's growing balance of payments surplus, which was recycled into U.S. government bonds, further contributing to the decline of interest rates there. China could not yet challenge U.S. dominance of the world economy but as its growth accelerated so it became the workshop of the world.[20]

America had won the Cold War, the ease of the coalitions' victory in Iraq proved its utter military dominance and its ability to operate outside of UN sanction. The international rules-based order did not apply to it. There appeared to be no limits on its ambition. Its hegemony expressed a key condition for an expansive long period, a dominant world power, with an interest in, and the capacity to, guarantee free trade. The first cycle of a long wave from 1991–2001 incorporated the former centrally planned economies into the world market. From the late 1990s the newly marketised former planned economies began to recover, the second cycle of the long wave was to be the strongest period of capitalist expansion in history the period of hyper-globalisation, 2001–2008.

Hyper-globalisation was a label coined by Dan Rodick of Harvard University[21] who attributed the hyper-expansion of trade to everything except the growth of the world market. His *Globalization Paradox* neglected to mention the end of the Cold War. He was in good company, Paul Krugman, the Nobel Prize winner's celebrated article *Growing World Trade: Causes and Consequences*[22] attributed the expansion of world trade

[19] Jefferies, W. 2021. China's Accession to the WTO and the Collapse That Never Was. *Review of Radical Political Economics,* 53(2), pp. 300–319.

[20] Baldwin Richard 2024. *China is the world's sole manufacturing superpower: A line sketch of the rise.* VoxEU, CEPR. https://cepr.org/voxeu/columns/china-worlds-sole-manufacturing-superpower-line-sketch-rise.

[21] Rodrik Dani 2011. *The Globalization Paradox; Democracy and the Future of the World Economy.* Oxford, Oxford University Press.

[22] Krugman Paul 1995. Growing World Trade: Causes and Consequences. Brookings Papers on Economic Activity 1.

to technology, tariff reductions and changes to factor prices, wages and raw materials, ignoring the physical expansion of the world market across one third of the globe and half its population just four years prior. In 2003 Kei-Mu Yi,[23] in the "most influential"[24] academic paper on trade policy and tariffs, was at a loss to explain the doubling of U.S. manufactured exports as a proportion of GDP in the 1990s. This "puzzle" bamboozled both standard and adjusted trade models which "cannot explain the magnitude of trade growth" they "fell short". Kei-Mu considered other relevant factors, but not the most relevant factor, the growth of the world market with the transition of centrally planned economies to the market. In 2023 Pinelopi Koujianou Goldberg the former Chief Economist of the World Bank Group analysed hyper-globalisation and de-globalisation, without mentioning the end of the Cold War. Communism was a bad dream, it was over, the less said the better.

The increase in trade with globalisation, not only reflected the outsourcing of the products of final demand, but what Richard Baldwin, the Harvard economist, dubbed the "second unbundling".[25] The unrestricted trade in intermediate parts, due to the dicing and slicing, and the fragmentation of the value chain, to reduce costs and turnover times. Baldwin claimed that the unbundling of economic power and development from industrialisation meant that industrialisation was "easier", "faster" and "less meaningful". The geographical separation of the stages of the value chain, and particularly the offshoring of production, meant industrialisation could not be equated with development. This "technology lending" could almost immediately revolutionise developing nation industry. Offshored factories were transplanted wholesale, now all that exports showed was "that the nation is located along a particular segment of an international value chain". This made industrialisation substantially less complex, quicker and better integrated, as "rich-nation firms" offshored segments of their value chains to developing nations.

[23] Yi Kei-Mu 2003. Can Vertical Specialization Explain the Growth of World Trade? *Journal of Political Economy,* 111 (1), pp. 52–102, p. 65, p. 85.

[24] Koujianou Goldberg Pinelopi with Larson Greg 2023. *The Unequal Effects of Globalization*. The Ohlin Lectures.

David Domeij, series editor. Cambridge, Massachusetts, MIT Press.

[25] Baldwin Richard 2011. Trade and Industrialisation After Globalisation's 2nd Unbundling: How building and Joining a Supply Chain are Different and Why it Matters. *NBER Working Paper 17,716*. http://www.nber.org/papers/w17716.

No longer was the development of a wholesale industrial base necessary, quite the opposite, it was undesirable, now rather, select capacity could be transplanted into any given nation, where the outsourced industries meshed with pan-border off shored production capacity but, not ownership. Ownership meant control and control meant that the "combination of rich-nation technology and low-wage labour could be very profitable".

Baldwin attributed this development to the combination of technology and low wages. He, like Rodick and Krugman, did not notice the end of the cold war.[26] Baldwin noted that China was the physical centre of "factory Asia", but he claimed, it barely used Chinese factors of production, nor technology, nor did it guarantee open access for the exports from it. While the ICT revolution meant that "technology no longer requires that successive stages of manufacturing production be physically contiguous or proximate". The geographical separation of manufacturing stages—the unbundling of factories from the supply chain that fed them and the final consumption of their output, was now "inevitable" due to economies of scale and comparative advantages.

Baldwin had drafted a manifesto for the deindustrialisation of Western imperialism. Finance was separate and so no longer dependent on manufacturing. This new form of imperialism broke the symbiosis of banking and manufacturing capital or finance capital as Hilferding had described it in 1910.[27] The separation of this class of fictional assets from production obscured the material basis for their extraction of rents, the mobilisation of vast financial resources, the ownership and control of key, necessarily scarce technologies, and access to the rich Western markets for the premium products based on them. The redistribution of value, not according to the organic composition of capital, or the contribution of labour to production, but according to monopoly control of vital technologies and markets, was what Stan Shih, the CEO of the Taiwanese Acer Group,[28] manufacturer of personal computers, labelled the Smiling Curve. Value was disproportionately appropriated before and after manufacturing. By the owner of key technological inputs, in this case

[26] Baldwin Richard 2006. *The Great Unbundlings*. Geneva, Graduate Institute of International Studies.

[27] Hilferding Rudolf 1981 [1910]. *Finance Capital. A Study of the Latest Phase of Capitalist Development*. Editor Tom Bottomore, London, Routledge and Kegan Paul.

[28] Shih Stan 1996. *Me Too Is Not My Style*. Acer Foundation.

microchips, and to the distributor of premium, technologically cutting-edge products to rich Western markets or "the share of value added in manufactured products is shifting from the fabrication stages to pre- and post-fabrication services".[29] These Smiling Curves became "much deeper and wider over time" reflecting the "deepening vertical specialization and the expanding cross-border fragmentation of production in the corresponding value chains during the data period".[30] Manufacturing was outsourced to the lowest cost supplier, but nonetheless, remained physically dependent on the commissioner multinational corporation, which controlled key input technology, oversaw production and undertook marketing, the distribution of the product in high value markets.

Western corporations became "Factoryless Goods Producers"[31] (FGPs) who designed the goods they sold, but did not necessarily undertake production activities, which were shifted to contract manufacturing services (CMS). After 2004 Apple divested itself of production line ownership. Apple now designed, engineered, developed, marketed and sold consumer electronics, software and computers, but manufacture was only indirectly controlled by it. By 2023 It directly employed 14,000 people in China but "monitors the weekly hours of 1.5 mn workers" the "vast majority in China"[32] where, by 2023, "more than 95% of iPhones, AirPods, Macs and iPads are made".[33] Mainly by Foxconn, a Taiwanese manufacturer, but located in mainland China, that produced the outputs that used the inputs, which were then marketed and sold by Apple or Taiwan's chip manufacturer TSMC, which provided services to Fabless, meaning without a directly owned Fabrication (Fab) microchip manufacturing facilities, for chip design companies like Nvidia, AMD and Apple. TSMC's output, owned by the commissioning MNC Apple, provided

[29] Baldwin Richard and Ito Tadashi 2021. The smile curve: Evolving sources of value added in manufacturing. *Canadian Journal of Economics/Revue Canadienne* d'economique, 54(4), pp. 1842–1880.

[30] Ming YE, Meng Bo and Wei Shang-jin 2015. Measuring Smile Curves in Global Value Chains. *IDE Discussion Paper No. 530*. JETRO Institute of Developing Economies.

[31] Bernard Andrew B. and Fort Teresa C. 2013. *Factoryless Goods Producers in the US*. NBER Working Paper 19,396. http://www.nber.org/papers/w19396.

[32] McGee Patrick 2023. *What it would take for Apple to disentangle itself from China*. https://www.ft.com/content/74f7e284-c047-4cc4-9b7a-408d40611bfa.

[33] McGee Patrick 2023. *How Apple tied its fortunes to China*. https://www.ft.com/content/d5a80891-b27d-4110-90c9-561b7836f11b.

the inputs for the CMS, like Foxconn, who manufactured the outputs for the marketeer, Apple. This lowered costs by enabling economies of scale, through increasing capacity utilisation, so spreading fixed capital and research and development costs across a larger amount of output. The rise of the internet and reduction of transportation and trade costs reduced relative costs and allowed the FGPs to swallow the bulk of value added, in 2015/2016 Apple claimed 73% of total profits across all premium models.[34] China claimed just 1% of the overall cost of an iPhone 7.[35] Increasing their share of value added, claiming more of the profits that they produced, defined China's economic policy from here on in.

These smiling curves produced what Ben Bernanke the Governor of the Federal Reserve described as a savings glut.[36] The U.S. off shored its production, lowering domestic investment, increasing its balance of payments deficit, while harvesting the savings or profits "glut" from abroad. From the early 1990s Foreign Direct Investment (FDI) in greenfield subsidiaries, buying existing foreign companies or mergers and acquisitions, flooded into the new market economies of CEE and China. Global FDI increased from 1990 $205bn to 2000 $1356bn, peaking at 2007 $1906bn with the global financial crisis, it then fluctuated and peaked again at 2015 $2056bn before declining to 2022 $1295bn.[37] Before China's WTO membership from 1997 to 2002 the share of foreign value added in China's manufactured exports was about 50%, in 2007, after 5 years of its WTO membership it had risen to over 60%,[38] before it subsequently declined with the growth of Chinese multinationals.

[34] Kraemer Kenneth L., Linden Greg, and Dedrick Jason 2011. *Capturing Value in Global Networks: Apple's iPad and iPhone*. Component (economiadeservicos.com).

[35] Dedrick Jason and Kraemer, Kenneth L. 2017. *Intangible Assets and Value Capture in Global Value Chains: The Smartphone Industry*. World Intellectual Property Organization (WIPO) Economic Research Working Paper Series No. 41. https://ssrn.com/abstract=4430090.

[36] Bernanke Ben S. 2005. *The Global Saving Glut and the U.S. Current Account Deficit, Remarks by Governor Ben S. Bernanke*. Federal Reserve Board. https://www.federalreserve.gov/boarddocs/speeches/2005/200503102/.

[37] UNCTAD 2023. World Investment Report. Geneva, UNCTAD. https://unctad.org/publication/world-investment-report-2023.

[38] Koopman Robert, Wang Zhi and Wei Shang-Jin 2009. How Much of Chinese Exports is Really Made in China? Assessing Domestic Value-Added When Processing Trade is Pervasive. *NBER Working Paper 14,109*. http://www.nber.org/papers/w14109.

The repatriation of these revenues and the rise of financial assets separate from physical manufacturing was reflected in the growth of services trade, which has no product and so is not trade as strictly defined. It adds no value as it provides nothing useful, rather it is a renamed form of financial parasitism the repatriation of revenues yielded abroad. This services trade increased as a proportion of total trade from about 17% of world trade in 1980 and about 20% in 2008 and even more so in value added terms 30% and 43%.[39] Financial institutions used the international rules-based system as a means of capture value created elsewhere. Manufacturing profits were replaced with intangible assets or legally defensible rents like "patents, copyrights and brands".[40] These intangible assets could not be valued with any certainty, they were akin to the valuations of land based on multiples of expected ground rents but extended to any class of asset, a claim on benefits without any tangible physical or financial embodiment, expressed as their Net Present Value (NPV) the discounted aggregate of the future revenues to be yielded by them. The same basis as the valuations of the fixed capital stock in the SNA.[41] Asset Backed Securities (ABS), like Mortgage-Backed Securities (MBS) or Collateralised Debt Obligations (CDOs), drew no distinction between the source of revenue, whether mortgage interest, or profits. This conceptually irrational value form expressed the alienated nature of surplus value in a capitalist society, where profits appear to arise from nothing, without direct reference to their physical or social basis.

The general economic laws of capital accumulation determine that the doubling of the world working class through the extension of the world market into the centrally planned economies must have lowered the labour to capital ratio or the organic composition of capital, as vast amounts of means of production were transferred to capitalists at no cost through theft or the expropriation of their state owners. This was reinforced by the mid-1990s onward technological revolution, sparked by the generalisation of internet and computer technology. The rapid rise in

[39] Subramanian Arvind and Kessler Martin 2013. The Hyperglobalization of Trade and Its Future. *Working Paper Series WP*, pp. 13–6. Washington DC, Peterson Institute.

[40] Mudambi Ram 2008. Geography and the Cultural Economy. Journal of Economic Geography 8(5), pp. 699–725.

[41] OECD 2008. *Measuring Capital—OECD Manual 2009*. Paris, OECD. https://www.oecd.org/en/publications/measuring-capital-oecd-manual-2009_9789264068476-en.html.

productivity depreciated existing capital and enabled manufacturing to be shifted to former centrally planned economies with a highly skilled labour force, low pay rates and integrated production networks across national borders. The sale of Russian oil at market prices held down raw materials prices until 2001, while U.S. hegemony lowered tariff rates, guaranteed the free movement of air and shipping and so lowered the cost of transportation and raised the rate of turnover. As turnover accelerated less capital was needed to be advanced in wages and raw materials as costs were paid through revenue received, while rising productivity reduced the cost of reproduction of labour power, raised what wages could buy even as their value fell, enabling wages to fall as a proportion of national income even as living standards outside of the countries facing the trauma of restoration rose. Rising profits were reflected in soaring income inequality. The combination of these factors massively increased the rate of profit.

Daron Acemoglu and James A. Robinson, archetypal economics professors from MIT and Harvard,[42] denied the existence of the general economic laws described by David Ricardo, Karl Marx and more recently Thomas Piketty. They claimed that the,

> quest for general laws of capitalism is misguided because it ignores the key forces shaping how an economy functions: the endogenous evolution of technology and of the institutions and the political equilibrium that influence not only technology but also how markets function and how the gains from various different economic arrangements are distributed.

Marx's identification of "certain hard-wired features of capitalism— what Marx called general laws of capitalist accumulation" was basically misconceived. The professors described three exemplar laws to illustrate the point. First the "General Law of Capitalist Accumulation" was in a "Strong Form: Real wages are stagnant under capitalism. Weak Form: The share of national income accruing to labour would fall under capitalism". Nonetheless, in "either its strong or weak form, this law implies that any economic growth under capitalism would almost automatically translate into greater inequality—as capitalists benefit and workers fail to do so". Their objection laughably fails the empirical test, the 2022 World Inequality Report observed "Global multimillionaires have captured a

[42] Acemoglu Daron and Robinson James A. 2015. The Rise and Decline of General Laws of Capitalism. *Journal of Economic Perspectives*, 29(1), pp. 3–28.

disproportionate share of global wealth growth over the past several decades: the top 1% took 38% of all additional wealth accumulated since the mid-1990s, whereas the bottom 50% captured just 2% of it",[43] but what about the theoretical one?

The law of capital accumulation is the process through which capitalists accumulate capital. They advance capital (M) to buy labour, machinery and raw materials (C), to produce a different product (P) with a higher value (C'), which they sell on a market (M') to realise a profit (M'-M) in the circuit M…C…P…C'…M'. This law is only indirectly connected to wage levels insofar as they alter costs. The capitalist necessity for surplus value extraction, the source of all profits, provides an absolute upward limit on the rise of wages in any given period, while the need of the working class to reproduce itself, provides an absolute lower limit, so that,

> either the price of labour keeps on rising, because its rise does not interfere with the progress of accumulation…or, on the other hand, accumulation slackens in consequence of the rise in the price of labour, because the stimulus of gain is blunted …the price of labour falls again to a level corresponding with the needs of the self-expansion of capital, whether the level be below, the same as, or above the one which was normal before the rise of wages took place.[44]

Wages may rise or fall or remain the same, depending on the exigencies of the accumulation process, but within the limits necessary to ensure expanded reproduction. The explanation is perfectly clear, completely accurate, hard wired, and not in the least like that claimed by the professors. The social law applies universally in the capitalist economy.

The second law was the "General Law of Declining Profit: as capital accumulates, the rate of profit falls". On the whole the rate of profit has been rising during the period of globalisation does this exception disprove the rule?[45] Marx discussed the "Law of the Tendency of the Rate of Profit

[43] Chancel Lucas, Piketty Thomas, Saez Emmanuel and Zucman Gabriel 2022. *World Inequality Report 2022*. World Inequality Lab. https://wir2022.wid.world/www-site/uploads/2022/01/Summary_WorldInequalityReport2022_English.pdf, p. 15.

[44] Marx Karl 1995 [1867]. *Capital; A Critique of Political Economy Volume I*. Moscow, Progress, p. 435.

[45] Jefferies William 2023. The U.S. rate of profit 1964–2017 and the turnover of fixed and circulating capital. *Capital & Class*, 47(2), pp. 267–289.

to Fall"[46] in *Capital III*. He explained the tendency for falling profit rates was "just an expression peculiar to the capitalist mode of production of the progressive development of the social productivity of labour", but Marx continued, the explanation of,

> the falling rate of profit, gives place to its opposite, namely to explain why this fall is not greater and more rapid. There must be some counteracting influences at work, which cross and annul the effect of the general law, and which give it merely the characteristic of a tendency, for which reason we have referred to the fall of the general rate of profit as a tendency to fall.

Five offsetting factors reduced the law to tendency; increasing the intensity of exploitation, reducing wages below their value, cheapening elements of constant capital, expanding the population that could be exploited by capital, and foreign trade. The upward long wave of globalisation saw them play out with striking in effect during hyper-globalisation phase. They were an astonishingly prescient description of the key factors shaping the world capitalist economy between 2001 and 2008 but, Marx's point was, and the reason the tendency was a law, was that they could not endure indefinitely. Rising productivity both produces and offsets the increase in the physical mass of capital by increasing its scale but reducing its value. Eventually, however, the infinite potential for the accumulation of the mass of capital, exceeds the finite potential for productivity to offset it. The pace of technological advance must continually accelerate faster than the growth in the mass of means of production, to deflate the cost of fixed and circulating capital, machinery, labour and raw materials, and to ensure that the value of wages becomes cheaper, so living standards rise, even as income inequality, the key product of capital accumulation, increases. The expansion of the system into new undeveloped sectors and nations expressed in urbanisation, the transformation of small farmers into proletarians wage earners dependent on the market for their means of subsistence, increasing demand and productivity, must grow faster than the accumulation of capital and demand of the existing population for improved living standards. This will not continue forever,

[46] Karl Marx 1959 [1894] *Capital A Critique of Political Economy Volume III*. Moscow, Progress, p. 152, 166, 165.

there are limits to the *Sturm und Drang*.[47] Hence, the transition from an expansionary long wave to a period of decline is inevitable, even if gradual, given the scale of the impetus provided by the extension of the world market across the globe in the 1990s.

Thus, the tendency of the rate of profit to fall is, even if, not the most essential and basic law of capitalist political economy, universal commodity exchange, nonetheless, its most important law. It points to the finitude, historically contingent nature of the capitalist system itself. It means that capitalist accumulation will not smoothly proceed forever but contains the seeds of its own destruction. The global capitalist accumulation process eventually undermines the economic and geopolitical foundations for capitalist globalisation, its own existence. It creates new powers that threaten the established order of nations. As free trade requires the monopoly of a world power, national rivalry leads to restrictions on trade, proxy wars and wars. Restrictions on the scope of the market, reduce economies of scale, disrupt integrated production networks, slow the rate of turnover, in turn lowering profit rates and exacerbating national rivalries. These limits are hard wired into the system, general economic laws of its functioning, a direct product of the capital accumulation process itself, not initially a product of falling profit rates, but of rising ones. Eventually they combine to choke off high profit rates, and with them, the upward wave.

The third law was the "General Law of Decreasing Competition: capital accumulation leads to increased industrial concentration" and the professors explain, the failure of this law is particularly evident in the U.S. due to the break-up of monopolies like Standard Oil, once again this is a frankly preposterous assertion given the dominance of monopolies in the U.S. economy. The growth of FGPs like Apple, with a low organic composition of capital, but huge valuations, revenues and profits, is dependent on their monopoly power. The top 10 companies in the Fortune 500 list of largest U.S. corporations make up 20% of its revenues. The top 200 companies account for 85% of the Fortune 500's revenues and 70% of profits. Amazon and Walmart together employ

[47] Parvus Alexander (Helphand) 1901 [2024]. *Die Handelskrisis und die Gewerkschaften, nebst Anhang: Gestzentwurf über den achtstündigen Normalarbeitstag*, München: Druck von M. Ernst, translated by Daniel Gaido.

3.2 mn workers.[48] The point is such concentration does not lead to decreasing competition and there is no such law enunciated anywhere in Marx as "unlimited competition is therefore not the presupposition for the truth of the economic laws, but rather the consequence—the form of appearance in which their necessity realizes itself",[49] so much for the theoretical denial of the laws of political economy.

But the impact of globalisation on profit rates is also denied empirically. Marxian economists, starting from the opposite end to Acemoglu and Robinson end up in the same place. They deny the empirical functioning of the economic laws which determine capitalist accumulation through the period of globalisation. Applying neo-classical datasets from official agencies like the World Bank, IMF and United Nations, they claim that globalisation in general, and hyper-globalisation in particular, was and is a period of deep, enduring and existential crisis for capitalist growth and profitability. Michael Roberts, a British Marxian catastrophist, labelled hyper-globalisation a Great Depression.[50] A period of crisis which has endured for many decades since at least the early 1970s, notwithstanding the absence of class struggle, revolutions and indeed, crises of capitalism since the early 1990s. Crisis becomes a chronic condition, not so much akin to a heart attack as an arthritic knee or bunion.

These catastrophist economists develop estimations of the rate of profit, which show profitability collapsing from the 1970s on. A typical 2023 example from Thomas R. Michl,[51] a U.S. political economist, showed the U.S. rate of profit plummeting from 1995, crashing with the onset of hyper-globalisation, before settling in a perpetual slump significantly below even the crisis years of 1980–82. Michael Roberts and Guglielmo Carchedi,[52] a veteran Marxian economist, produced rate of

[48] Oxfam 2024. *How do the largest US corporations contribute to inequality? Oxfam's corporate inequality framework*. https://www.oxfamamerica.org/explore/research-publications/corporate-inequality-footprint/.

[49] Marx Karl 1973. *Grundrisse*. Translated by Martin Nicolaus. London, Penguin, p. 476.

[50] Roberts Michael 2016. *The Long Depression: Marxism and the Global Crisis of Capitalism*. Chicago, Haymarket.

[51] Michl Thomas R. 2023. The Falling Rate of Profit as a Research Program. *The New School Economic Review*, 12, pp. 36–51. https://nsereview.org/index.php/NSER/article/view/112.

[52] Carchedi Guglielmo and Roberts Michael 2021. The Economics of Modern Imperialism. *Historical Materialism*, 29(4), pp. 23–69.

profit estimates that similarly demonstrated a collapse of profitability in the early 1980s, from which it never recovered. According to them the greatest most rapid period of capitalist growth ever was actually a period of stagnant collapse.

This implausible outcome is shared by similar papers based on data from the Penn World Tables (PWT).[53] These authors use statistics that apply Hulten and Wykoff[54] valuations of the fixed capital stock derived from the UN System of National Accounts[55] (SNA) this explained that valuations of the fixed capital stock "may be determined by the present value of its future earnings". This is further developed in the OECD's *Measuring Capital*[56] and *Measuring Productivity*.[57] The OECD's manuals, produced in partnership with the U.S. Bureau of Economic Analysis (BEA), EU, UN, World Bank and IMF, provide a catalogue of the methods used to construct valuations of the fixed capital stock in the various SNAs across the world. All their formulations "build on the idea that the price of an asset equals the discounted value of the net benefits that it is expected to generate in the future" its Net Present Value NPV. This market equilibrium condition forms the conceptual link between the age price profile and the depreciation pattern. It is specifically and explicitly not a measure of the fixed capital advanced of past costs incurred but an estimate of future, not yet yielded profits, an aggregate of what are labelled discounted services. These capital values whether historic, the discounted services from installation, or current, the discounted services at present, are a future guestimate. Following

[53] Basu Deepankar, Huato Julio, Jauregui Jesus Lara, and Wasner Evan 2022. World Profit Rates, 1960–2019. *Economics Department Working Paper Series 318*, Amherst, University of Massachusetts.

[54] Wykoff Frank C. and Hulten Charles R. 1979. Tax and Economic Depreciation of Machinery and Equipment: A Theoretical and Empirical Appraisal, Phase II Report. In: *Economic Depreciation of the U.S. Capital Stock: A First Step*; Washington DC, U.S. Department of the Treasury, Office of Tax Analysis.

[55] United Nations 2008. *System of National Accounts*. New York, United Nations, p. 415.

[56] OECD 2009. *Measuring Capital; OECD Manual Second Edition*. Paris, Organisation of Economic Cooperation and Development. https://unstats.un.org/unsd/nationalaccount/docs/oecd-capital-e.pdf.

[57] OECD 2001. *Measuring Productivity*. OECD, p. 54. https://unstats.un.org/unsd/nationalaccount/docs/OECD-Productivity-e.pdf.

Walras,[58] the SNA do not measure the value of capital by its physical amount, which is incommensurate, or its labour cost, which is ideologically unacceptable, but rather, by the revenue it creates, which is a circular mess. The profit of capital depends on the value of capital multiplied by the profit yielded, but the value of capital is a multiple of the profit yielded. The OECD's *Measuring Capital* noted "a possible circularity when the rate of return is computed endogenously"[59] as "a rate of return is needed to compute the age-price profile and hence depreciation. But the rate of depreciation is needed to compute the endogenous rate of return". This can be solved by a system of nonlinear equations, or more pragmatically the valuations are a "plausible" made-up number.

In 1926 Wassily Leontief, who collaborated with Simon Kuznets in developing the U.S. SNA, had criticised "Irving Fisher's contraposition of capital and income" in his PhD dissertation on the circulation of capital. Fisher precisely valued capital as an aggregate of future revenues, but Leontief's objection was dismissed by his PhD supervisor von Borkiewicz as "largely misguided".[60] As a Soviet exile in the U.S. from Leningrad University, who had worked on the Soviet *Balance*, the original state estimate of national income, and in need of a job, Leontief was in no position to argue with Fisher the President of the Econometric Society overseeing the appointment of economists for the development of the U.S. SNA. Neither was Simon Kuznets, similarly a Soviet exile, who recommended Leontief for a job with the National Bureau of Economic Research (NBER). Hence, income measures of capital were used in the SNA and provided the foundation for the fixed capital stock applied in the SNA. Capital valuations are the opportunity cost of future investments.[61]

58 Walras Leon 1954. *Elements of Pure Economics*. Translated by W. Jaffé of the Edition Définitive (1926) of the Eléments d'économie pure, first edition published in 1874, Homewood, Illinois Richard D. Irwin.

59 OECD 2009. *Measuring Capital; OECD Manual Second Edition*. Paris, Organisation of Economic Cooperation and Development. https://unstats.un.org/unsd/nationalaccount/docs/oecd-capital-e.pdf, p. 102.

60 Bjerkholt Olav 2016. Wassily Leontief and the discovery of the input–output approach. *University of Oslo, Department of Economics* Memorandum, 18/2016, p. 37.

61 Fabricant Solomon 1938. *Capital Consumption and Adjustment*. Cambridge, MA: National Bureau of Economic Research (NBER).

This method of valuation, which treats profits as a cost, was criticised by Joan Robinson during the Cambridge Capital Controversy (CCC).[62] Robinson observed that the standard production function of neo-classical economics, the formula that seeks to explain growth and profitability, attributes revenue to two sources, labour and capital. The measure of labour is straightforward, labour time, but what is the measure of capital? Physically capital consists of heterogenous masses of different machines, technology and raw materials. Its separate parts are incommensurate; yards of cloth, tonnes of steel, litres of milk, cubic metreage of buildings, gigahertz of computer processors, etc., have no common unit, and so defy common measurement. The solution of the classical economists, to measure capital by the amount of labour time it costs to produce, was rejected as it implied labour is the source of all value and so of all profit.

These imaginary NPV estimations of future services when multiplied by their imaginary service lives form the valuations of the "real" fixed capital stock. Hence, as the mass of profits rises, so does the valuation of the fixed capital stock, but by more as the increase is multiplied by the service life, so an increase in the mass of profit, leads to a fall in the rate of profit. As the mass of profits rose during the period of globalisation, so the rate of profit, using these imaginary valuations, fell. A period of expansion was transformed into a period of contraction. Just as the SNA statistics measured the expansion of the world market (with the transformation of planned economies into market ones) as the reduction of national income (confusing the expansion of the market with the decline of the plan) so they measure an increase of the rate of profit as a fall of it.

The Great Doubling of the world's capitalist workforce,[63] China's almost limitless low-wage population and the highly skilled but poor populations of Central and Eastern Europe and Russia, the physical infrastructure paid for by the busted speculators of the Dot-Com bubble, and American global hegemony which dismantled barriers to trade and the export of finance capital, together meant that "in the late 1990s....

[62] Robinson Joan 1953. The production function and the theory of capital. *The Review of Economic Studies* 21(2), pp. 81–106.

[63] Freeman Richard 2007. The Great Doubling: The Challenge of the New Global Labor Market. In *Ending Poverty In America: How to Restore the American Dream*. New York, The New Press.

economic growth took off across the world, a phenomenon that is best described as convergence with a vengeance…at around the same time, perhaps just preceding this convergence phase, world trade surged, ushering in an era of hyper-globalization".[64]

[64] Subramanian Arvind and Kessler Martin 2013. The Hyperglobalization of Trade and Its Future. *Working Paper Series WP*, pp. 13–16 Washington DC, Peterson Institute.

CHAPTER 6

Rising Profits and the Great Recession

"Frankly, if I had perfect foresight, I would never have taken this job in the first place". Hank Paulson, U.S. Secretary of the Treasury 2008.

In 2001, in the aftermath of the Dot-Com crash and Twin Towers attack, the Fed slashed interest rates by five percentage points to historically low levels. The collapse in the price of money was not only the result of a policy decision. Domestic profits soared, while from around 2002, foreign surpluses poured into the U.S. and UK. After Putin's Presidential election in 2000 Russian oligarchs recycled their ill-gotten gains abroad. Roman Abramovich bought Chelsea FC in 2003. The Gulf Cooperation Council (GCC) of Middle Eastern oil producers grew very rich as rising oil and raw materials prices flooded their coffers, while China parked its foreign trade surpluses which rose from 2001 $28bn to 2008 $349bn[1] in U.S. government debt. In January 2008 Goldman Sachs summarised the trend,

[1] World Bank 2024. China Net trade in goods and services. https://data.worldbank.org/indicator/BN.GSR.GNFS.CD?locations=CN.

W. Jefferies, *War and the World Economy*, Palgrave Insights into Apocalypse Economics,
https://doi.org/10.1007/978-3-031-85236-7_6

> The past five years have seen a spectacular boom in global profits. The boom has been driven by strong sales growth and by a rapid expansion in corporate profit margins. After reaching 5% in the first quarter of 2000 net profit margins among publicly listed companies worldwide plunged below 2% in 2002. Since then, margins have staged a remarkable comeback. By 2007, global profit margins have risen to about 7%. Not only was this considerably above the previous cyclical peak it was about 3 percentage points above the average over the previous 20 years.[2]

The U.S. Internal Revenue Service[3] (IRS) provide an alternative data source to the BEA's fictional neo-classical Hulten and Wykoff valuations of the fixed capital stock. The rate of profit is the most important indicator of the capitalist economy as it provides both the funds and the motivation for capital accumulation. It measures the ratio of the mass of profits to the mass of costs, the amount of capital advanced. The mass of profits the numerator of the rate of profit calculation is straightforward, it is the aggregate of what Kuznets called property income, profit, interest and rent. The denominator which measures capital advanced or costs is more complicated and depends on the ratio between fixed and circulating capital, unproductive and productive capital, inventories, variable capital or wages and the rate of turnover of the respective parts.[4]

Figure 6.1 shows the U.S. rate of profit from 1964 to 2020. The shift in periods is very striking. The post-war long boom faded during the 1970s before the rate of profit crashed in the recession of 1980–82. The Reaganite offensive of the 1980s made little headway in restoring it. The 1990s was the first phase of the long wave, established the conditions for the restoration of profitability, but it took several years before the impact of the extension of capitalism into the former Soviet Union and Central and Eastern Europe and China became evident.

Profit rates rose slightly up to 1998 but after the East Asian Crisis declined again. The Dot-Com Bubble up to 2000 was precisely a bubble as asset prices rose while profit rates fell. The bubble burst and a recession

[2] Goldman Sachs 2008. The end of the Global Profit Boom? *Global Economics Weekly* 8(2) January the 16th 2008.

[3] Jefferies William 2023. *U.S. Rate of Profit Capital and Class Updated dataset*. https://www.researchgate.net/publication/354477964_Capital_and_Class_Rate_of_Profit_Calculation_1964_to_2019_Updated_Dataset.

[4] Jefferies William 2023. The U.S. rate of profit 1964–2017 and the turnover of fixed and circulating capital. *Capital & Class,* 47(2), pp. 267–289.

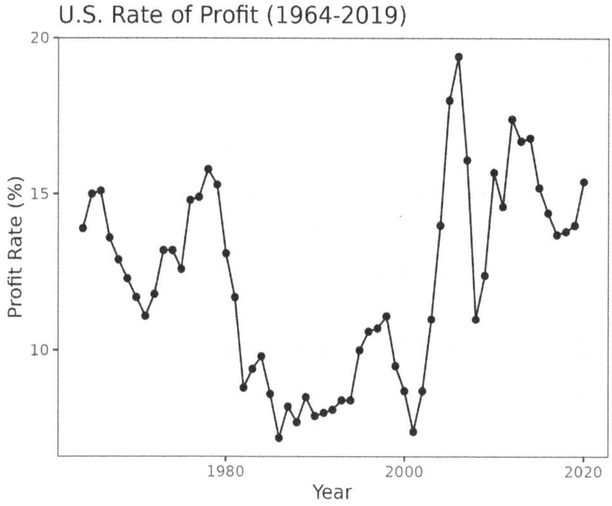

Fig. 6.1 US rate of profit, 1964–2020

ensued which bottomed in 2001 before the very striking surge in profit rates until 2006, peaking with the next bubble but now in residential property. The rise in profitability during hyper-globalisation was exaggerated by the strength of demand, which meant that for the only year in the entire series, the ratio between accounts payable and accounts receivable reversed, capitalist producers had to pay for their inputs in advance, so the rate of turnover dramatically accelerated, reducing the cost of circulating capital. The bursting of the housing bubble in 2007 was compounded by the collapse of Lehman Bros on 15 September 2008, with the financial crisis dramatically escalating into the Great Recession. The Federal Reserve's bail-out of the banks meant there was no repeat of the 1930s with profit rates rapidly recovering, not to the peaks of hyper-globalisation but a sustained high level.

The enterprise rate of profit in Fig. 6.2 reflects the appearance of profits to the capitalist of the individual sector or enterprise, where what are in aggregate surplus, rents and interest, are for the individual capitalist treated as costs. It nonetheless, reflects the general rise in profit rates between 2001 and 2006.

Although there are marked differences between sectors, the graph also shows the tendency towards the equalisation of profit rates between

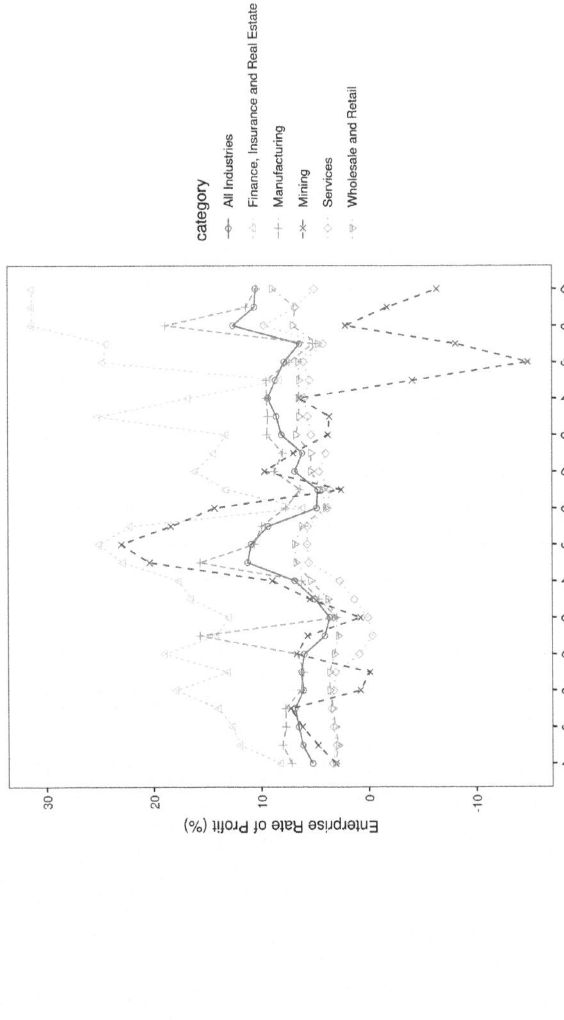

Fig. 6.2 Enterprise rate of profit—key sectors, 1994–2020

sectors, with only finance and mining immune. Mining shows strongest sectoral fluctuations in profit rates as it is demand dependent and so profitability is strongly influenced by the phases of the business cycle. It rose particularly strongly in the run up to the 2008 Great Recession; the Baltic Dry Index (BDI) provides a benchmark for the price of moving major raw materials by sea. It peaked in May 2008 at 11,793, ten times its 1990s' average before collapsing never to recover, while the oil price rose fourfold between 2003 and 2008[5] peaking at $147/barrel in July 2008.

Finance is also noticeable as it stands separate from the tendency to profit rate equalisation. It benefitted from the windfall of the housing bubble and the repatriation of foreign profits and has become more significant as a proportion of total U.S. profits through the period of globalisation.

Although the Fed began raising interest rates to eventually reach 5.25% by June 2006 the cascade of cash meant it made little practical difference. As Reagan had taught, America's trade and budget deficits did not matter. Stagnant wages did not either. The value of bonds or securities (Asset Back Securities (ABS) either Mortgage-Backed Securities (MBD) or Collateralised Debt Obligations (CDO) and the interest rate are inversely related. If interest rates go down then the price of existing bonds or securities typically increases, as newer bonds or securities with low interest rates pay less and vice versa. The price of private houses and flats are also responsive to demand, when interest rates fall, mortgages become more affordable and so house prices rise. From 2000 to 2006, the peak of the housing bubble, U.S. house prices increased by around 85% while manufacturing goods fell in price and overall inflation was just 17%. After the bubble burst in 2007/8, house prices then fell by around a third up to 2015, before doubling again by 2024.[6]

The UK experienced an extreme version of the rise in house prices typical across the West. Thatcher's 1975 promise of a "property-owning democracy" was, on announcement, little more than an attempt to sweeten the privatisation of state assets including council housing. In the

[5] EIA 2024. *West Texas Intermediate Spot Price*. U.S. Energy Information Administration. https://www.eia.gov/outlooks/steo/data/browser/#.

[6] S&P Dow Jones Indices LLC 2024. *S&P CoreLogic Case-Shiller U.S. National Home Price Index [CSUSHPINSA]*. FRED, Federal Reserve Bank of St. Louis. https://fred.stlouisfed.org/series/CSUSHPINSA.

1990s it inadvertently came true for millions of people.[7] Anyone who had accidentally owned a home, bought at a low price when interest rates were high suddenly became better off, as their mortgage payments fell, and the value of their home rose. Their house now represented not just a place to live, but an unrealised windfall. Millions of people across the West, whole social strata, experienced this wealth effect. As house prices soared why engage in the risky endeavour of the class struggle when all you had to do was sit at home and get rich?

Financial deregulation lowered lending standards to so-called sub-prime, or more accurately poor, and so not prime borrowers, without the pay levels or job security to repay a mortgage to term. Teaser rates, temporary introductory low interest rates were used to tempt sub-prime buyers into the mortgage market. When these low interest rates jumped after a couple of years there was no realistic prospect that the mortgagee could meet the higher payments. From 1994 to 2006, sub-prime lending increased from an estimated 4.5% or $35bn to 20% or $600bn[8] of originations with a near tripling in the value of Large Complex Financial Institutions' (LCFI) assets between 2001 and 2007.[9] Mortgage brokers had a positive incentive to lower lending standards, to sell as many NINJA mortgages, no income, no job, no assets, as possible to these sub-prime borrowers. Mortgage brokers issued mortgages to mortgagees and then promptly resold them as packages ABS. This reduced risks for the mortgage broker, lowered their gearing, and meant they could earn commission selling further mortgages so broadening the base of demand, now anyone who wanted was permitted a mortgage. The year 2007 was slated to see a particularly dramatic increase in the expiry of low interest so-called teaser rates, but by then the risk would have been sold on, the question then became who would be holding the bomb when it went off?

[7] Moore Rowan 2015. *Margaret Thatcher began Britain's obsession with property. It's time to end it.* The Guardian. https://www.theguardian.com/society/2014/apr/06/margaret-thatcher-britains-obsession-property-right-to-buy.

[8] Bernanke Ben S. 2008. *Fostering Sustainable Homeownership.* National Community Reinvestment Coalition Annual Meeting, Washington, D.C. https://www.federalreserve.gov/newsevents/speech/bernanke20080314a.htm.

[9] Bank of England 2008. *Financial Stability Report.* Issue 24. London, Bank of England.

After the 1987 Savings and Loans crisis, the 1989 Basel I accord[10] established Tier 1 and Tier 2 bank capital definitions with a minimum ratio of capital to risk weighted assets of 8% based on internal value-at-risk models. The 2004 Basel II refined the weighting of Risk Weighted Assets (RWA). The higher the credit rating the less of the assets needing to be held. The RWA's were ranked as AAA for long-term investment prime mortgage packages falling to BBB- for sub-prime. These ratings were purportedly an objective assessment of the assets risk, but they became increasingly less objective due to competition between the ratings agencies for the fees attached to the ratings process. The claim of the securitisation process was that the combination of low and high, prime and sub-prime securities, reduced overall risk, by diluting the proportion of risky lending in the ABS packages. As every asset held is an asset not loaned and so interest not made, the banks lent on the ratings agencies to provide AAA ratings. The willingness of the ratings agencies Fitch (not fined), Moody's (later fined $864 m)[11] and Standard and Poors (S&P) (later fined $1.375bn) which together controlled more than 90% of the ratings market, to respond to market demands, enabled banks to effectively circumvent the Basel II 8% capital adequacy ratio. A Congressional hearing later heard they had a positive incentive to ensure that "junk bonds based on subprime mortgages receive AAA ratings". S&P increased its share of revenue for rating MBS from 2002 24% to 2006 37%, Fitch 35% and Moody's more than half.[12] The American insurance giant AIG was the largest insurer against losses on ABS or for "regulatory capital relief".[13] From 2005 to 2008 AIG's insurance of MBS for Wall St firms led by Goldman Sachs, rose from 2 to 95% sub-prime.[14]

[10] BIS 2020. *A History of the Basel Committee*. Bank of International Settlements. https://www.bis.org/bcbs/history.htm.

[11] Reuters 2017. *Moody's $864 m penalty for ratings in run-up to 2008 financial*. The Guardian. crisishttps://www.theguardian.com/business/2017/jan/14/moodys-864m-penalty-for-ratings-in-run-up-to-2008-financial-crisis.

[12] House of Representatives 2008. *Credit Rating Agencies and the Financial Crisis*. Serial No. 110–155. U.S. Government Publishing Office. https://www.govinfo.gov/content/pkg/CHRG-110hhrg51103/html/CHRG-110hhrg51103.htm.

[13] Tooze Adam 2018. *Crashed: How a decade of financial crises changed the world*. New York, Allen Lane.

[14] Greenberg Hank. *AIG Hank Greenberg Fact Sheet on AIGFP*. Stanford University https://fcic-static.law.stanford.edu/cdn_media/fcic-docs/0000-00-00%20AIG%20Hank%20Greenberg%20Fact%20Sheet%20on%20AIGFP.pdf.

The UK particularly benefited from the City of London's role in providing financial services, so acting as a hub for recycling funds from abroad. Financial services as a proportion of total UK GDP increased from 6.1% in 1990 to 9.1% in 2009 before falling slightly to 8.3% in 2021.[15] This underestimated their impact on the wider economy. In 2007 the market value of the June 2008 $673tn[16] Over The Counter (OTC) derivatives market was eight times larger than exchange-listed derivatives, which were in turn 25 times the turnover of traded cash equities. London conducted 43% of the worldwide derivatives trade compared to 24% in New York, and less than 15% for France, Germany and Japan combined.[17] After including services to the rich, property deals and money laundering through offshore accounts, financial services dominated an economy that did little else. It provided more than enough revenues for the UK Prime Minister Blair to buy social peace.

For as long as brokers could pass these ABS up the chain, to sell them for securitisation as CDO and MBS on financial markets, then the liquidity of loans increased. This was fine while house prices were rising. If mortgagees failed to pay mortgages it meant that property was repossessed and then sold at higher prices than it had originally been purchased for. The repossessor could then repay any outstanding debts and even make a profit on any excess yielded. Not so when house prices were falling. Now the repossessor made a loss on their MBS when they sold the homes, as they did so, they became more reluctant to take packages of securities off mortgage brokers, as they did so, brokers became more reluctant to lend to sub-prime borrowers, as they did so, demand for housing fell, as they did so, prices fell faster, as they did so, losses on mortgage backed securities increased and so on. House price rises stalled in 2006 and then fell, and so the MBS and CDO that underwrote them began to unravel, far from diluting risk they spread it. The uncertainty inherent in the capitalisation of ground rent, an illogical and intangible

[15] Hutton Georgina 2022. *Financial services: contribution to the UK economy*. House of Commons Library. https://researchbriefings.files.parliament.uk/documents/SN06193/SN06193.pdf.

[16] BIS 2011. *BIS Quarterly Review*. December. Bank of International Settlements https://www.bis.org/publ/qtrpdf/r_qt1112.pdf.

[17] Smith Terry 2009. *Facts belie the diagnosis on credit derivatives*. Financial Times. https://www.ft.com/content/86ca64ae-328e-11de-8116-00144feabdc0#axzz3oLEYFiMF.

asset, meant then entire package of assets went bad. Mark to market accounting, introduced to ensure that changes to the imputed values, instantly re-priced securities to their current market price and meant the value of ABS were marked down automatically, eventually to zero. They had no value, as no one would buy them, as no one knew their value. Banks which had relied on these assets to meet capital requirements, withdrew risky assets from the market, causing their price to fall. A general credit crunch ensued.

3 January 2007, the first mortgage issuer to fail was the aptly named Ownit Mortgage Solutions, linked to Merrill Lynch. On July 31st the American Home Mortgage Investment Corp[18] the 10th largest U.S. mortgage lender failed. On 2nd August IKB, a small German bank, was the first European bank to fall. On August 9th BNP Paribas froze three funds exposed to US sub-prime mortgages. In September UK bank Northern Rock, not exposed to the U.S. sub-prime market but dependent on short-term debt refinancing, first received Bank of England's support before being nationalised in February 2008. In October Switzerland's UBS bank announced a $4bn loss on sub-prime mortgages, increasing to $10bn in December. In December 2007 the Fed established a Term Auction Facility (TAF) of $40bn which enabled banks to borrow directly from it using ABS as collateral as liquidity dried up. In March the Federal Deposit Insurance Corporation (FDIC), which provided insurance on the first $250,000 of assets for depositors in all participating banks or systemically important banks, oversaw the forced sale of Californian bank IndyMac to OneWest Bank. By August nine banks had failed. Eventually from 2008 to 2013 almost 500 banks did so, at a cost of approximately $73bn to the Deposit Insurance Fund (DIF).

In spring 2008 US investment bank Bear Stearns was bailed out by the Federal Reserve and forcibly sold to JPMorgan for $10/share down from January 2007 $172/share. In May the Fed established the Term Securities Lending Facility (TSLF) a 28-day term loan facility. This was expanded in September and peaked on 1st October with $236bn outstanding.[19]

[18] Brunnermeier Markus K. 2008. *Deciphering the Liquidity and Credit Crunch 2007–8*. NBER working Paper 14612. www.nber.org/papers/w14612.

[19] Leon Hoyos, Manuel 2020. Term Securities Lending Facility () (U.S. GFC). *Journal of Financial Crises*, 2(3), pp. 202–228. https://elischolar.library.yale.edu/journal-of-financial-crises/vol2/iss3/8.

In July the iPhone was launched and the Bank of America bought Countrywide, a mortgage lender for around $500bn of mainly sub-prime loans, for $4 billion. Hank Paulson the U.S. Secretary of the Treasury told a Senate Banking Committee that "if you have a bazooka in your pocket and people know it, you probably won't have to use it"[20] he wished, more tellingly confessing, "frankly, if I had perfect foresight, I would never have taken this job in the first place". Paulson's blank panicked stare was an enduring image of the crisis, his subjective failings became crucial to its development.

As the value of securities became uncertain so interbank lending dried up. The Libor-OIS spread, the difference between the Overnight Interest Rate Swap (OIS) rate, generally fixed by the central bank, and so deemed less risky, and the London Interbank Offered Rate (LIBOR) (fraudulently[21]) fixed by a panel of banks chosen by the British Bankers Association (BBA), widened. LIBOR determined the cost of around $150tn of interbank lending. In the summer of 2007, it was typically around 5 or 6 basis points, by December it had risen to 100 before peaking at 400 basis points in October 2008.[22] To fill the LIBOR gap the Fed established the Primary Dealer Credit Facility (PDCF) an overnight banking loan facility widely used by mainly U.S. and UK banks which borrowed astonishing amounts; Merrill Lynch $2tn, Citigroup $1.75tn, Morgan Stanley $1.3tn, Citigroup London $263bn, Morgan Stanley London $548bn, Barclays $410bn, BNP Paribas $66bn, UBS $35bn. The Fed was bailing out the world, or at least New York and London, with total lending from the PDCF eventually reaching $8.5tn.[23]

In August Russia invaded Georgia.

In September 2008 the US government bailed out or nationalised or put into "conservatorship" the two Government-Sponsored Enterprise

[20] Barr Colin 2009. Paulson readies the 'bazooka'. CNN. https://money.cnn.com/2008/09/06/news/economy/fannie_freddie_paulson.fortune/index.htm.

[21] SFO 2019. *SFO concludes investigation into LIBOR manipulation*. Serious Fraud Office. https://www.sfo.gov.uk/2019/10/18/sfo-concludes-investigation-into-libor-manipulation/.

[22] Kwan Simon 2009. Behavior of Libor in the Current Financial Crisis. *FRBSF Economic Letter 2009–04*, Federal Reserve Bank of San Francisco. https://www.frbsf.org/research-and-insights/publications/economic-letter/2009/01/libor-financial-crisis/.

[23] Fed 2020. *Primary Dealer Credit Facility (PDCF)*. Board of Governors of the Federal Reserve System. https://www.federalreserve.gov/regreform/reform-pdcf.htm.

(GSE) mortgage providers Fannie Mae and Freddie Mac to the tune of $100bn each. Larry Summers, Clinton's Treasury Secretary, claimed that the U.S. deficit and American implicit dependence on China created a Balance of Financial Terror.[24] China held $2.3tn of foreign assets with U.S. assets around 70% of the total, including an estimated $760bn of treasuries and $489bn of GSE or MBS assets.[25]Hank Paulson worried that "if China had suffered losses on its vast holdings of Fannie or Freddie securities, there could have been a huge political problem and loss of confidence in the government".[26] Nonetheless, GSE "conservatorship" was seen as a line crossed.

Alongside Paulson the U.S. Treasury Secretary, Tim Geithner, the CEO of the New York Fed, and Ben Bernanke the Chair of the Fed formed the triumvirate who coordinated the response of the financial authorities. Paulson was the former CEO of Goldman Sachs, Bernanke was a historian of the Great Depression while Geithner had undertaken stress tests on New York banks which served as a model for the eventual restructuring of the banks. Paulson baulked at comparisons of his bank nationalisations with Lenin and Mussolini and resisted the appellation "Mr Bailout". The triumvirate vehemently opposed nationalisation; capital must be provided by the private sector they insisted.

When Lehman Bros, the fourth largest investment bank, (behind Goldman Sachs, Morgan Stanley, and Merrill Lynch), with 25,000 employees and $639bn of assets required $6bn over the weekend of the 13/14th September, Paulson's preference was to draw a line in the sand. His judgement was further coloured (it was rumoured) by long-term animosity harboured against the Lehman CEO Dick Fuld, who garnered $484.8 million in salary and bonuses between 2000 and 2008 and who, ten years previously had refused to join the bail-out Long-Term Capital Management (LCTM) during the East Asian Crisis. Paulson attempted to persuade Tony Blair's chancellor Alistair Darling to strong

[24] Summers Larry 2004. The United States and the Global Adjustment Process. Institute for International Economics. https://www.piie.com/events/united-states-and-global-adjustment-process.

[25] Setser Brad W. and Pandey Arpana 2009. *China's $1.5 Trillion Bet; Understanding China's External Portfolio*. Council for Foreign Relations (CFR). https://cdn.cfr.org/sites/default/files/book_pdf/CGS_WorkingPaper_6_China_update0509%20%282%29.pdf.

[26] Setser Brad 2024. Power and Financial Interdependence. IFRI Papers, *French Institute of International Relations*.

arm Barclays into buying the bank for £5bn. A steal, but too much for Darling, who declined Lehman's rescue. On Monday 15th September, Lehman collapsed and the instant meltdown of the world financial system followed. If Lehman's was not too big to fail nothing was.

On Tuesday 16th Paulson earnt his appellation when the US government nationalised AIG loaning it $85bn for 79.9% of its equity at an interest rate of 14% guaranteed against all its $600bn in assets.[27] Inadvertently triggering default clauses in outstanding (OTC) derivative contracts. By November 2008 the highest AAA rated CDS debt was discounted by two-thirds, while all other lower rated tranches were trading just above zero.[28] Under Basel II banks had to raise reserves to maintain core capital ratios and settle outstanding CDS including an estimated US$1tn, connected to the debt of Fannie Mae, Freddie Mac and Lehman Brothers. Gross foreign exposure to ABS was roughly $2.5tn, around 60% of the value of U.S. ABS and 17% of total foreign claims on the U.S.[29] Foreign owned assets lost some $1.3tn about $160bn linked to ABS, and the rest due to the collapse of stocks, the DJIA fell by 51%.

As the Fed bought up MBS its balance sheet doubled to about $2tn. This dramatically understated the scale of its intervention which, including liabilities, reached $6.8tn.[30] On September 19th the Department of the Treasury guaranteed money market mutual funds worth $3.5tn. On 29th September Paulson frantically negotiated a general bail-out, pleading with Nancy Pelosi, the Democratic Congressional leader on one knee, to agree to his $700bn three-page begging letter or bail-out proposal or the Emergency Economic Stabilization Act (EESA). It was rejected, Congress refused to recognise the scale of the pending disaster and repeated clichés about bankers facing moral hazard. They clung onto the absurd and outdated notion that the financiers should pay when their

[27] Greenberg Maurice R. 2013. *The AIG Story (Chapter 18, Nationalization)*. George Washington University Law School.

[28] Brunnermeier Markus K. 2008. Deciphering the Liquidity and Credit Crunch 2007–8. *NBER working Paper 14612*. www.nber.org/papers/w14612. p. 9.

[29] Kamin Steven B. and DeMarco Laurie Pounder 2010. How Did a Domestic Housing Slump Turn into a Global Financial Crisis? *International Finance Discussion Papers 994*. Board of Governors of the Federal Reserve System.

[30] SIGTARP 2009. *Office of the Special Inspector General for the Troubled Asset Relief Program (SIGTARP) Quarterly Report to Congress*. https://www.sigtarp.gov/sites/sigtarp/files/Quarterly_Reports/July2009_Quarterly_Report_to_Congress.pdf.

bets on the future went bad. The DJIA fell 777 points its sharpest ever collapse to teach them a lesson. 3rd October $700bn Troubled Asset Relief Program (TARP), emergency bail-out became law.[31] According to Paulson the $700bn was "the biggest number we thought we could ask for without spooking Congress".[32] The Capital Purchase Program Facility (CPPF) took stakes worth $125bn in the nine largest banks and two of the nation's Big Three automakers—General Motors (GM) and Chrysler Group (FCAM). About $245bn went to shore up the capital of financial institutions. 13th October the FDIC announced its Temporary Liquidity Guarantee Program (TLGP), which eventually guaranteed more than $600bn in debt. It was not enough.

Almost immediately TARP evolved into 12 separate programmes involving up to approximately $3tn.[33] It was not enough. The Treasury then "interpreted" the $699bn maximum TARP funding as a cap on the daily amount "outstanding". Alistair Darling commented "the world banking system was on the brink of collapse", intervention was necessary to keep bank "cash machines operating".[34] The Fed and Bank of England oversaw a rapid series of nationalisations Lloyds acquired Halifax/Bank of Scotland, the Bank of America took over Merrill Lynch and JPMorgan bought Washington Mutual. Federal support eventually reached an estimated $23.7tn. Although once these financial measures were unwound the Fed made a profit of around $109bn.[35]

As the ABS were dominated in dollars, borrowers of whatever nationality required dollars to reschedule their debts. The dollar rose as the demand for dollars far exceeded dollar reserves or holdings, leaving the Fed as the only source of dollars. As the crisis deepened the financial power of the U.S. grew, but not without some bumps in the road.

[31] FDIC 2019. Crisis and Response. FDIC.

[32] Vice 2020. *Panic: The Untold Story of the 2008 Financial Crisis 2018—Transcript. HBO.* https://scrapsfromtheloft.com/movies/panic-the-untold-story-of-the-2008-financial-crisis-transcript/.

[33] SIGTARP 2009. *Office of the Special Inspector General for the Troubled Asset Relief Program (SIGTARP) Quarterly Report to Congress.* https://www.sigtarp.gov/sites/sigtarp/files/Quarterly_Reports/July2009_Quarterly_Report_to_Congress.pdf.

[34] Darling Alistair 2009. *Indemnity to Bank of England.* Hansard 501. https://hansard.parliament.uk/Commons/2009-11-25/debates/09112522000002/IndemnityToBankOfEngland.

[35] Kiel Paul and Nguyen Dan 2020. *Bailout Tracker; Tracking Every Dollar and Every Recipient.* ProPublica. https://projects.propublica.org/bailout/.

The Great Recession signalled the end of hyper-globalisation and with it China's peak dependence on globalised trade. The recession briefly traced or exceeded the falls in trade and output following the 1929 Wall Street Crash.[36] The stock market fell faster and so did trade and industrial production. Insurance companies could not insure shipping so trade halted and with it industrial production as inventories piled up, but the analogy with the Great Depression was false. In 1929 around 9,000 or between a third and half U.S. banks were allowed to go to the wall, output fell by a third, and trade took twenty years to recover after a world war. The Great Recession was more akin to the 1907–1908 Wall Street Crash. In 1907–1908 financial grandees led by JPMorgan backed a general banking bail-out, the crisis was contained even though industrial output fell 1908 17%, the economy then recovered quickly, there was no Great Depression, although there was a world war.

In November China's State Council announced 4 trillion Yuan of spending, this was combined with far larger amounts of increased bank lending and local government spending. By January 2009 China's trade had fallen by 27% but its industrial production only 1%.[37] High Speed Railways more than doubled each year between 2008 and 2012[38] and continued to grow strongly afterwards. Steel production, which had reached 45% of world output by 2008 continued to grow. Investment as a proportion of GDP peaked at 2010, 47%, and so 2009 GDP growth continued at 9.4%. China would eventually rid itself of most of holdings of Treasuries, GSEs and MBS, but these Communists had no intention of bringing down capitalism. China's reserves provided the financial power of China's turn towards its domestic market, its financial sector remained almost entirely Chinese owned state banks. In 2006 the IMF estimated foreign ownership of China's banks amounted to 1.8%.[39] It was not

[36] O'Rouke Kevin and Eichengreen Barry 2012. *A tale of two depressions redux*. VoxEU, CEPR. https://cepr.org/voxeu/columns/tale-two-depressions-redux.

[37] CPB 2024. *World Trade Monitor January 2024*. https://www.cpb.nl/en/world-trade-monitor-january-2024.

[38] Lawrence Martha, Bullock Richard, and Liu Ziming. 2019. *China's High-Speed Rail Development. World* Bank. https://documents1.worldbank.org/curated/en/933411559841476316/pdf/Chinas-High-Speed-Rail-Development.pdf.

[39] Leigh Lamin and Podpiera Richard 2006. *The Rise of Foreign Investment in China's Banks—Taking Stock*. IMF Working Paper WP/06/292. https://www.imf.org/external/pubs/ft/wp/2006/wp06292.pdf.

reliant on access to US liquidity, or FDI or exports, it could reflate its own economy and stimulate domestic consumption, albeit in the form of investment, which further accelerated its move away from dependence on exports, which fell as proportion of GDP from here on in. The development of China's domestic market meant that China alongside the U.S. (and to a lesser extent the UK) was the other great beneficiary of the Great Recession.

By December 2008 the Fed had cut U.S. interest rates from 5.25% to near zero, more significantly, in March 2009 the Fed initiated Quantitative Easing (QE) 1. Between March 2009 and March 2010, they purchased $200 billion in GSE debt (Fannie Mae, Freddie Mac and Ginnie Mae), $1.25tn in MBS and $300bn in long-term Treasury debt. QE effectively shifted the costs of reflation to foreign owners of U.S. debt.[40] QE prints money and so creates currency without equivalent, interest-bearing assets owned by foreigners are bought for no cost, transferring dollars to the former owner, and saving the U.S. the amount of interest they would have paid. Adam Tooze commented after November 2010 "there is a near one-for-one identity between the expansion of the Federal Reserve balance sheet and the expansion of dollar cash balances held by non-US banks with the Fed".[41] QE2 followed in November 2010 $75bn for eight months of GSE MBS and QE3 in December 2012, or unlimited "QE infinity" purchasing between $40-$75bn a month. The UK followed the Fed's lead with QE purchases of government debt by November 2021 £895bn owning a third of government debt worth around 40% of GDP.[42] This expansion of U.S. financial power, and the alignment of U.S. and UK financial interests, stood in stark contrast to the Eurozone, where the ECBs balance sheet contracted.[43]

[40] Federal Reserve 2010. *Assets and Liabilities of Commercial Banks in the United States*. H.8. https://www.federalreserve.gov/releases/h8/current/default.htm.

[41] Tooze Adam 2018. *Crashed: How a decade of financial crises changed the world*. New York, Allen Lane.

[42] Smith Chris 2021. *Quantitative easing*. House of Lords Library. https://lordslibrary.parliament.uk/quantitative-easing/#.

[43] Richter Wolf 2024. *ECB Balance Sheet QT: -€2.2 Trillion from Peak, to €6.61 Trillion. Shed 25% of Total Assets, 53% of Pandemic QE*. https://wolfstreet.com/2024/04/07/ecb-balance-sheet-qt-e2-2-trillion-from-peak-to-e6-61-trillion-shed-25-of-total-assets-53-of-pandemic-qe/.

In 2001 the Euro came into full effect it was backed by a single European Central Bank (ECB) and the Stability and Growth Pact. This limited deficits to 3% and debt ceilings to 60% of GDP, but crucially, the EU had no comparable institution to the Fed. After 2000 European banks undertook a "remarkable expansion" of US dollar MBS and CDOs that "exposed these banks to foreign currency funding risk" of "at least $1.0–1.2 trillion by mid-2007".[44] The U.S. ratings agencies, which had been so reluctant to downgrade domestic MBS, had no such qualms about Europe. The refusal of the European financial authorities and particularly Germany's insistence that the Maastricht Treaty banned QE, bail-outs, up front cuts in debt load or haircuts. Instead it preferred to reschedule debt into the far future and inadvertently called into question the entire Euro project as it particularly impacted the PIIGS (Portugal, Ireland, Italy, Greece and Spain). Only after much arm twisting from the IMF and U.S. as well as the universally negative, apocalyptic consequences of Grexit modelling, did Germany agree something approaching a bail-out in May 2010. Even so the Euro crisis rumbled on until Greece's Syriza capitulated to austerity in 2015. The ECB did not begin QE until after the risk of Grexit had ended in 2015. The ECBs hesitancy, and the stark dependency of the City of London on Fed bail-outs, explains its subsequent lack of opposition to Brexit.

Obama's 2009 reappointment of Ben Bernanke as Chair of the Fed and elevation of Timothy Geithner to Treasury Secretary signalled the continuity between the new and old regimes. The Dodd-Frank legislation purported to regulate finance, while new Basel III regulations were developed and enacted in November 2011. Oversight of the banks amounted to forcing them to increase their core capital and allowing financial authorities a free hand to take necessary action independently of democratic oversight. Geithner and Bernanke were clear, there would be no limitations of bankers' bonuses and nationalisation would not be countenanced, as Tooze euphemistically put it, "pursuing maximum freedom from congressional interference, Geithner's Treasury had pushed for the agencies to have the widest possible latitude in their regulatory efforts".[45]

[44] McGuire Patrick and Peter Götz von 2009. The US dollar shortage in global banking and the international policy response. *BIS Working Papers No 291*, Monetary and Economic Department. https://www.bis.org/publ/work291.pdf.

[45] Tooze Adam 2018. *Crashed: How a decade of financial crises changed the world*. New York, Allen Lane.

Financial regulation would be left to the FED experts. This was after all the difference between the U.S. and Europe during the crisis and was the reason the U.S. avoided the post-crisis conflicts that wracked the Eurozone. In 2012 a self-satisfied Obama boasted that the U.S. was exceptional "the one indispensable nation in world affairs",

> I see it everywhere I go, from London and Prague, to Tokyo and Seoul, to Rio and Jakarta... there is a new confidence in our leadership... I see an American century because no other nation seeks the role that we play in global affairs, and no other nation can play the role that we play in global affairs.[46]

The 2008 Great Recession brought hyper-globalisation to a crashing halt. The deepest financial crisis since the 1929 Wall Street Great Crash provided dramatic evidence of the financial instability that underpinned the hollowed-out core of the major Western economies, but it reconfirmed U.S. financial power, and in forcing China to turn towards the domestic market, set the scene for the conflict to come.

[46] Klein Kent 2012. *Obama: US 'The One Indispensable Nation in World Affairs'*. https://www.voanews.com/a/obama_tells_air_force_academy_us_is_one_indispensable_country_world_affairs/940158.html.

CHAPTER 7

China—The New Great Power

"I believe in American exceptionalism with every fibre of my being". Barak Obama 2014.[1]

Donald Trump's 2016 Presidential election made manifest the shift in U.S. policy from free trade to protectionism. Trump's slogan of America First was and is presented as a conflict between populism and liberalism, right and left, but it is more accurately viewed as a matter of timing. There are no substantive differences between the U.S. establishment, but the transition to a new policy regime requires debate. For Kristina Spohr, a German historian who yearned for the days of the statesman George Bush, the U.S.-China trade war was the product of Trump's unpredictability and his "aggressive economic nationalism" even though inevitably for Spohr the U.S. was provoked by "Beijing's predatory economic policies".[2] Any economic policy that threatens U.S. interests is predatory. The trade war

[1] Obama Barak 2014. *Remarks by the President at the United States Military Academy Commencement Ceremony*. The White House. https://obamawhitehouse.archives.gov/the-press-office/2014/05/28/remarks-president-united-states-military-academy-commencement-ceremony.

[2] Spohr Kristina 2022. Post Wall, Post Square; How Bush, Gorbachev, Kohl, and Deng Shaped the World after 1989. New Haven, Yale University Press.

W. Jefferies, *War and the World Economy*, Palgrave Insights into Apocalypse Economics,
https://doi.org/10.1007/978-3-031-85236-7_7

was not a result of Trump's subjective predilections, it was deepened and extended by the Biden administration, rather it reflected, but did not create, the transition to a multi-polar world which was mainly a result of, but not limited to, China. The other nemesis of the international rules-based order was Putin's Russia.

Larry Summers evoked the idea of secular stagnation[3] to describe the new period. Interest rates, investment and growth were low, government debt to GDP high, such that "greater saving has been driven by increases in inequality and in the share of income going to the wealthy". Secular stagnation, the relative slowdown of Western economic growth, was the necessary consequence of Bernanke's so-called savings glut,[4] the accumulation, but not investment, of vast surplus capitals. As the poor spent a higher proportion of their income than the rich, and as the rich were not investing at least in the West, there was a shortage of aggregate demand in the domestic Western economies. Savings, Adam Smith's euphemism for profits, were flooding to the top, while the offshoring of production to China, the former centrally planned economies, and so-called emerging markets, meant that high paid secure jobs and investment were surplus to the requirement of capital accumulation. It was almost as if Bernanke and Summers were unaware that the purpose of a capitalist economy was to maximise profits. Income inequality is the very essence of capitalist production. The poor are poor so that the rich may be rich or as Pharrell Williams' 2013 hit, the highest selling track of the decade, put it they were "Happy".

Steven Pinker, the Harvard philosopher, channelled the spirit of Dr. Pangloss[5] and hailed the new enlightenment—peace now prevailed as people were rational. Even Israel "has acceded to international pressure to relinquish most of the territory it has occupied in the various wars since then, and within our lifetimes it will probably withdraw from the

[3] Summers Larry 2016. *The Age of Secular Stagnation: What It Is and What to Do About It.* Foreign Affairs. https://larrysummers.com/2016/02/17/the-age-of-secular-stagnation/.

[4] Bernanke Ben S. 2005. *The Global Saving Glut and the U.S. Current Account Deficit, Remarks by Governor Ben S. Bernanke.* Federal Reserve Board. https://www.federalreserve.gov/boarddocs/speeches/2005/200503102/.

[5] Gould Stephen J. and Lewontin Richard C. 1979. The Spandrels of San Marco and the Panglossian Paradigm: A critique of the Adaptationist Programme. *Proceedings of the Royal Society of London*, B 205(1161), pp. 581–598.

rest".[6] In 2019 Israel's Prime Minister Benjamin Netanyahu was to disappoint Pinker's forecast explaining that "Israel is not a state of all its citizens... [but rather] the nation-state of the Jewish people and only them".[7] Israel's apartheid expansion expelled the Palestinian peoples to make way for Israeli Jewish settlers in the West Bank, while viciously oppressing the Palestinians in Gaza. Hyper-globalisation was over, but in every other respect the new normal, of the post-credit crunch world, was the old normal.

For the financial authorities of the U.S. and UK that was the point. Having come out of the melt down of the housing crisis in the 2008 Great Recession they had achieved their nirvana. The collapse of the USSR in 1991 and the transition of China to the market in the mid-1990s, restored U.S. global domination and ushered in the period of globalisation; a monopolar world economy of financialised, free trade capitalism.[8] The period of hyper-globalisation from 2001 to 2008 supported the illusion that, in the West at least, profits arose without equivalent from thin air. This was also the high point of China's export-oriented economy and its corollary U.S. world hegemony. The collapse of trade after the September 2008 credit crunch forced China away from dependence on Western markets, accelerated its independent development and inevitably eroded the preconditions upon which its initial rise was built.

China stimulated domestic investment from 2009 on to avoid the disproportion threatened by the Great Western Recession. 16 Megaprojects were accelerated[9] henceforth exports, while remaining important, were no longer the focus of its development. It used rents from nationalised land to fund investment in infrastructure. This created a construction boom, accelerated urbanisation, transformed farmers into wage workers, raised productivity, stimulated domestic demand and increased overall wealth alongside rising wages. As productivity rose faster than wages, the value of wages as a proportion of national income fell,

[6] Pinker Steven 2011. *The Better Angels of Our Nature: Why Violence Has Declined*. London, Viking. p. 259.

[7] Amnesty International. 2022. *Israel's Apartheid Against Palestinians*. 2022. MDE 15/5141/2022, London, Amnesty International.

[8] Johnson Nathan. 2020. Empirical Evaluation of Long Waves of Capitalist Development. *Critique*, 48 (2–3), pp. 149–168.

[9] Naughton Barry 2021. *The Rise of China's Industrial Policy 1978 to 2020*. Universidad Nacional Autónoma de México.

even as their purchasing power increased. The IMF explained that as "labour productivity was higher than wages, capital owners received excess returns, while the labour income share has fallen over time".[10] This resulted in growing income inequality, luxury consumption and the creation of a middle or capitalist class. Finally, China began to export finance, mainly loans although with some foreign direct investment, initially to secure sources of key raw materials and trade routes, but latterly to guarantee spheres of influence.

Barry Naughton, a veteran free market Western China expert, described the transition to capitalism from the market reforms of the late 1970s as a process of growing out of the plan.[11] Planned production was fixed while private production above a set minimum permitted, so that as private production expanded it rapidly supplanted planned. China's GDP per capita grew from 2001 $1053 to 2011 $5614 and 2022 $12,720[12] reflecting the shift from a rural to an urban society, such that by 2020 China had abolished absolute poverty for 800 million people according to World Bank definitions. This accounted for the vast bulk of the worldwide reduction in poverty during the period.[13] At the same time, however, inequality grew, between, workers and the rural poor, and a growing capitalist class. Rising wages and urbanisation meant "ordinary workers have benefited…factory wages in China were far ahead of rural incomes, and those wages doubled over 15 years" and this explained the "impressive decline of absolute poverty in China" nevertheless, "the really big benefits in China accrued to the small number of high-skilled workers and to the owners of capital, including foreign investors".[14]

[10] Zhang Longmei, Brooks Ray, Ding Ding, Ding Haiyan, He Hui, Lu Jing and Mano Rui 2018. China's High Savings: Drivers, Prospects, and Policies. *International Monetary Fund (IMF) Working Paper, WP/18/277*. New York, IMF.

[11] Naughton Barry 2008. Growing Out of the Plan: Chinese Economic Reform, 1978–1993. Cambridge, Cambridge University Press.

[12] World Bank 2024. People's Republic of China. datacatalog.worldbank.org.

[13] WB 2020. *Four Decades of Poverty Reduction in China*. The World Bank Development Research Center of the State Council,the People's Republic of China. https://openknowledge.worldbank.org/server/api/core/bitstreams/e9a5bc3c-718d-57d8-9558-ce325407f737/content.

[14] Bo Meng, Ming Ye and Shang-Jin Wei 2020. Measuring Smile Curves in Global Value Chains. *Oxford Bulletin of Economics and Statistics*, 82, 5. pp. 961–1237. P. 1104.

After 1978 income inequality measured in the Gini index soared[15] with the official estimate from the National Bureau of Statistics (NBS) at 47.3 Gini points.[16] After China's entry into the WTO in 2001, savings, i.e. profits as a share of national income, peaked at 52% in 2008. Between 1978 and 2015 the income share of the top 10% rose from 27 to 41% while the bottom 50% fell from 27 to 15%. In 2015 the top 1% received 14% of national income in China compared to 20% in the U.S. and 10% in France.[17] The recovery from the Covid-19 virus has further exacerbated income inequality.[18]

The Fifteenth Party Congress in 1997 completed the transition to a market economy through the reform of State-Owned Enterprises (SOE) on market lines. Larger SOE were forced to make profits, while smaller ones were privatised or went bust. Around 27 mn workers were fired and lost the benefits of the iron rice bowl, health care, education, housing and pensions.[19] The decollectivisation of agriculture after 1978 meant the rural population similarly lost access to low-cost basic health care. The sustained cuts to the welfare state have been partially reversed over the last years through initiatives like Healthy China 2030,[20] to levels typical of, albeit still slightly lower on the whole than, those of most developed capitalist economies. Overall public service delivery has increased especially for pensions and health insurance.[21] By 2022 there were more than 4.43 mn

[15] Ding H. and He H. 2018. A Tale of Transition: An Empirical Analysis of Economic Inequality in Urban China, 1986–2009. *Review of Economic Dynamics*, 29, pp. 106–137.

[16] Jain-Chandra S, Khor N, Mano R., Schauer J., Wingender P. and Zhuang J. 2018. Inequality in China—Trends, Drivers and Policy Remedies. *IMF Working Paper* 18/127, New York, IMF.

[17] Piketty T., Yang L. and Zucman G. 2017. Capital Accumulation, Private Property and Rising Inequality in China, 1978–2015. NBER Working Paper 23368. NBER.

[18] Yu Sun and Yuan Yang. 2020. *Why China's economic recovery from coronavirus is widening the wealth gap*. Financial Times. https://www.ft.com/content/e0e2940a-17cb-40ed-8d27-3722c9349a5d. Accessed 15/09/2020.

[19] He H., Huang F., Liu Z. and D. Zhu, 2018. Breaking the 'Iron Rice Bowl:' Evidence of Precautionary Savings from the Chinese State-Owned Enterprises Reform. *Journal of Monetary Economics*, 94, pp. 94–113.

[20] Tan Xiaodong, Xiangxiang Liu and Haiyan Shao. 2017. Commentary; Healthy China 2030: A Vision for Health Care. *Value in Health* 12(C), pp. 112–114.

[21] Wingender Phillipe. 2018. Intergovernmental Fiscal Reform in China. International Monetary Fund *(IMF) Working Paper*, WP/18/88 New York, IMF.

primary medical personnel and more than 970,000 primary medical institutions an increase of over 1.05 mn persons and nearly 60,000 institutions compared to 2011.[22] In 2022 the Chinese government spent 3.3% of GDP on Education, 1.9% on Healthcare and 3% on Public Security and Employment.[23]

Marx observed that a capitalist economy is characterised by "an immense accumulation of commodities" so that in "societies where capitalist production is fully developed, the commodity appears there as both the constant elementary presupposition of capital and…as the direct result of the capitalist production process". This universal commodity production extends to the labour market so that "commodity production necessarily leads to capitalist production, once the worker has ceased to be a part of the conditions of production…from the moment at which labour power itself in general becomes a commodity".[24] In a capitalist economy a working class sells its labour power to a class of capitalists. By the late 1990s around 98% of China's output was at market prices.[25]

China's transition to capitalist Great Power status is contested. It is claimed that continued Communist Party rule is incompatible with capitalism. President Xi Jinping commented in 2014 that "promoting the modernization of the national governance system and capacity is definitely not Westernization or capitalism".[26] Zhonglin Li and David Kotz, both radical economists, noted the growth of private-sector employment from 18% in 1998 to 82% in 2018 of total employment and necessarily concluded that "the economic base in China today is capitalist". Yet, they perversely claimed, "there is no evidence that capitalists now control the CCP or can dictate state policy", so that "as long as the CCP is not controlled by the capitalist class in China, we do not expect China to

[22] KPMG 2023. *Takeaways of China's 2023 Two Sessions*. KPMG China. https://kpmg.com/cn.

[23] NBS 2024. National Data. China National Bureau of Statistics. https://data.stats.gov.cn/english/tablequery.htm?code=AC07.

[24] Marx Karl. 1976 [1867]. *Capital a Critique of Political Economy Volume I*. London: Penguin.

[25] OECD 2005. *OECD Economic Surveys China*. Paris, OECD.

[26] U.S. DoD 2023. *Military and Security Developments Involving the People's Republic of China*. Department of Defense. https://media.defense.gov/2023/Oct/19/2003323409/-1/-1/1/2023-MILITARY-AND-SECURITY-DEVELOPMENTS-INVOLVING-THE-PEOPLES-REPUBLIC-OF-CHINA.PDF.

operate as an imperialist power".[27] From the other end of the political spectrum Ronald Coase[28] (the Nobel prize winning economist and originator of the notorious Coase theorem, that no government intervention whatsoever in the economy is ever justified) disagreed. Although Coase had previously asserted during the privatisation of the Soviet Union that the abolition of Communist Rule was the sine qua non of capitalist restoration, now he had second thoughts. Notwithstanding Chinese Communist Party rule Coase was in no doubt of China's capitalism. Insofar as there remains any dispute it revolves around the extent of the integration between state and society and the significance of the relationship between the CCP and the economy, in what may be designated a state capitalist system,[29] a capitalist economy dominated by an outsized state sector, which is atypical of contemporary neo-liberal capitalism.

Barry Naughton and Briana Boland, a senior analyst for the CSIS, consider that this state capitalism[30] has transmuted into a more all-encompassing system, they designated "CCP Inc."[31] They attributed this to Xi Jinping's determination to achieve the China Dream through an "intentionally designed hierarchical structure" which includes controlling directly and indirectly both state-owned and private firms to prioritise and achieve CCP goals.[32] Plus ça change.

[27] Li Zhongjin, Kotz David M. 2020. *Is China Imperialist? Economy, State, and Insertion in the Global System.* Paper written for a session of the Allied Social Sciences Association entitled "The Political Economy of China: Institutions, Policies, and Role in the Global Economy," sponsored by the Union for Radical Political Economics, January 3–5, 2021.

[28] Coase Ronald and Wang Ning. 2012. *How China Became Capitalist.* New York, Palgrave McMillan. p. 154.

[29] Li Minqi. 2016. *China and the Twenty-first-Century Crisis.* London, Pluto.

[30] Naughton Barry, Tsai Kellee S. 2015. *State Capitalism, Institutional Adaptation, and the Chinese Miracle.* Cambridge, Cambridge University Press.

[31] Naughton Barry and Boland Briana 2023. CCP Inc. *The Reshaping of China's State Capitalist System.* Report of the Centre for Strategic and International Studies, Freeman Chair in China Studies. https://csis-website-prod.s3.amazonaws.com/s3fs-public/2023-01/230131_Naughton_Reshaping_CCPInc_0.pdf.

[32] Naughton Barry. 2017. Is China Socialist? *Journal of Economic Perspectives*, 31 (1). pp. 3–24.

In 2016 China challenged the EU and U.S. refusal to designate it as a "market economy" in the WTO.[33] In a curious inversion of the norm, China was effectively arguing it was a capitalist economy and the EU and U.S. were arguing it was not. The Western failure to grant China market economy status enabled the application of "punitive tariffs" in "anti-dumping cases". It was a hangover from the punitive conditions that marked China's WTO accession in 2001. The original terms of the accession treaty required that China enacted market reforms, to the satisfaction of other WTO members, as a condition for reaching market economy status. Irrespective market status was automatically granted from December 2016, after a maximum of 15 years membership.[34] The refusal of the EU and U.S. to follow the treaty protocols anticipated the U.S.-China trade war begun under the Trump administration.

The CCP allowed the entry of capitalists in 2001.[35] In 2018 the net worth of the 153 members of China's National People's Congress and its advisory body was $650bn.[36] By 2023 there were over 80 billionaire delegates. The fortunes of the 41 billionaire NPC deputies totalled $191bn, paupers compared to the 40 advisory committee billionaires worth $313bn.[37]As Trotsky dryly observed when considering how the Soviet Union may undertake its transition to the market, "privileges have only half their worth, if they cannot be transmitted to one's children. But the right of testament is inseparable from the right of property".[38] In

[33] Donnan Shawn, Hornby Lucy and Beesley Arthur. 2016. *China challenges EU and US over market economy status.* Financial Times, 12 December, https://www.ft.com/content/6af8da62-bf5d-11e6-9bca-2b93a6856354. Accessed 07/10/2020.

[34] Puccio L. 2015. *Granting of market economy status to China—An analysis of WTO law and of selected WTO Members' policy—In-depth analysis.* European Parliament, Directorate-General for Parliamentary Research Services. https://data.europa.eu/doi/10.2861/22416.

[35] Guiheux Gilles. 2006. The Political "Participation" of Entrepreneurs: Challenge or Opportunity for the Chinese Communist Party? *Social Research*, 73(1), pp. 219–244.

[36] Wee Sui-Lee. *China's Parliament Is a Growing Billionaires' Club.* New York Times. www.nytimes.com/2018/03/01/business/china-parliament-billionaires.html.

[37] Leahy Joe and Liu Nian 2023. *Three-day weekends and more time for love: China's elite dream up policies for Xi.* Financial Times. https://www.ft.com/content/4149ecc5-53c2-4890-97b9-29a7c8c0aa8d.

[38] Trotsky, Leon. 1936 [2004]. *The Revolution Betrayed.* Dover Publications.

2020 President Xi, who's family share in the riches of the new elite,[39] affirmed that while "we should not ignore the blindness of the market, nor should we return to the old path of a planned economy".[40] The 2023 14th National People's Congress (NPC) and the National Committee of the Chinese People's Political Consultative Conference (CPPCC) sought to improve the "modern capital market with Chinese characteristics"[41] such that "the market plays a better role in resource allocation".[42]

In 2003 the State-owned Assets Supervision and Administration Commission of the State Council[43] (SASAC) was established. By 2023, after mergers, it grouped the largest 96[44] SOE. In 2018 SASAC SOE accounted for 28% of industrial assets and 18% of industrial profit and owed RMB 100tn of debt equivalent to 120% of national income[45]. As SOE traditionally accept lower than market profit rates[46] they subsidise the private sector by providing inputs at below market prices. Recent market reforms have sought to increase their profitability but, SOE "do

[39] Guevara Marina, Ryle Gerard, Olesen Alexa, Cabra Mar, Hudson Michael, Giesen Christoph, Williams Margot and Donald Donald 2014. *Leaked Records Reveal Offshore Holdings of China's Elite. International* Consortium of Investigative Journalists. https://www.icij.org/investigations/offshore/leaked-records-reveal-offshore-holdings-of-chinas-elite/.

[40] Bloomberg, 2020. *Xi Says China Won't Return to Planned Economy.* Bloomberg News. www.bloomberg.com/news/articles/2020-05-23/xi-says-china-won-t-return-to-planned-economy-urges-cooperation. Accessed 25/08/2020.

[41] KPMG 2023. *Takeaways of China's 2023 Two Sessions.* KPMG China. https://kpmg.com/cn.

[42] Xinhua 2022. *Securities regulator details construction of modern capital market with Chinese characteristics.* China.org.cn. http://www.china.org.cn/china/Off_the_Wire/2022-11/21/content_78530707.htm.

[43] SASAC 2024. SASAC Financial Overview. SASAC. http://www.sasac.gov.cn/n16582853/n16582888/index.html.

[44] SASAC 2024. *The State-owned Assets Supervision and Administration Commission (SASAC) has clarified the focus of a new round of reform to improve the core competitiveness of state-owned.* SASAC. https://www.gov.cn/xinwen/2023-02/25/content_5743240.htm.

[45] Rosen Daniel, Leutert Wendy and Guo Shan. 2018. Missing Link: Corporate Governance in China's State Sector. Asia Society Special Report in Collaboration with Rhodium Group. Northern California: Asia Society.

[46] Sandlund William and Harding Robin 2024. China reforms its unloved state-owned enterprises to win back investors. Financial Times. https://www.ft.com/content/65ed3767-7b6d-4f80-b91a-c1b478117482.

Table 7.1 SASAC firms' key financial information, 2014–2023

Year	*Operating income Yuan bn*	*Total profit Yuan bn*	*Taxes payable Yuan bn*	*Asset liability ratio*	*GDP Yuan bn*	*Taxes/ GDP*	*Profits/ GDP*
2023	85,730.61	4,633.28	5,874.58	65%	126,058.20	4.66%	3.68%
2022	82,569.74	4,314.82	5,931.57	64%	120,472.40	4.92%	3.58%
2021	75,554.36	4,516.48	5,355.99	64%	114,920.00	4.66%	3.93%
2020	63,286.77	3,422.27	4,611.13	64%	101,356.70	4.55%	3.38%
2019	62,552.05	3,596.10	4,609.63	64%	99,086.50	4.65%	3.63%
2018	58,750.07	3,387.77	4,608.97	65%	91,928.10	5.01%	3.69%
2017	52,201.49	2,898.59	4,234.55	66%	82,712.20	5.12%	3.50%
2016	45,897.80	2,315.78	3,807.61	66%	74,360.00	5.12%	3.11%
2015	45,470.41	2,302.75	3,859.87	66%	68,885.82	5.60%	3.34%
2014	48,063.64	2,476.54	3,786.08	65%	64,356.31	5.88%	3.85%

not necessarily consider maximising economic returns to be their primary goal"[47] other social priorities[48] remain important for them, not least reinvesting profits to create national champions, as is evident in Table 7.1.

The relative constancy of the ratios for assets to liabilities, taxes and profits to national income suggests that these totals are manipulated to support the SASAC defined objectives. Profits are not paid to private shareholders or even the state but used by the SASAC corporations for their developmental priorities. In 1994 when SOE established profits were small and many loss-making, it was decreed that firms retained after-tax profits.[49] In 2007 the State Council instructed non-financial SOE to pay over their dividends, but by 2019 only 2.4% of their after-tax profits were so paid. The SASAC opposed these transfers and insisted that profits are retained for investment at the firm level[50] so transfers to the state are

[47] KPMG 2023. *Takeaways of China's 2023 Two Sessions*. KPMG China. https://kpmg.com/cn.

[48] Qi H. and Kotz D. M. 2020. The Impact of State-Owned Enterprises on China's Economic Growth. *Review of Radical Political Economics*, 52(1), pp. 96–114.

[49] Naughton Barry 2008. Claiming Profit for the State: SASAC and the Capital Management Budget. *China Leadership Monitor* 18.

[50] Hianlei Huang 202. *Chinese SOEs should help fund China's response to pandemic*. Peterson Institute for International Economics (PIIE). https://www.piie.com/blogs/china-economic-watch/chinese-soes-should-help-fund-chinas-response-pandemic.

effectively limited to taxes. In 2023 SASAC taxes[51] accounted for around 32% of total tax revenue, reducing the contribution of individual taxes to a mere 8.9%.[52] The growth in the mass of profit accruing to SASAC firms and invested by them, has reduced the share of private investment in total investment, which had grown from 51% in 2010 to 64% in 2014 and 62% in 2018 before declining to 54% in 2022.[53] Meanwhile, between 2000 and 2019, the amount of private firms with direct state investment increased around 50-fold,[54] of the thousand largest private firms 65% had state investment, totalling around 15% of their capital. These large firms invest in turn invest in around 3.5 million smaller firms and joint ventures.

The growth in the power of SOE and wider state investment, coincided with China's Research and Development (R&D) priorities, which are in turn the prerequisite for reducing unequal exchange with the U.S. Between 1995 and 2009 China's ICT industry was concentrated in low value-added assembly,[55] most notoriously exemplified by the iPhone 8, and the trivial revenues, only $6.5, or about 3.6% of the total production cost, that accrued to the Chinese. By 2018 the total manufacturing cost of the iPhone X was $409.25 and Chinese firms added around $104 or 25.4%[56] by 2024 Chinese rival firms were eating into Apple's sales.[57] As China has moved up the value chain it has reduced, although not

[51] SASAC 2024. *Economic performance of state-owned and state-holding enterprises nationwide from January to December 2023*. State-owned Assets Supervision and Administration Commission. http://www.sasac.gov.cn/n16582853/n16582888/c29924008/content.html.

[52] NBS 2024. National Data. China National Bureau of Statistics. https://data.stats.gov.cn/english/tablequery.htm?code=AC07.

[53] KPMG 2023. *Takeaways of China's 2023 Two Sessions*. KPMG China. https://kpmg.com/cn.

[54] Bai Chong-En, Hsieh Chang-Tai, Song Zheng Michael and Wang Xin 2020. *The Rise of State Connected Private Owners in China*. NBER Working Paper 28170. http://www.nber.org/papers/w28170.

[55] Meng Bo, Ming Ye, and Shang-Jin Wei 2020. Measuring Smile Curves in Global Value Chains. *Oxford Bulletin of Economics and Statistics*, 82(5), pp. 988–1016.

[56] Xing Yuqing. 2019. *How the iPhone Widens the US Trade Deficit with China: the Case of the iPhone X*. National Graduate Institute for Policy Studies (GRIPS) Discussion Paper, pp. 19–21.

[57] Bradshaw Tim and Acton Michael 2024. *Apple loses smartphone crown to Samsung as Chinese rivals gain ground*. Financial Times. https://www.ft.com/content/2c13254b-9995-4408-b02b-6ff07ce706b8e.

Table 7.2 Patent Cooperation Treaty (PCT) applications by country of origin, 2009 and 2023

	China	*France*	*Germany*	*Japan*	*UK*	*U.S*
2009	7906	7163	16,732	29,807	5326	46,079
2019	58,990	7934	19,353	52,660	5786	57,840
2023	69,610	7916	16,916	48,879	5586	55,678

eliminated, the excess profits flowing to U.S. corporations in general and tech giants in particular. U.S. nervousness about this trend, predicated on retaining its technological advance, explains the trade war, the inevitable result of China's challenge to the West.

In 2023 R&D expenditures increased by 8.1% to 3,328bn Yuan or 2.64% GDP with 221bn Yuan on basic research up 9.3% or 6.65%[58] of GDP targeted to rise to 8% by 2025. Importantly over 90% of China's basic research funding comes from the government and universities, while the proportion of investment contributed by enterprises accounts for a mere 3.8%.[59]

A key indicator of this movement up the value chain is the ownership of patents. Patents are a claim on future revenues for the use of a technology. In 2020 China had 3.6 million science, technology, engineering and maths (STEM) graduates, the U.S. 820,000. BYD employs nearly 100,000 people in research and development averaging 19 patents every working day.[60] The growth in Chinese patents is shown in the WIPO Statistics Database in Table 7.2.[61]

[58] NBS 2024. *Statistical Communiqué of the People's Republic of China on the National Economic and Social Development.* National Bureau of Statistics of China. https://www.stats.gov.cn/english/PressRelease/202402/t20240228_1947918.html#.

[59] KPMG 2023. *Takeaways of China's 2023 Two Sessions.* KPMG China. https://kpmg.com/cn.

[60] White Edward 2024. The ambitions of China's BYD stretch well beyond electric vehicles. Financial Times. https://www.ft.com/content/b8bde0b5-7484-45bf-a1e0-475a3ac91bd6.

[61] WIPO, 2024. *WIPO Statistics Database.* World Intellectual Property Organization (WIPO). https://www.wipo.int/ipstats/en/.

Only a small minority of patents become products, and there is a further delay between issuance and production, but the trend is obvious, China's patents overtook the U.S. for the first time in 2019, increasing nine-fold between 2009 and 2023. The bridging of the unbridgeable technological gap is not consequent on "reverse engineering, industrial espionage, and, in particular, cyber espionage"[62] it is the inevitable result of the passage of time.

The Forbes 2000 is a list of the top global 2000 corporations, Fig. 7.1 records the ascent of China's corporate power.

The growth of Chinese firms is striking, rising from 106 in 2008 to 319 firms in 2024. However, the divergence of the U.S. from the rest of the West is also evident. In the immediate aftermath of the credit crunch the number of U.S. firms in the top 2000 fell from 551 in 2008 to 523 in 2012, it then recovered up to 671 in 2024 primarily due to

Fig. 7.1 Forbes (2000)[63] (Total China is China and Hong Kong)

[62] Gilli, Andrea and Gilli Mauro 2019. Why China Has Not Caught Up Yet; Military-Technological Superiority and the Limits of Imitation, Reverse Engineering, and Cyber Espionage. *International Security*, 43 (3), pp. 141–189.

[63] Forbes 2024. *Forbes 2000*. Forbes. https://www.forbes.com/lists/list-directory/.

the strength of the dollar after Covid-19. This growth was not at the expense of China but of the UK, France, Germany and Japan, increasing their dependency on the U.S. The UK 2016 Brexit vote and eventual departure in December 2020 expressed the dependency of the City on the U.S. and relative decline of the Eurozone. While the chaotic threat of, Greek exit from the EU or Grexit was only eventually resolved by Syriza's 2015 capitulation to the Troika of Greece's creditors, the European Commission (EC), the European Central Bank (ECB) and the IMF, who implemented the disastrous austerity driven Economic Adjustment Programmes (EAPs) for Greece.[64]

China's economic development is analogous to the U.S. in the latter part of the nineteenth century. U.S. development was not exceptional, notwithstanding Obama's claims to the contrary, rather it was necessary and inevitable. As is China's now. As a continental size emerging power, China continues to have much room for domestic investment. The CCP's priority, in line with its national interest, is the development of its domestic market, yet inevitably, as its power grows it must exert its influence abroad. Initially over its geographical neighbours, such as in the South China Sea, before extending to the world stage. Except China's rate of development is much faster than nineteenth-century U.S. China's alleged over-capacity problem is not one for China but the U.S. where industry is uncompetitive, weighed down by unproductive services and a neo-liberal ideology which abjures effective coordination between monopolies and the state.

The efficiency of Chinese industry became manifest in the large trade surpluses it began to accrue from the late 1990s. At the outset these were primarily invested in U.S. government debt, treasuries and agencies but, the huge growth in these assets, exceeding $3tn, and worries about their security during the 2007/8 Credit Crunch (notwithstanding the attempts of Treasury Secretary Hank Paulson to provide reassurance) caused a shift in China's foreign investment. The Central Bank Governor Zhou Xiaochuan amongst other top policymakers questioned the opportunity cost of these investments. The ownership of such large amounts of dollar debt also posed a potential conflict of interest if or when China sought to repossess Taiwan, so that between 2008 and

[64] Visvizi Anna 2014. From Grexit to Grecovery: The Paradox of the Troika's Engagement with Greece. *Perspectives on European Politics and Society*, 15(3), pp. 335–345.

2013 China's central authorities reduced their ownership of U.S. Treasuries from around $200bn to nothing and Mortgage-Backed Securities (MBS) or Agencies from around $550bn to $200bn, where they remain today.[65] Even though other state banks continue to hold significant amounts of U.S. government debt.[66] The People's Bank of China (PBoC) foreign exchange management arm, the State Administration of Foreign Exchange (SAFE) oversees the investment of foreign exchange assets. The creation of a sovereign wealth fund, the Chinese Investment Corporation (CIC), in 2007 reflected the authorities' desire to, as Liu put it, "use China's financial power to shape global markets. The goal is to transform China's foreign exchange reserves into strategic overseas assets and seek higher financial and political returns on investments".[67] This shift of investment away from the U.S. was not limited to purchases of debt.

Chinese FDI grew from 2011 $48bn to 2016 $216bn, but this included many unregulated investments in property, sport and entertainment. Responding to this trend the National Development and Reform Commission (NDRC) determined that all sensitive projects and all projects more than US$300 mn needed their approval,[68] such that, since August 2017 there have been no recorded Chinese investment in these sectors. This also reflected the developing U.S.-China trade war, as the U.S. restricted Chinese investment in technologically advanced sectors. By 2019 two-way capital flows between the U.S. reflecting "persistent capital controls and other pressures on outbound investors in China, but US regulatory tightening and an uncertain outlook for US-China relations are creating additional headwinds".[69]

[65] Setser Brad 2024. Power and Financial Interdependence. IFRI Papers, *French Institute of International Relations*.

[66] U.S. Treasury Dept. 2024. Table7.1: *Major Foreign Holders of Treasury Securities*. U.S. Treasury Department. https://ticdata.treasury.gov/resource-center/data-chart-center/tic/Documents/slt_table5.html.

[67] Liu Zongyuan Zoe 2023. *Sovereign Funds How the Communist Party of China Finances Its Global Ambitions*. Cambridge Massachusetts, Harvard University Press.

[68] Kaiding Wang, Huang Mengting, Tang Xinran 2018. *China's NDRC Issued New Outbound Investment Rules*. China Law Insight, King & Wood Mallesons. https://www.chinalawinsight.com/2018/01/articles/foreign-investment/chinas-ndrc-issued-new-outbound-investment-rules/.

[69] Hanemann Thilo, Gao Cassie, Lysenko Adam and Rosen Daniel 2019. Sidelined: US-China Investment in 1H 2019. *US-China Investment Project*. Rhodium Group and National Committee on US China relations.

Rather China has shifted towards a foreign investment strategy that favours emerging nations over advanced Western ones.[70] The 2015 Belt and Road Initiative (BRI)[71] formalised this trend. By 2022, at least 147 countries had signed BRI cooperation documents, up from 146 in 2021, 138 in 2020, and 125 in 2019. China sought to secure access to and ownership of, key raw materials and supplies, provide a market for its construction sector firms and road, rail and steel industries, and access to the key technologies necessary for both military strength and the move into higher value-added sectors. By 2021 the China Development Bank and the Export–Import Bank of China alone had loaned BRI participants investments worth around a trillion dollars. China uses direct loans and FDI directed towards the raw materials sector and the transport and energy. In 2016 investment into BRI nations increased to 12% of total FDI from 8%.[72] This understates the extent of China's investments as the activity of Chinese construction SOEs does not appear in FDI or loan statistics as this "type of overseas loan is not actually transferred abroad, there is nothing to report to the BIS, which could explain part of China's large reporting gaps".[73] China's state-owned banks extend direct loans at market rates of interest. Payments may be in resource deliveries and backed by collateral in physical quantities of those raw materials or occasionally feature debt right offs in exchange for extended leases on key strategic assets, such as in Sri Lanka and Pakistan. By the end of June 2018, unpublished data from the Bank of International Settlements (BIS) reported Chinese cross-border loans worth $919bn with emerging

[70] Horn Sebastian, Reinhart Carmen and Trebesch Christoph 2019. China's Overseas Lending. *NBER Working Paper Series WP 26050*, Cambridge, MA. National Bureau of Economic Research (NBER).

[71] Cerutti Eugenio, Koch Catherine and Pradhan Swapan 2018. The growing footprint of EME banks in the international banking system. *Bank of International Settlements (BIS) Quarterly Review*, (December), pp. 27–37.

[72] Huang Betty and Le Xia 2018. China FDI from the Middle Kingdom: What's next after the big turnaround? *BBVA Research China Economic Watch*, 1 February, pp. 1–10.

[73] Horn Sebastian, Reinhart Carmen and Trebesch Christoph 2019. China's Overseas Lending. *NBER Working Paper Series WP 26050*, Cambridge, MA. National Bureau of Economic Research (NBER).

market economies.[74] This was around 64% of so-called emerging market economy lending which totalled $1,442bn. This was "more than twice the amount of $400bn" that was traceable through official sources at the end of 2017. Unpublished data from the World Bank Debtor Reporting System and data on BIS reported bank claims found that "50% of China's lending is 'hidden'" having grown "to more than $200bn as of 2016". This was "unreported by the IMF, World Bank, and credit rating agencies".[75] China's direct loans and trade credits have climbed from almost zero in 1998 to more than $1.6tn by 2018. By 2023 SAFE reported that the value of its foreign holdings had reached around $3tn, although Brad Setser, the leading U.S. expert on China's foreign exchange holdings estimated the real figure was around twice as high, $6tn measured in dollars, but not necessarily denominated in them.[76]

Estimates suggest that the Chinese state now accounts for a quarter of total bank lending to so-called emerging markets. This has "transformed China into the largest official creditor, easily surpassing the IMF or the World Bank". From 2010 to 2020, Chinese state lending was equivalent to the total of the world's multilateral development banks in seventy years.[77] The China in Africa Research Initiative (CARI), part of John Hopkins University, identified "a total of $135bn of Chinese loan commitments between 2000 to 2018" to "40 African low-income countries listed" with the "outstanding debt to China in 2018 is about 48% of that commitment" as many loans were not disbursed.[78] As of 2018 the 72 low-income countries covered in the World Bank's Debtor Reporting

[74] Cerutti Eugenio, Koch Catherine and Pradhan Swapan-Kumar 2018. The growing footprint of EME banks in the international banking system. *Bank of International Settlements (BIS) Quarterly Review December*. https://www.bis.org/publ/qtrpdf/r_qt1812e.pdf.

[75] Horn Sebastian, Reinhart Carmen and Trebesch Christoph 2019. China's Overseas Lending. *NBER Working Paper Series WP 26050*, Cambridge, MA. National Bureau of Economic Research (NBER).

[76] Setser Brad 2023. *Shadow reserves—how China hides trillions of dollars of hard currency.* The China Project. https://thechinaproject.com/2023/06/29/shadow-reserves-how-china-hides-trillions-of-dollars-of-hard-currency/.

[77] AidData 2023. *Global Chinese Development Finance Dataset, Version 3.0.* AidData. www.aiddata.org.

[78] Huang Yufan and Brautigam Deborah 2020. *Putting a Dollar Amount on China's Loans to the Developing World.* The Diplomat. https://thediplomat.com/2020/06/putting-a-dollar-amount-on-chinas-loans-to-the-developing-world/.

System (DRS) owed Chinese creditors $104bn out of a total disbursed and outstanding debt of $514bn. $64bn of this Chinese debt, or 62% was disbursed in Africa, "overall China made up only 20% of the 72 countries' total public external debt. In Africa, that proportion is 22%". Interest-free loans were probably under 5% of China's overall lending to Africa from 2000 to 2018.[79] The World Bank's Debtor Reporting System (DRS) shows a detailed breakdown of debt for 68 countries eligible for the 2020 Debt Service Suspension Initiative (DSSI).[80] Li and Kotz noted that loan decisions are channelled through state banks in order to bolster their claim that these loans are "largely development-oriented and policy-oriented…rather than originating from private capitalists in pursuit of profit".[81] Certainly, the bulk of China's foreign investments are state directed but are they for profit? Horn, Trebesch, Reinhart noted that the terms and characteristics of China's state-driven overseas loans are akin to commercial lending, loans generally denominated in U.S. dollars, at interest rates "that resemble private bank loans".[82] They claimed that "in low income countries, China's loans are generally repayable at interest rates of 2% to 3%, in contrast to the interest-free loans and grants LIDCs usually receive from most other bilateral and multilateral creditors", albeit China's loans form a far higher total amount. Comparisons of returns against the nominal value of the loans to the most indebted countries show no significant difference between the rates of return charged by the U.S. or China.

The CCP directs China's state, major corporations, and banks, through initiatives like President Xi Jinping's 2015 Made in China 2025 (MIC) development strategy, which formed the successor to its Megaprojects.

[79] Acker Kevin, Brautigam Deborah and Huang Yufan 2020. Debt Relief with Chinese Characteristics. Working Paper No. 2020/39. China Africa Research Initiative, School of Advanced International Studies, Washington DC, Johns Hopkins University.

[80] World Bank 2024. *International Debt Statistics*. World Bank. https://www.worldbank.org/en/programs/debt-statistics/idr-pages.

[81] Li Zhongjin, Kotz David M. 2020. *Is China Imperialist? Economy, State, and Insertion in the Global System*. Paper written for a session of the Allied Social Sciences Association entitled "The Political Economy of China: Institutions, Policies, and Role in the Global Economy," sponsored by the Union for Radical Political Economics, January 3–5, 2021.

[82] Horn Sebastian, Reinhart Carmen and Trebesch Christoph 2019. China's Overseas Lending. *NBER Working Paper Series WP 26050*, Cambridge, MA. National Bureau of Economic Research (NBER).

The MIC targets 10 key sectors encompassing 40% of China's entire industrial value-added manufacturing and seeks to direct the production of next generation large aircraft, aircraft engines, new energy vehicles, smart grids and high-end medical devices to improve indigenous research and development. It aims to double self-sufficiency rates for core infrastructure components and key raw materials. According to Thilo Hanemann and Daniel Rosen, in a report for the US-China Economic and Security Review Commission the MIC "is the clearest example of the nexus between strategic high-tech policy and outbound investment in today's China".[83] The US Chamber of Commerce observed in 2017 that,

> MIC 2025 raises significant concerns not only for China's domestic economy but its economic partners. MIC 2025 aims to leverage the power of the state to alter competitive dynamics in global markets in industries core to economic competitiveness. By targeting and channelling capital to specific technologies and industries, MIC 2025 risks precipitating market inefficiencies and sparking overcapacity, globally.[84]

The CoC continued that the "US CoC is concerned about the growing risk that policies such as MIC 2025 pose for China's relationships with its key economic and commercial partners, including the United States". The criticism of MIC by Western governments meant that from June 2018, China largely refrained from using the term but, according to the U.S. Department of Defense at least, "despite the adjustments in its narrative, China has largely continued implementing the policies behind 'Made in China 2025'".[85] Combined with the Internet Plus Program and Industrial Guidance Funds by 2020 this investment amounted to

[83] Hanemann, Thilo and Daniel Rosen. 2016. *Chinese Investment in the United States; Recent Trends and Policy Agenda*. US-China Economic and Security Review Commission, December. New York, Rhodium Group. p. 22.

[84] US CoC. 2017. *Made in China 2025: Global Ambitions Built on Local Protections*. Washington, United States Chamber of Commerce (US CoC). pp. 7, 41.

[85] U.S. DoD 2023. *Military and Security Developments Involving the People's Republic of China*. Department of Defense. https://media.defense.gov/2023/Oct/19/2003323409/-1/-1/1/2023-MILITARY-AND-SECURITY-DEVELOPMENTS-INVOLVING-THE-PEOPLES-REPUBLIC-OF-CHINA.PDF.

around 11.27tn Yuan or approximately $1.6tn.[86] Barry Naughton considered that the problems with this wave of investment included "a bigger and more dangerous bubble, to say nothing of future over-capacity problems" but these funds are state funds that do not earn the rate of profit or even the rate of interest. A bubble arises when valuations are too high for a given level of returns. The SASAC do not pay returns, so SASAC investments do not drive down the rate of profit, as these firms do not pay profits, capital owned by them is not private property. As Bukharin, the Soviet Communist, commented in 1925, state investment in industry would enable economies of scale, and technological advance such that SOE would "produce and to sell cheaper and better" than private-sector rivals.[87] The Chinese were no communists as traditionally understood, but the combination of state-directed investment and its status as the world's workshop had transformed China's economy. Its burgeoning economic might posed a challenge to U.S. hegemony in the world market by its very existence over the next years what was incipient became manifest.

[86] Naughton Barry 2021. *The Rise of China's Industrial Policy 1978 to 2020*. Universidad Nacional Autónoma de México.

[87] Ball Alan 1987. *Russia's Last Capitalists: The Nepmen, 1921–1929*. Berkeley: University of California Press.

CHAPTER 8

Russia's Collapse and Recovery and Iran and the Middle East

> "Putin has big plans for Russia. He wants to edge out its neighbours so that Russia can dominate oil supplies to all of Europe", Trump said. "I respect Putin and Russians but cannot believe our leader (Obama) allows them to get away with so much…Hats off to the Russians". Donald Trump 2011.

In December 2010 the self-immolation of a Tunisian street vendor Mohamed Bouazizi sparked the Arab Spring. The destabilisation of the 2008 credit crunch had called into question the legitimacy of the international rules-based order. A movement for democratic rights of the urban poor and dispossessed swept North Africa and the Middle East including Bahrain, Egypt, Libya, Syria, Tunisia and Yemen. In New York, and then across the world, the Occupy movement followed their lead and sought to challenge the rule of the 1%. As normalcy returned to the world economy, its momentum faded, as did that of the Arab Spring. Libya, Syria and Yemen entered civil war.[1] In October 2011 Libya's President Gaddafi

[1] Robinson Kali and Merrow Will 2020. *The Arab Spring at Ten Years: What's the Legacy of the Uprisings?* Council Foreign Relations (CFR) https://www.cfr.org/article/arab-spring-ten-years-whats-legacy-uprisings.

W. Jefferies, *War and the World Economy*, Palgrave Insights into Apocalypse Economics,
https://doi.org/10.1007/978-3-031-85236-7_8

was murdered by NATO supported rebels. Egypt briefly escaped dictatorship. Only Tunisia achieved any lasting democracy. The Syrian war rumbled on eventually embroiling Russia, the U.S., Kurdistan, Turkey and Saudi Arabia that anticipated the Great Power struggle to come. President Trump's backhanded compliments to Putin were deliberately provocative, but the chaos of Syria and the conflicts it created echoed the unresolvable Balkan national questions and proxy wars in the lead up to the First World War.

The period after 2010 largely completed Russia's alienation from the Western international rules-based order. In 1988 the USSR's military expenditure was 41% of the U.S. by 2010 Russia's military expenditure was 6%.[2] The collapse of the Soviet Union in 1991 removed the alternative, albeit non-capitalist, pole to U.S. hegemony. In 1990 during the reunification of Germany James Baker, then U.S. Secretary of State, told CPSU General Secretary Mikhail Gorbachev that there would be "no extension of NATO's jurisdiction for forces of NATO one inch to the east".[3] As the collapse of the central plan destroyed the manufacturing and military base of the Russian Federation, Bill Clinton felt no particular obligation to remember Baker's promise "at preliminary bilateral talks in Helsinki in March 1997, Clinton refused to respond to Yeltsin's call for binding restrictions on the establishment of NATO security infrastructure in new member states. Yeltsin's attempt to introduce a Russian veto into the Act—to be directed against a future round of expansion in the ex-Soviet republics, 'particularly Ukraine'—also failed". Russia's interpretation of not an inch East was a misunderstanding, "a myth" indeed.[4]

Clinton was determined to embrace former Soviet Republics, like Latvia, Lithuanian and Estonia and Central and Eastern European (CEE) Allies, like Poland and the Czech and Slovakian republics, preferably with Russia's permission but not necessarily so. Russia was to be reduced to a source of minerals and oil for Western extractivist multinationals and

[2] SIPRI 2024. *Military Expenditure Database*. Stockholm International Peace Research Institute. https://www.sipri.org/databases/milex.

[3] Speigel 2009. *NATO's Eastward Expansion: Did the West Break Its Promise to Moscow?* Spiegel, 26 November.

[4] Spohr Kristina 2022. *Exposing the myth of Western betrayal of Russia over NATO's eastern enlargement*. LSE. https://blogs.lse.ac.uk/politicsandpolicy/exposing-the-myth-of-western-betrayal-of-russia/.

riches for the Russian inheritors of the remnants of the plan's wealth, the criminal oligarchs of the restoration period. This putative relationship was codified in the May 1997 Paris NATO-Russia Mutual Relations Treaty[5] which duly floundered as NATO enlargement progressed, including plans for missile defence in Russia's former allies of the CEE. Russian involvement in the wars of Bosnia, Kosovo and Chechnya further eroded the relationship as did the U.S. invasion of Iraq. It was finally killed off by the 2008 Russian-Georgian and the 2014 Russian-Ukrainian conflicts.

U.S. assertiveness was predicated on the collapse of the Russian centrally planned economy after the restoration of capitalism in 1991. The collapse of the plan was the creation of the market. As national income is a measure of market prices so it was the creation of national income. The UN and World Bank national income statistics note that these measures are not applicable to the plan period. Theoretical consistency demands that was there was no national income in an economy without national income so the measure of national income in 1991 should be nil. Nonetheless, the conflation of physical output with national income, does trace the decline and subsequent recovery of the Russian economy. Between 1991 and 1997 output fell by around half, while working-class incomes fell more, by around 60% to 70%.[6] Figure 8.1 shows World Bank[7] estimates of Russian national income in billions of current US $ from 1991 to 2022.

This chart is also influenced by the level of the Rouble, which collapsed after the East Asian crisis of 1997/8 and then rose until 2014 before falling again until 2021. The implied growth of the economy after 1999 implied here overstates the recovery of production during the capitalist period. In 1990 the Russian Federation produced 1082 Terawatts (TW)

[5] NATO 1997. *Founding Act on Mutual Relations, Cooperation and Security between NATO and the Russian Federation signed in Paris, France*. NATO. https://www.nato.int/cps/su/natohq/official_texts_25468.htm.

[6] Milanovic Branko 2022. *Russia's War Shows the Chaos in the World Order; An Interview with Branko Milanovic*. Jacobin. https://jacobin.com/2022/03/russia-war-ukraine-sanctions-world-order-global-economy.

[7] World Bank 2024. *GDP (current US$)—Russian Federation*. World Bank. https://data.worldbank.org/indicator/NY.GDP.MKTP.CD?locations=RU.

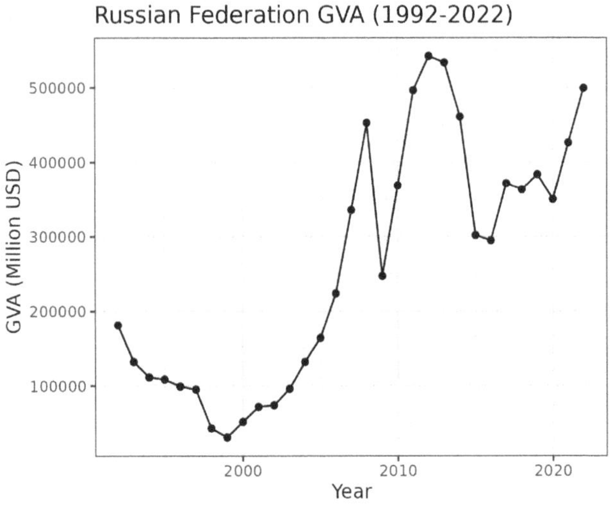

Fig. 8.1 Russia Total Value Added Current US $ 1992-2022

of electricity, which fell to 827TW in 1998, and only eventually recovered to 1091TW in 2016 and 1167TW in 2022,[8] an increase of 8% in 32 years. Other physical indicators have never recovered. Hydraulic concrete production, a proxy for the construction of residential housing and infrastructure was 68,000[9] thousand metric tonnes in 1992, by 2018 it had fallen to 53,678.[10] Steel production fell from 89.6 mn tonnes in 1990 when Russia was the second largest producer in the world after Japan, to 48.5 mn tonnes in 1997, by 2007 it had recovered slightly to 72 mn tonnes[11] and continues to fluctuate around that level.

The destruction of Russia's industrial base, and the military might that rested upon it, was the prerequisite for Russia's subjection to the

[8] Energy Institute 2024. *Statistical Review of World Energy 2023*. Energy Institute. https://www.energyinst.org/statistical-review.

[9] Bureau of Mines 1992. Minerals yearbook: Mineral industries of Europe and central Eurasia 1992. Washington, D. C.: Bureau of Mines: United States Government Printing Office, 1992 https://digital.library.wisc.edu/1711.dl/PPYAWXJZXOESO8L.

[10] USGS 2018. 2018 Minerals Yearbook. *United States Geological Survey*.

[11] Fortescue Stephen 2009. The Russian Steel Industry, 1990–2009. *Eurasian Geography and Economics*, 50(3), pp. 252–274.

West. President Putin's 2000 election was its unravelling. Susan Glasser the Washington Posts former Soviet bureau chief explained "from the start" Putin "was both clear and acted on with breathtaking speed" he waged war on "Chechnya with unforgiving force... reinstated the Soviet national anthem, ordered the government takeover of the only independent television network in Russia's history, passed a new flat tax on income and required Russians to actually pay it, and exiled powerful oligarchs". Putin reconstituted the Russian now capitalist state outside of the orbit of Western control. Nationalising key industries, limiting Western investment, and asserting a Russian sphere of influence over the former Soviet republics of central Asia and Europe. The post-restoration economic collapse had reached its nadir after the East Asian financial crisis of 1997. Market prices then began to function as a mechanism for allocating the productive resources and oil prices, which had fallen as Russian supplies became available to the world market after 1991, began to recover. Russian oil exports were just under 4 mn barrels (bbl) a day from 1993 to 2000, then rose to nearly 8 mn bbl/day by 2007 to 2014, peaked at 9 mn bbl/day in 2017 before falling under the impact of U.S. sanctions to 2023 just under 7 mn bbl/day. The revenues this production yields fluctuates sharply due to changes in the oil price and the dollar/rouble exchange rate. The Russian Federation also exported around 200bn cubic metres of gas to Western Europe by pipeline, only falling sharply to 50bn cubic metres in 2023 after the invasion of Ukraine. The similarity between changes to Russian GDP and its oil revenues shown in Fig. 8.2 is striking.[12]

As oil prices accelerated after China's accession to the WTO in 2001 and the recovery of the West after the hi-tech recession of 2001, so Russia's oil revenues funded its economic recovery. BP, Shell, Total and Chevron had investments in the Russian oil and gas sector and in 2007 the German electricity company E.ON invested $25bn in Russian gas and electricity including 6.43% of Gazprom. Oil revenues dipped after the 2008 Great Recession but then rose again as oil prices approached previous highs before U.S. fracking output and the development of the U.S. into the largest gas and oil exporter in the world, capped the oil price after around 2010.

[12] EIS 2024. *Energy Institute Statistical Review of World Energy*. https://www.energyinst.org/statistical-review/home.

Fig. 8.2 Russian Federation oil revenues US $bn/year

In 2012 oil and gas accounted for more than 50% of Russian federal budget revenues and over 70% of total exports. In 2013 Russian state-owned banks used EU capital markets for nearly half of their bond borrowings, but the growth of China provided Russia with an alternative market for its resources, and a supplier to, and replacement for, the remnants of its industrial base.

Russia's renewed confidence was expressed in its desire to exercise control over what it deemed to be its natural sphere of influence across the former Russian empire, as it did so, it separated itself from the West. Putin opposed the "colour revolutions" of the post-Soviet states, the 2003 Georgian Rose Revolution that deposed Eduard Shevardnadze, the final foreign minister of the Soviet Union, the 2004 Orange Revolution in Ukraine where the pro-Western Viktor Yushchenko saw off at least temporarily, the pro-Russian Viktor Yanukovych, and the 2005 Tulip Revolution in Kyrgyzstan where Kurmanbek Bakiyev deposed Askar Akayev.[13]

[13] Glasser Susan B. 2019. Putin the Great. *Foreign Affairs,* 98(5), pp. 10–17.

In 2005 Ukraine had entered into "Intensified Dialogue" with NATO, so that by April 2008 at the Bucharest NATO summit the membership of Ukraine and also Georgia was supported by Jaap de Hoop Scheffer, the NATO Secretary General.[14] Negotiations towards membership continued, even as the Russia-Georgia war of August 2008 broke out. This was connected with separatist conflict around Abkhazia and South Ossetia with fighting continuing until December. Meanwhile, Ukraine continued high-level negotiations including with the EU until on 21 November 2013 before, in an abrupt volte-face, Ukraine's President Yanukovych, who won a closely contested election in 2010, suspended EU trade and began association talks in favour of Russia.

Protests in favour of the West began in Kyiv's Independence Square (Maidan). Ignoring the protestors on 6th December Yanukovych met with Putin to develop a new "strategic partnership". This included Russia loaning the Ukrainian government $3bn. Nonetheless, anti-government protests continued and turned violent. At the end of February, an EU mediated peace treaty that scheduled elections before the year end was agreed then immediately broken. Ukraine's parliament impeached Yanukovych who fled to Russia. In Crimea Pro-Russian separatists and Russian troops then occupied government buildings and on the 21 March 2014 Putin formalised Russia's takeover. In a subsequent Russian referendum, not internationally recognised, 95.5% of voters in Crimea supported union with Russia.[15] Despite the Minsk ceasefire agreements of 2014/2015 fighting between Russian-supported separatists and Ukrainian government forces continued in the Donbas around the status of Donetsk and Luhansk.[16] On 17th July the MH17 Malaysian Airlines airliner was shot down, probably by Russian separatists. On 25th July the EU Council adopted "tier three" sanctions against Russia which were the

[14] HoC 2008. Hansard Ministerial Statement c111WS. House of Commons Hansard Ministerial Statements for 24 Apr 2008 (pt 0001) (parliament.uk).

[15] Walker Nigel 2023. *Conflict in Ukraine: A timeline (2014 - eve of 2022 invasion)*. Research Briefing, House of Commons Library. https://researchbriefings.files.parliament.uk/documents/CBP-9476/CBP-9476.pdf.

[16] Smith Ben and Mills Claire 2014. *Ukraine: towards a frozen conflict*? House of Commons Library. https://researchbriefings.files.parliament.uk/documents/SN06978/SN06978.pdf.

hardest since the Cold War.[17]The United Nations estimated that a total of 2,729 dead, rising to over 3,000 if the 298 who died on the Malaysia Airlines flight were included died in the fighting.[18]

The December 2014 Rouble collapse followed this crisis. It was sparked by international sanctions from Western institutions and the nationalisation of Western oil assets by the Russian government. In 2013 Rosneft Russia's state-owned and largest oil producer, accounting for around a third of Russia's total output,[19] borrowed about $40 billion to buy out BP's 50% share in TNK-BP to Rosneft, in exchange for $12.5bn in cash and a 19.75% BP stake in Rosneft. Anxiety in Western financial centres was heightened in July by a U.S. $8.9bn fine on the French bank BNP Paribas for sanctions violations.[20] At the end of 2014 the initial tranche of the Rosneft loan, around $10bn was due, with $20bn more in 2015.[21] In October, Rosneft issued $11bn worth of rouble-denominated bonds equivalent to around 70% of total Russian annual corporate bond issuance. In effect the Russian state was printing Roubles to pay off its dollar denominated loans, which called into question the value of a further $300bn such debt. On "Black Monday" December 15th, the rouble and the stock-price indices crashed falling 30%. The Central Bank of Russia (CBR) hiked interest rates from 10.5% to 17% but to no avail. The fall of the Rouble paradoxically reduced the value of oil sales, priced in dollars, but increased their purchasing power in Roubles, and meant that exports of capital were more expensive, heightening the separation of the economy from the West, which anticipated the eventual rupture of Russia with the West over the next decade.

[17] European Council 2024. *Timeline—EU sanctions against Russia*. European Council. https://www.consilium.europa.eu/en/policies/sanctions-against-russia/timeline-sanctions-against-russia/.

[18] UN 2014. *Ukraine death toll of more than 3,000 'alarming'*. New York, United Nations.

[19] Wilson Tom and Chazan Guy 2022. *BP to divest stake in Russian state-oil company Rosneft*. Financial Times.
https://www.ft.com/content/8b4968fa-40d8-40ae-b2f9-f12cd8b23f9c.

[20] Parker George, Stacey Kiran and Fleming Sam 2014. *Osborne warns UK on financial impact of Russian sanctions*. Financial Times. https://www.ft.com/content/3c544fce-10f6-11e4-94f3-00144feabdc0#.

[21] Guriev Sergei 2014. *What caused the ruble to fall?* World Economic Forum. https://www.weforum.org/agenda/2014/12/what-caused-the-ruble-to-fall/.

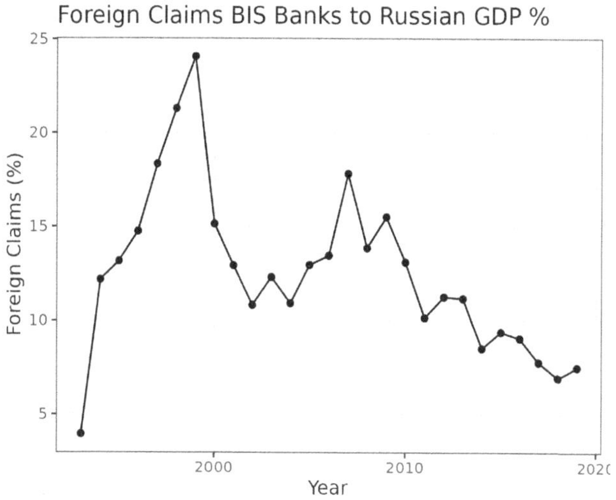

Fig. 8.3 Foreign claims BIS banks to Russian GDP %

The collapse of the central plan was simultaneously the opening of the Russian Federation to Western banks who sought cheap assets in Russia and facilitated oligarchs moving their capital abroad. By 2000 foreign banks owned Russian assets equivalent to 25% of Russian national income as shown in Fig. 8.3.[22]Putin's reassertion of Russian nationalism sharply reduced this trend to 7.5% by 2019.

The renewed outbreak of the Ukraine-Russian war in 2023 and consequent Western sanctions will have reduced these numbers to practically zero. Figure 8.4 shows Russian FDI outflows.[23]

After 2000 as oligarchs sought to harvest their fortunes abroad FDI outflows peaked in 2008 and then fell, rose again before the Ukrainian war in 2014, and then fell sharply except for a Covid-19 spike in 2021.

[22] World Bank 2024. *Consolidated Foreign Claims of BIS-Reporting Banks to GDP for Russian Federation* [DDOI12RUA156NWDB], retrieved from FRED, Federal Reserve Bank of St. Louis; https://fred.stlouisfed.org/series/DDOI12RUA156NWDB.

[23] World Bank 2024. *Foreign direct investment, net outflows (% of GDP) - Russian Federation*. World Bank. https://data.worldbank.org/indicator/BM.KLT.DINV.WD.GD.ZS?locations=RU.

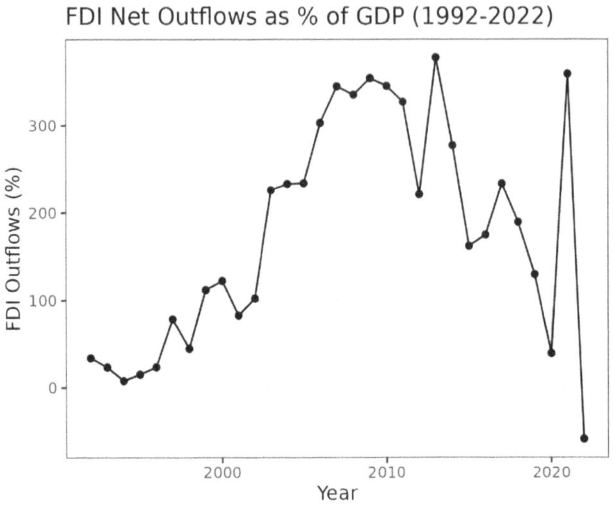

Fig. 8.4 Russia FDI net outflows % GDP

By the time of the second Ukrainian war of 2024 net outflows had completely halted.

As Russia shifted towards a resource extraction economy, so manufacturing fell from 24% of output in 1992 to 2022 14% while mining and utilities rose from 12% in 1992 to 14% in 2022.[24] Even these figures conceal the extent of the shift. In 2012 Russia commissioned new hydroelectric and nuclear power schemes to reduce the domestic consumption of fossil fuels for electricity[25] to enable their export abroad. The sustained surplus of exports over imports or balance of payments[26] meant Russia built up large currency reserves from almost nothing in 1998 to a peak of nearly 2008 $600bn, they fell after the Russia-Georgia conflict to

[24] World Bank 2024. *GDP (current US$) - Russian Federation*. World Bank. https://data.worldbank.org/indicator/NY.GDP.MKTP.CD?locations = RU.

[25] World Nuclear Association 2024. *Nuclear Power in Russia, Russian Nuclear Energy 2024* https://world-nuclear.org/information-library/country-profiles/countries-o-s/russia-nuclear-power.aspx.

[26] World Bank 2024. *Exports of goods and services (current US$) - Russian Federation*. World Bank. https://data.worldbank.org/indicator/NE.EXP.GNFS.CD?locations=RU.

2009 $400bn and the Ukraine-Russia conflict to 2014 $300bn[27] before rising to 2024 $600bn. Meanwhile their composition also changed from 2013/14 Russia sold its almost $180bn of U.S. treasuries almost entirely extinguishing its holdings in 2018.[28] These foreign exchange surpluses enabled it to replace the output of the manufacturing sector destroyed in the transition to the market with imports. Russia was still dependent on Europe as a market, particularly for gas, but China now provided an alternative, as the Atlantic Council explained "Russia is now heavily dependent on China and has a similar model of trade with China as Iran: Russia exports oil to China and imports technology. In 2022, Russia received $88bn from Beijing from energy exports and paid $71.7bn for Chinese goods. Since Russia and China have switched to the use of national currencies, rouble-renminbi trade increased 80-fold between February and October 2022".[29]

The Russian intervention in the Syrian civil war presaged subsequent conflicts in the Middle East and elsewhere. Towards the end of 2015, Syrian opposition forces including ISIS appeared capable of defeating Assad and establishing an Islamic republic. This had serious implications for Russia's internal security in Chechnya it had fought a civil war against similar forces and it also threatened its geo-strategic interests. The Syrian Tartus port is an important naval base originally established in 1971 but made permanent in 2017 which provided Russia with access to the Mediterranean sea and supported its growing collaboration with Turkey and Iran.[30] Russia's force was limited to several thousand troops on the ground and the Wagner mercenary group, and focussed on "airpower, missile strikes, and unmanned systems" to break up, degrade and destroy "capabilities and fighting formations of the anti-Assad opposition, rather

[27] Bank of Russia 2024. *International Reserves of the Russian Federation (End of period). Bank* of Russia (cbr.ru). https://cbr.ru/eng/hd_base/mrrf/mrrf_m/.

[28] Setser Brad 2024. *Mobilizing Russia's Immobilized Reserves.* Council on Foreign Relations (CFR).

[29] Donovan Kimberly and Nikoladze Maia 2024. T*he axis of evasion: Behind China's oil trade with Iran and Russia*. Atlantic Council. https://www.atlanticcouncil.org/blogs/new-atlanticist/the-axis-of-evasion-behind-chinas-oil-trade-with-iran-and-russia/.

[30] Smagin Nikita 2023. *Moscow's Original "Special Operation": Why Russia Is Staying in Syria*. Carnegie Corporation. https://carnegieendowment.org/russia-eurasia/politika/2023/01/moscows-original-special-operation-why-russia-is-staying-in-syria?lang=en.

than on occupying territory".[31] The "subsequent reoccupation of much of Syria's territory by Assad's military was a byproduct of the massive pounding the opposition took, rather than the initial purpose of the intervention, which was to stave off Assad's collapse". Russia's offensive included collaboration with the U.S. against the common enemy,[32] but the narrow rapprochement in Syria remained separate from the wider and more fundamental conflict of interests between the U.S. and Russia.[33]

Since the Iranian revolution of 1979 Iran has been an opponent of U.S. policy in the Middle East and as the Carnegie peace institute noted "both Republican and Democratic administrations have effectively followed the same blueprint"[34] towards it. Not only there.

In the aftermath of the 2003 American invasion of Iraq, Iran began to develop a nuclear defence programme, which lead to U.S. and Western sanctions. In 2015 the 5 + 1, the UK, China, France, Germany, Russia, the U.S. and Iran (the P5 + 1 with Iran as the appendage to the deal that concerned them) agreed the Joint Comprehensive Plan of Action (JCPOA) wherein Iran limited its nuclear programme in exchange for sanctions relief.[35] Provided Iran complied then all the 2023 restrictions on ballistic missile and sensitive technologies expired. As the U.S., UK and France (the E3) did not want to lift these restrictions, they found that Iran had incrementally refused to comply with its treaty obligations. In 2018 the Trump administration reimposed sanctions, which were inevitably, continued and deepened by Biden. The impact of these

[31] Gvosdev Nikolas K. 2022. D*oes Russia's Syria Intervention Reveal Its Ukraine Strategy?* The National Interest. https://nationalinterest.org/feature/does-russia%E2%80%99s-syria-intervention-reveal-its-ukraine-strategy-200527.

[32] Graham Thomas E. and Saradzhyan Simon 2015. *ISIS' Worst Nightmare: The U.S. and Russia Teaming Up on Terrorism*. Foreign Affairs. https://nationalinterest.org/feature/isis-worst-nightmare-the-us-russia-teaming-terrorism-12216.

[33] Scherbakov Eugene 2015. *Five Questions: Russia's Goals in Syria and Ukraine*. Carnegie Corporation. https://www.carnegie.org/news/articles/five-questions-russias-goals-syria-and-ukraine/.

[34] Chivvis Christopher S., Maloney Suzanne and Sadjadpour Karim 2024. *Why Washington Has Struggled to Find the Right Policy Formula for Iran*. Carnegie Corporation. https://carnegieendowment.org/posts/2024/03/why-washington-has-struggled-to-find-the-right-policy-formula-for-iran?lang=en.

[35] Mills Claire 2024. *What is the status of the Iran nuclear deal?* Research Briefing House of Commons library. https://researchbriefings.files.parliament.uk/documents/CBP-9870/CBP-9870.pdf.

sanctions is substantially mitigated however, as China now provides an alternative market for Iranian oil such that in the first quarter of 2024 its oil exports had recovered to average 1.56 million bbls/day "almost all" of which was sent to China earning Tehran some $35 billion. In 2018 Iran exported nearly 3 million bbls/day with around 750,000 to China, in 2020 that had fallen to around 500,000 bbls/day but, due to increased Chinese sales has subsequently recovered.[36] The very existence of China limits the U.S. international rules-based order.

In 2023 Iran's military spending was a mere 0.8% of the U.S. but around a quarter of Israel's spending. Support for Israel forms the pivot around which U.S. Middle-Eastern policy revolves. Karim Sadjadpour for Carnegie summarised what Western analysts consider to be the three pillars of the Iranian worldview "number one is to evict America from the Middle East. Number two is to replace Israel with Palestine. Number three is to help defeat the U.S.-led world order", what is positive for Iran is negative for the U.S. The U.S. seeks to defend the U.S. led world order by replacing Palestine with Israel in order to guarantee its position in the Middle East. The 2020 Abraham Accords between Israel and Bahrain, Morocco and the UAE sought to normalise relations between Israel and its Arab neighbours to form an anti-Iranian alliance including Saudi Arabia. As the US Secretary of State Blinken explained in December 2023 "normalization would join Israel to a regional security architecture, unlock economic opportunities across the region, and isolate Iran and its proxies".[37]

According to Ben Aluf of *Foreign Affairs* on 7 October 2023 "Hamas surprised Israel's famed military and intelligence agencies"[38] like Mossad. Incompetent Israeli spies, Aluf claimed, "failed to believe" Hamas "would dare or succeed to execute such an unprecedented operation" in which 1,200 Israelis died. By the first anniversary in October 2024 Israel had wrought a terrible revenge; killing at least 42,000 Palestinians, around

[36] CRS 2024. *Iran's Petroleum Exports to China and U.S. Sanctions.* Congressional Research Service. https://crsreports.congress.gov/product/pdf/IN/IN12267.

[37] Blinken Antony J. 2024. *America's Strategy of Renewal, Rebuilding Leadership for a New World.* Foreign Affairs. https://www.foreignaffairs.com/united-states/antony-blinken-americas-strategy-renewal-leadership-new-world.

[38] Benn Aluf 2024 Israel's Paradox of Defeat; How the Country's Military Success Is Producing Political Failure. Foreign Affairs. https://www.foreignaffairs.com/middle-east/israel-paradox-defeat-aluf-benn.

half women and children, displacing about 90% of Gaza's 2.3 million population and destroying 92% of roads, more than 84% of health facilities and over 70% of water and sanitation facilities, producing 40 million tonnes of debris.[39]Blinken is no simple hypocrite, for the U.S. and their proxy Israel, conflict arises when others wage war against their war for peace, that is, when they defend themselves against Israeli and U.S. attack. Netanyahu elaborated "Israel is fighting on seven fronts. Amongst Tel Aviv's enemies are Iranian-backed Hezbollah, Hamas, the Houthis in Yemen, Shiite militias in Iraq and Syria, and terrorists in the West Bank, states Israeli Prime Minister Benjamin Netanyahu"[40] or more precisely, the U.S. proxy Israel is fighting what Blinken labels Iranian proxies. In September 2024 Mossad illustrated its reach by exploding thousands of Hezbollah pagers loaded with explosive in "an audacious piece of tradecraft"[41] according to the *Financial Times*. This was almost immediately followed by the murder of Hezbollah leader Hassan Nasrallah. In July Israel killed Hamas's chief negotiator Ismail Haniyeh and in October 2024 they killed the Hamas leader Yahya Sinwar. John Sawers, former chief of MI6 and UK ambassador to the UN, described the killings as "a gamble for Israel but one it seems ready for"[42] and not only Israel. Nasrallah had sought to limit the spread of the conflict by limiting Hezbollah's response to token actions in tune with Iran's "telegraphed" April 2024 drone strike.[43]Iran's far stronger October 2024 180 ballistic missile strike was the inevitable escalated response Nasrallah's murder. The ever-extending scope of the conflict, extending to the collapse of Syria in early December, as Assad's regime was undermined by Hezbollah's truce with Israel and Russia's focus on Ukraine, reflects its strategic importance for the U.S. the underwriter of Israel's war materiel and finance. The

[39] Al Jazeera 2024. A year of Israel's devastating war on Gaza Al Jazeera. https://www.aljazeera.com/gallery/2024/10/7/a-year-of-israels-devastating-war-on-gaza.

[40] Zimko Oleksandra 2024. *Netanyahu: Israel is fighting on seven fronts.* RBC Ukraine. https://www.msn.com/en-gb/news/world/netanyahu-israel-is-fighting-on-seven-fronts/

[41] Fletcher Tom 2024. Israel's pager attack has raised the stakes in the Middle East. Financial Times. https://www.ft.com/content/ff638e9a-0a20-4d56-ae59-128dfaf762a3.

[42] Sawers John 2024. *Middle East's power scales tip as Israel senses Iran's weakness.* Financial Times. https://www.ft.com/content/fbce0418-efc5-4055-a4ca-c60580bf43e2.

[43] Rathbone John Paul, Bott Ian and Zilber Neri 2024. *How Israel's air defences withstood Iran's missile barrage.* Financial Times. https://www.ft.com/content/3fa784e6-3e5e-4f6c-8285-52b297c986da.

U.S. is fighting for, in Blinken's words, "the foundational principles of the international system" he continued "for many developing and emerging-market countries, great-power competition in the past meant being told to pick a side in a contest that felt far removed from their daily struggles. Many have expressed concern that today's rivalry is no different. And some worry that the United States' focus on domestic renewal and strategic competition will come at the expense of the issues that matter most to them. Washington must demonstrate that the opposite is true"[44], Israel must pre-empt Saudi's moves away from the U.S.

In a 2024 address to the UN Israeli Prime Minister Netanyahu produced a map of Israel which incorporated Palestine explaining "We are at the cusp of" a "dramatic breakthrough: a historic peace with Saudi Arabia"[45], this tied into other proposals for a possible rail deal with the U.S., India and Saudi Arabia, India to provide an alternative to China's BRI. The Gaza-Arish-Sderot Free Trade Zone would create an Israeli port in Gaza cleansed of its Hamas.[46] Israel's problem is, and the likely reason for the intensity of the assault of Gaza and its extension into Lebanon, that Saudi Arabia is being pulled towards China. In March 2023 in Beijing China brokered a Iran-Saudi deal to restore diplomatic relations in what was described as "the new 'post-American Gulf era'".[47] Saudi after some hesitation has joined the BRICS (Brazil, Russia, India, China, South Africa) in January 2024 and China is by far its largest trade partner. A member of the BRI there are strong Chinese investment in Saudi Arabia "this new China-Gulf energy interdependence is occurring against a backdrop of declining U.S. hegemony and increasing multipolarity, which is

[44] Blinken Antony J. 2024. *America's Strategy of Renewal, Rebuilding Leadership for a New World*. Foreign Affairs. https://www.foreignaffairs.com/united-states/antony-blinken-americas-strategy-renewal-leadership-new-world.

[45] Lazaroff Tovah 2024. *Netanyahu unveils 'new Middle East' with Israel-Saudi peace at UNGA*. Jerusalem Post. https://www.jpost.com/israel-news/article-760158.

[46] Roche Daniel Jonas 2024. Israel Prime Minister Benjamin Netanyahu unveils regional.

plan to build a "massive free trade zone" with rail service to NEOM. The Architects Newspaper. https://www.archpaper.com/2024/05/benjamin-netanyahu-unveils-regional-plan-free-trade-zone-rail-service-neom.

[47] Cafiero Giorgio 2024 *A year ago, Beijing brokered an Iran-Saudi deal. How does détente look today?* Atlantic Council. https://www.atlanticcouncil.org/blogs/iransource/iran-saudi-arabia-china-deal-one-year/.

also pushing them together".[48] Israel acting as the U.S. proxy seeks to "create a Jewish state from the river to the sea, extending limited if necessary but preferably no political rights to non-Jewish subjects, even those who hold Israeli citizenship".[49]

Blinken did not oppose Israel extending conflict from the ethnic cleansing of Gaza,[50] he opposed others extending the conflict to Israel and the U.S. Blinken's extension of the war follows a logical path, what Blinken labels "Great Power competition". The struggle for the U.S. against its "pacing challenge" China and its other enemies, Russia, Iran and North Korea. In the Middle East that means to "work toward greater integration and normalization in the region, including between Israel and Saudi Arabia". The war needs to be sufficiently extensive and vicious to discourage Saudi Arabia, the United Arab Emirates (UAE) from their flirtation with China and to ensure that they understand that support for the Western alliance really is in their best interest.

The third phase of globalisation ended with the Covid-19 pandemic of 2020–21.[51] The pandemic was the inevitable consequence of industrial farming techniques and systematic under investment in vaccines. Mike Davis, a U.S. Marxist, observed that "the collective revenue from *every* single vaccine is less 'than Pfizer's income from a single anti-cholesterol medication".[52] The U.S. experienced the highest excess mortality 420,000 deaths by 3 January 2021, Mexico followed with 270,000 by 13 December 2020 and then Russia with 270,000 by 30 November 2020. The world's official COVID-19 death count was 2.1

[48] Lons Camille 2024. *East meets middle: China's blossoming relationship with Saudi Arabia and the UAE.* European Council for Foreign Relations. https://ecfr.eu/publication/east-meets-middle-chinas-blossoming-relationship-with-saudi-arabia-and-the-uae.

[49] Aluf Benn 2024. Israel's Paradox of Defeat How the Country's Military Success Is Producing Political Failure. Foreign Affairs. https://www.foreignaffairs.com/middle-east/israel-paradox-defeat-aluf-benn.

[50] Albanese Francesca 2023. UN expert warns of new instance of mass ethnic cleansing of Palestinians, calls for immediate ceasefire. United Nations. https://www.ohchr.org/en/press-releases/2023/10/un-expert-warns-new-instance-mass-ethnic-cleansing-palestinians-calls.

[51] Tooze Adam 202. *Shutdown; How Covid Shook the World's Economy.* London, Penguin.

[52] Davis Mike 202. *The monster enters: COVID 19, avian flu, and the plagues of capitalism.* New York and London: OR Books.

million, the true toll could exceed 3.3 million.[53]GDP growth declined significantly due to the COVID-19 shock. The impact was approximately –6.45% across advanced countries. China –3.57% and India –13.63%. The impact in other emerging and developing regions ranged from –4.57 in E&D Sub-Saharan Africa to –8.96 in E&D Latin America and Caribbean.[54] Trade slumped and governments conducted fiscal and monetary stimulus to bail out their economies, with huge amounts of Quantitative Easing across the Western economies. U.S. Federal assets fluctuated between 15 and 20% of total government liabilities. After the 2008 Great Crash the Fed's assets doubled from $1tn to $2tn. It continued its loose monetary policy with assets slowing doubling again to $4tn. Then during Covid from 2020 to 2022 assets doubled again to $8tn.[55]The UK followed a similar pattern with assets amounting to £580bn by 2023[56] or 28% of total government debt. This increase in assets substantially offsets the growth in debt as "Federal Reserve Banks remit their profits to the Treasury, any interest earned on their federal debt is rebated to the federal government. Thus, debt held by Federal Reserve Banks constitutes liabilities that the federal government owes to itself".[57]

Although the response of Western governments to the pandemic was panicked and uneven, they nonetheless sought to mitigate its worst effects however inadequately and incompetently. Mandel observed "During an expansionist long wave... the priority for the capitalist class was to buy

[53] Karlinsky Ariel, Kobak Dmitry 2021. *The World Mortality Dataset: Tracking excess mortality across countries during the COVID-19 pandemic.* medRxiv. The World Mortality Dataset: Tracking excess mortality across countries during the COVID-19 pandemic - PubMed (nih.gov).

[54] Martin Fernando M., Sánchez Juan M., and Wilkinson Olivia 2023. The Economic Impact of COVID-19 around the World. *Federal Reserve Bank of St. Louis Review*, Second Quarter 2023, pp. 74–88.

[55] Board of Governors of the Federal Reserve System (US) 2024. Assets: Total Assets: Total Assets (Less Eliminations from Consolidation. FRED, Federal Reserve Bank of St. Louis; https://fred.stlouisfed.org/series/WALCL.

[56] UK DMO 2024. *Quarterly Review January to March 2024.* Debt Management Office. https://www.dmo.gov.uk/media/hmjfikgr/jan-mar-2024.pdf.

[57] Martin Fernando 2019. A lesson in measuring the federal debt. FRED blog. https://fredblog.stlouisfed.org/2019/12/a-lesson-in-measuring-the-federalddebt/?utm_source=series_page&utm_medium=related_content&utm_term=related_resources&utm_campaign=fredblog.

off the working class through reforms, among which full employment and social security policies played a key role. The economic expansion itself created the material conditions in which, by and large, the system could deliver these goods".[58] Capitalist governments of all nominal hues followed essentially the same policy prescription to limit the social impact of the pandemic through lock downs, wage and business subsidies, and accelerated vaccination programmes, while the enormous reserves accumulated during globalisation provided them with the resources to do it.

The point of the global system was to deliver more of the same. Social peace was the prerequisite for parasitism and income inequality, the rule of the 0.01%. But nothing good lasts forever. The end of globalisation was as inevitable as China's growth, Russia's recovery and their separation from Western financial capital. The recreation of a multi-polar world, undermining a key precondition for free trade (a single global hegemonic power) was the striking feature of the third phase of the upward long wave.

[58] Mandel Ernest 1995. *Long Waves of Capitalist Development*. London, Verso.

CHAPTER 9

The War Potential of China and the U.S

"Western countries led by the United States have implemented comprehensive containment, encirclement and suppression against us, bringing unprecedented severe challenges to our country's development". Xi Jinping 2023.[1]

In 1946 Nicholas Kaldor, a Keynesian Lord to be, undertook a detailed statistical survey of Germany's Nazi war economy to define its "war potential" or "the maximum war production which the country's available resources permit, once these resources have been fully adapted to the purpose of carrying on the war". In the short-run it was determined by four factors "the capital equipment of its industry, its available manpower, its supply of raw materials, and finally, the ability and skill of its industrial organisers, engineers and technicians" assuming that war did not occur overnight, that is that there was a period of rearmament, then in the long run "the ultimate limits to a country's war potential are set simply by the quantity and skill of its manpower, and by the richness of ores and

[1] U.S. DoD 2023. *Military and Security Developments Involving the People's Republic of China*. Department of Defense. https://media.defense.gov/2023/Oct/19/2003323409/-1/-1/1/2023-MILITARY-AND-SECURITY-DEVELOPMENTS-INVOLVING-THE-PEOPLES-REPUBLIC-OF-CHINA.PDF.

W. Jefferies, *War and the World Economy*, Palgrave Insights into Apocalypse Economics,
https://doi.org/10.1007/978-3-031-85236-7_9

minerals of the areas under its control or with which it is capable of trading". These were the two "ultimate bottlenecks" once other temporary restrictions were overcome.[2]

For analytical purposes China's economy is divided into three sectors, the primary sector agriculture, fishing and mining, the secondary sector manufacturing and the tertiary sector, services. By 1956 China had abolished market production completely. It was a centrally planned economy where nothing was bought or sold, so there was no national income insofar as national income measures market exchange or price. Output was measured through a Material Product System (MPS) similar to that of the USSR, which aggregated various non-monetary physical inputs and outputs to enable central planners to determine production decisions. After 1978 the introduction of market reforms eventually transformed the basis of the economy into one of universal commodity production. By roughly the end of the 1990s central planning had transitioned into a market economy. Even State-Owned Enterprises (SOE) now performed according to market criteria. Financial planning and investment were indirectly enacted through SOE retained profits, bank interest or loans financed by rents, national income Gross Domestic Product (GDP) replaced the MPS. China was a capitalist economy notwithstanding the rule of the Communist Party, so that by 2000 almost all exchanges were at market prices.

The absolute size of the workforce peaked in 2012 at 780 mn before (as a legacy of the one child policy eventually abolished in 2016) it slowly began to decline, falling to 734 mn in 2022.[3] As important as the absolute size of the workforce is the proportion of wage labourers, the working class who sell their labour to a capitalist employer and create surplus value. Agri-business has consolidated land holdings, raised rural productivity and transformed poor farmers into rural proletarians or migrant workers who have abandoned the countryside for the city in search of higher paid urban work. This process remains the key driver for China's growth as is shown in Fig. 9.1.

The agricultural sector peaked in 1990 to 389 mn before falling to 176 mn in 2022. The secondary manufacturing sector peaked in 2012 at

[2] Kaldor Nicholas 1946. The German War Economy. The Review of Economic Studies, 1945–1946, 13(1), pp. 33–52.

[3] China NBS 2023. Table 4.2. China National Bureau of Statistics. https://www.stats.gov.cn/sj/ndsj/2023/indexeh.htm.

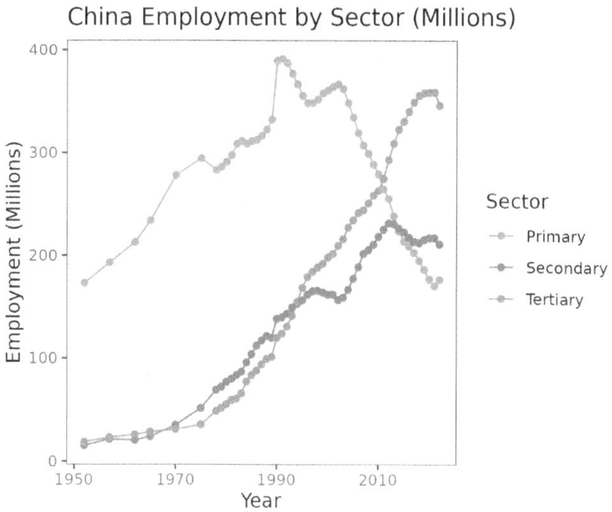

Fig. 9.1 China Employment by Sector (Millions)

231 mn or 30% of total employment before declining to 211 mn in 2022 or 29% of total employment. Current migration, around 16 mn people a year or about 1% of the population a year, is largely into the tertiary service sector which reached 346 mn in 2022. This inward migration the key driver of capital accumulation will be exhausted within the next decade.

U.S. manufacturing employment peaked at 1979, 19 mn which is 21% of all employment. It fell to 11 mn in 2009 before recovering slightly to 13 mn in 2024, just 8% of a larger workforce. Total employees were 90 mn in 1979 and 159 mn in 2024.[4] In 2022 21 mn were employed in the goods producing sector, 13% of total employment, 132 mn in the service sector and 2 mn in agriculture. The balance of 9 mn were self-employed. If the ultimate limit of a country's war potential is "the quantity and skill of its manpower" there is no contest.

Meanwhile the capital intensity of China's manufacturing sector is rapidly increasing. Installations of industrial robots, a proxy for general

[4] U.S. Bureau of Labor Statistics 2024. *All Employees, Manufacturing [MANEMP]*. FRED, Federal Reserve Bank of St. Louis. https://fred.stlouisfed.org/series/MANEMP.

increase in the technical composition of capital, explains the relative decline in Chinese manufacturing employment over the last decade. In 2022 China, U.S., Germany, South Korea and Japan accounted for 79% of all robot installations, China installed over half illustrated in Table 7.

Industrial Robot Installations 1000 s.[5]

	US	*China*	*Germany*	*South Korea*	*Japan*
2013	24	37	18	21	25
2014	26	57	20	24	29
2015	28	69	20	38	35
2016	31	97	20	41	39
2017	33	156	21	40	46
2018	40	154	27	38	55
2019	33	140	21	28	50
2020	31	168	22	31	39
2021	36	268	24	31	47
2022	40	290	26	32	50

In 2023 the U.S. installed 44,000 robots and China 316,000. Most installations were in the electrical and automotive sectors. China is rapidly increasing the intensity of robots per worker, in 2022 Korea had slightly over 1,000 robots per 10,000 manufacturing workers, Germany had slightly over 400, Japan slightly under. In 2020 China's intensity was 246 in 2021 it was 322, and in 2022 it was 392 while the U.S. was 285.[6] This trend towards an increasing technical and so organic composition of capital is accelerating. As China's property sector has slowed, with floor space construction falling "two-thirds below the peak in early 2021"[7] resources have been shifted into renewables manufacturing, solar, wind, batteries and electric vehicles. The expansion of the renewable sector has enabled the Chinese to offset the decline in the construction sector. Banking investment in manufacturing has risen from around $70bn a

[5] IFR 2024. *Industrial Robot Installations*. International Federation of Robotics. http://www.worldrobotics.org.

[6] Atkinson Robert D. 2024. *How Innovative Is China in the Robotics Industry?* ITIF Hamilton Center on Industrial Strategy. https://www2.itif.org/2024-chinese-robotics-innovation.pdf.

[7] Long Chen 2024. *China's big housing correction is not over*. Financial Times. https://www.ft.com/content/38f32adf-fc91-4f3c-a5df-69c676da646e.

quarter in 2019 to $700bn a quarter in 2023.[8] China's government has announced more than $800bn by 2030 investment in its electricity grid, compared with Biden's announced $3.5bn.[9] China installed 102GW (Gigawatts) of solar in the first half of 2024 the U.S. installed 40GW in the whole of 2023. This when combined with rapid technological advance, means the quality of renewables has risen as their costs have fallen.[10] Between 2010 and 2020 the cost of solar PV fell by 15% each year[11] and by 42% in 2023. China's 2023 output of solar cells exceeded 600GW rising from 375GW in 2022. In 2022 there were 240GW global solar installations, in 2023 China installed 216GW solar and 76GW[12] wind, 7GW hydro and 3GW of nuclear. China invested around $890bn in 423 Terawatt hours (TWh) clean energy.[13] The sharp reduction in the proportion of coal power generation to 53% in May 2024 down from 60% at the same time the year before, implies a rapid transition to free carbon-free electricity[14] far faster than most current estimates. Almost uniquely the installation of solar power creates its own market. Its use generates a saleable product, electricity, which can pay for, or at least offset its cost of installation. As this product costs nothing, eventually provided there is enough of it, the price of this electricity will fall to zero, but in the

[8] Graham Niels 2023. *China's manufacturing overcapacity threatens global green goods trade*. Atlantic Council. https://www.atlanticcouncil.org/blogs/econographics/sinographs/chinas-manufacturing-overcapacity-threatens-global-green-goods-trade/.

[9] White Edward and Ding Wenjie 2024. Gridlock in China: huge spending on network in shift to green energy. Financial Times. https://www.ft.com/content/2c0fa0d1-2902-440e-8677-d9f087c2e943.

[10] Myllyvirta Lauri 2023. *China's emissions set to fall in 2024 after record growth in clean energy*. Carbon Brief. https://www.carbonbrief.org/analysis-chinas-emissions-set-to-fall-in-2024-after-record-growth-in-clean-energy/.

[11] Nijsse Femke J. M. M, Mercure Jean-Francois, Ameli Nadia, Larosa Francesca, Kothari Sumit, Rickman Jamie, Vercoulen Pim and Pollitt Hector 2023. The momentum of the solar energy transition. *Nature Communications*, 14(1), pp. 1–10.

[12] Bloomberg 2024. *China Added More Solar Panels in 2023 Than U.S. Did In Its Entire History*. Bloomberg. https://www.bloomberg.com/news/articles/2024-01-26/china-added-more-solar-panels-in-2023-than-us-did-in-its-entire-history.

[13] Carbon Brief 2024. *Analysis: Clean energy was top driver of China's economic growth in 2023*. Carbon Brief. https://www.carbonbrief.org/analysis-clean-energy-was-top-driver-of-chinas-economic-growth-in-2023/.

[14] Carbon Brief 2024. *Analysis: China's clean energy pushes coal to record-low 53% share of power in May 2024*. Carbon Brief. https://www.carbonbrief.org/analysis-chinas-clean-energy-pushes-coal-to-record-low-53-share-of-power-in-may-2024/.

meantime, as China is a net importer of energy, it will reduce the costs of Chinese imports and provide China with a competitive advantage over its rivals.

Aside from the size of the working population, Kaldor considered the other long-term constraint on a nation's war potential was the richness of ores and minerals under its control. By 2022 Chinese investment in the 150 Belt and Road Initiative (BRI) nations[15] exceeded $1tn split $634bn in construction and $419bn in non-financial investments. China strongly invested in metals and mining, in particular copper, lithium, nickel and steel, minerals relevant for renewable electricity, but also in transport, renewable energy, mining and related technologies. The Middle East and Africa had the largest proportion of construction projects, East Asia and Latin America of investment projects.[16] In 2022, China produced 68% of the world's rare earth minerals, supplying 70% of products such as magnets and batteries, and it processed 100% of the world's graphite, 90% of rare earths and 74% of cobalt. China is the top source for 5 out of 12 of these critical minerals, and the second or third top source for an additional three: Fluorspar, Galium and Scandium. U.S. imports at least 50% of an additional 29 minerals including a 90% plus for titanium, 14 rare earths and bismuth.[17]

In 2023 NATO members spent $1341bn or 55% of total world military spending.[18] U.S. military spending was $916bn. The U.S. maintains a kind of ten-power standard, total military spending is greater than the nominal totals of the next 10 nations combined. Russia's $109bn saw a 24% increase due to the Ukraine war or 5.9% of Russian GDP. Ukraine

[15] Huang, Yufan and Deborah Brautigam. 2020. *Putting a Dollar Amount on China's Loans to the Developing World*. The Diplomat. https://thediplomat.com/2020/06/putting-a-dollar-amount-on-chinas-loans-to-the-developing-world.

[16] Nedopil Christoph 2024. *China Belt and Road Initiative (BRI) Investment Report 2023*. Griffith Asia Institute (GAI) at Griffith University, Brisbane, Australia. https://www.griffith.edu.au/__data/assets/pdf_file/0033/1910697/Nedopil-2024-China-Belt-Road-Initiative-Investment-report.pdf.

[17] Daniel Will 2024. *China has a 'near monopoly' on many critical minerals. JPMorgan says it could be the next battleground with the U.S.* Fortune. https://fortune.com/2024/06/10/china-near-monopoly-many-critical-minerals-jpmorgan-says-next-battleground-usa/.

[18] Tian Nan, Lopes da Silva Diego, Liang Xiao and Scarazzato Lorenzo 2024. *Trends in World Military Expenditure, 2023*. SIPRI. https://www.sipri.org/sites/default/files/2024-04/2404_fs_milex_2023.pdf.

increased its spending by 51% to $64.8bn supplemented by U.S. military aid of $35.7bn and $10.3bn from European allies. This mismatch of resources implies only one result. Presidential candidate Trump[19] has already alluded to the possibility of a peace deal and there is increasing reluctance by Ukraine's Western allies to underwrite military aid in perpetuity, not least as continued transfers of military materiel, no matter how technologically obsolete, impinges on the Wests own military capacity. China's spending was an estimated $296bn, which is generally considered an underestimate. China's domestic prices are lower than that of the U.S., so it receives more bang for its Yuan. The Stockholm International Peace Research Institute (SIPRI) estimates that the inflation adjusted Purchasing Power Parity (PPP) total should be 27% higher,[20] other estimates are higher still around $471bn.[21] But war potential measures how much military production there could be. China's manufacturing output exceeds that of the next nine industrial nations combined. China's share of gross production, including intermediates, is three times that of the U.S., six times Japan and nine times Germany.[22]

The concentration of U.S. employment in unproductive business services and administration means U.S. capitalism is structurally dependent on its ability to extract surplus from the world. It reveals both the U.S.' immense power and its vulnerability to a change in the international rules-based order, the source of its financial strength. In 2022 Professional and Business Services employed 23 mn and Financial Services 9 mn.[23] Financial services merely redistribute value they do not create it.

[19] Foy Henry 2024.Donald Trump has 'well-founded plans' for Russia-Ukraine peace talks, Viktor Orbán claims. Financial Times. https://www.ft.com/content/44493fa9-d8f2-4407-94ac-a072c1976ca2.

[20] Nan Tian and Fei Su 2021. *A New Estimate of China's Military Expenditure.* SIPRI. https://www.sipri.org/publications/2021/other-publications/new-estimate-chinas-military-expenditure.

[21] Fravel Taylor M., Gilboy George J. and Heginbotham Eric 2024. *Estimating China's Defense Spending: How to Get It Wrong (and Right).* Texas National Security Review 7(3), University of Texas. https://tnsr.org/2024/06/estimating-chinas-defense-spending-how-to-get-it-wrong-and-right/.

[22] Baldwin Richard 2024. *China is the world's sole manufacturing superpower: A line sketch of the rise.* VOXEU. https://cepr.org/voxeu/columns/china-worlds-sole-manufacturing-superpower-line-sketch-rise1/11.

[23] U.S. BLS 2024. *Employment by major industry sector.* Bureau of Labor Statistics. https://www.bls.gov/emp/tables/employment-by-major-industry-sector.htm.

They may enrich the individual law firm or bank but only by appropriating value from other productive sectors or countries. After the 2008 crash regulators oversaw the concentration of banking into four mega-banks—JPMorgan Chase, Bank of America, Wells Fargo and Citigroup. In 2023 JPMorgan Chase the U.S.' largest bank was worth over $400bn. In 2021 the combined market capitalisation of U.S. banks was $2.6tn. The Big Three Asset Management firms BlackRock, Vanguard and State Street were combined the largest or second largest shareholders in firms comprising nearly 90% US market capitalisation.[24] U.S. owned 70% of asset management funds include the top 7 firms and 16 of the top 20 with Assets under Management (AuM) of $65tn, a 300% rise since 2007. The licensing of online services appears to produce money from nothing and 7 of the 8 companies which have achieved a $1tn market capitalisation are tech firms.

Financial accounting databases, such as Orbis and Compustat, understate the power of financial corporations as they exclude the enormous profits transferred to tax havens. In 2023 tax evasion by giant corporations was estimated at $480bn every year. UK tax havens were responsible for $169bn of that and OECD members $374bn.[25] In 2017 an estimated $15tn of Foreign Direct Investment (FDI) was not real investment, but rather "into empty shell corporations with no real activities". Indeed "close to 40% of multinational profits defined as profits made by multinational companies outside of the country where their parent is located are shifted to tax havens" such that $600bn of profits were shifted to tax havens annually.[26] The share of Phantom FDI has grown from slightly above 30% in 2009 to almost 40% in 2017.[27] The scale of this financial manipulation is so large that of "the $4.2tn in offshore earnings visible

[24] Maher Stephen and Aquanno Scott M. 2024. The Fall and Rise of American Finance From J. P. Morgan to BlackRock. London, Verso.

[25] Tax Justice Network 2023. *State of Tax Justice*. London, Tax Justice Network. https://taxjustice.net/wp-content/uploads/SOTJ/SOTJ23/English/State%20of%20Tax%20Justice%202023%20-%20Tax%20Justice%20Network%20-%20English.pdf.

[26] Tørsløv, Thomas, Wier Ludvig and Zucman Gabriel 2018. The Missing Profits of Nations. *National Bureau of Economic Research (NBER) Working Paper Series 24701*, Cambridge Massachusetts MA, NBER.

[27] Damgaard Jannick, Elkjaer Thomas and Johannesen Niels 2019. *What Is Real and What Is Not in the Global FDI Network?* International Monetary Fund (IMF) Working Paper WP/19/274. https://www.imf.org/en/Publications/WP/Issues/2019/12/11/what-is-real-and-what-is-not-in-the-global-fdi-network.

in the US country-by-country data, $3.0tn of which is in known havens or countries with effective tax rates below 10%".[28] While there is a structural limit to the amount of real FDI an economy can absorb phantom FDI is unbounded. The profits shifted to tax havens are so large that when output, net exports and profits recorded in non-haven countries are redistributed to the country of origin "the rise in the European corporate capital share since the early 1990s is twice as large as recorded in the national account data". The wealth of the rich is based on the indebtedness of the poor, nearly half the rise of debt since the 1980s is owned by the top 1%. The savings of the rich, less consumption, had reached around 20% of US national income by 2016. In the U.S. the consumption share of the top 1% has risen from 4 or 5% in the 1960s and 1970s to 7% by 2016. While the total global volume of sovereign and corporate bond debt was almost USD 100tn, of which OECD governments held 54tn. These financial profits predicated financial speculation, unequal exchange or tax evasion are the fruit of the international rules-based order,[29] they will not be surrendered willingly.

The huge debts of these governments form the assets of the financial sectors, recycling surplus value to the financiers. The status of the U.S. dollar as a proxy world currency enables dollar seigniorage, the demand for dollars for use in trade as a proxy world currency, keeps U.S. interest rates down and so enables the U.S. exploitation of the world. This depends on U.S. control of key high value components of the value chain, the ownership of assets in foreign countries, often oil and raw materials, some manufacturing located offshore and trade through the mechanism of unequal exchange. Dollar seigniorage in turn stimulates the moves towards de-dollarisation, the attempt to trade without the U.S. dollar through the use of alternative currencies, gold or the direct exchange of commodities.

While the international rules-based order was unquestioned, consumers have no option but to pay for the unproductive expenses foisted on them. Once commodities and services are produced outside of the purview of these international rules, then these superfluous legal costs form an insuperable barrier to competitiveness. As there is no state

[28] Clausing, Kimberly. 2020. *Profit Shifting Before and After the Tax Cuts and Jobs Act*. SSRN 3 June, https://ssrn.com/abstract=3274827. Accessed 15/08/2020.

[29] Mian, Atif, Ludwig Straub, Amir Sufi. 2020. *The Saving Glut of the Rich*. Cambridge Massachusetts (MA), National Bureau of Economic Research (NBER).

to enforce international law, once the convention which demands their payment falls into abeyance, they will not be paid. China's manufacturing dominance provides an alternative non-Western supplier of key commodities, not reliant on Western technology or distribution, reducing general dependence on international financial mechanisms, and that of the world, threatening to choke off the financial sources of Western imperial wealth, while providing impetus to de-dollarisation, the by-passing of the dollar as the international reserve currency.

Gold is the universal equivalent in a commodity economy, the only element that does not degrade in normal atmospheric conditions, with a set of unique physical qualities that enable it to act as money directly without translation into a national currency. It may be mined but it may not be manufactured, in contrast with for example diamonds the value of which is collapsing as manufactured diamonds supplant mined diamonds. Gold initially functioned as the direct equivalent in exchange, however, as it is a symbol of social value, it may be replaced by symbols of itself. Intrinsically valueless paper currency supplanted it within the domestic capitalist economies during the nineteenth century, its role restricted to settling balances on international trade. The Bretton Woods treaties followed the British banking acts based on Ricardo's invariable equivalent fixed currencies relative to gold. By the late 1960s these relationships no longer reflected the relative productive capacities of different capitalist powers, so Bretton Woods collapsed and gold was further relegated by the use of the U.S. dollar as a proxy international currency. As the innate symbol of private property gold can never be supplanted as the universal equivalent by a national currency however marginal it may be to the day-to-day functioning of the economy.

In the run up to the Second World War, after the 1929 Wall Street Crash and during the Great Depression, as trade barriers and autarchy dominated the world economy, the proportion of gold in central banks foreign exchange reserves increased from 1929–30 64% to 1931 81%, 1932 92% and 1939 98%. Gold as a scarce mined commodity is valued at the margin, so as central banks increase the proportion of gold in their reserves its price rises, as it rises, it reflects a higher proportion of reserves and so there is an incentive to buy more of it.[30] The trend towards an

[30] Eichengreen Barry and Flandreau Marc 2008. *The Rise and fall of the Dollar, or when di the Dollar Replace Sterling as the Leading International Currency?* NBER WP 14154. http://www.nber.org/papers/w14154.

increasing proportion of gold in reserves becomes mutually reinforcing. In 2022 gold averaged 17% of official reserves for advanced economies (down from 80% in 1950) and 7% for Emerging Market and Developing Economies (EMDEs) down from 30% in 1950 but the outbreak of trade and direct wars between the major powers mean that the downward trend has reversed.[31]

In January 2018 the first Trump administration-imposed import duties of 25% on $250 bn of Chinese manufactured goods.[32] By October 2018 the proportion of U.S. imports facing duties exceeding 10% rose from 3.5% in December 2017 to 10.6%. During 2018 this reduced the real income of U.S. retailers and consumers by an estimated $23.8bn consisting of $8.2bn in price rises and $15.6bn in government in tariff revenues. As Chinese manufacturers sell their goods at cost, so U.S. tariffs have reduced the profits of US corporations and raised prices for US consumers "the Trump administration's tariff changes have been almost entirely passed through into domestic prices, leaving exporter prices unchanged".[33] In April 2024 the Biden administration exceeded Trump's total for punitive tariffs hitting 319 Chinese firms.[34] By June 2024 total duties assessed on Chinese goods under Sect. 301 were $219.6bn from $41.6bn in 2018.[35] The Chinese State Administration of Foreign Exchange (SAFE) showed that FDI from China into the U.S. has fallen

[31] Arslanalp Serkan, Eichengreen Barry, and Simpson-Bell Chima 2023. *Gold as International Reserves: A Barbarous Relic No More? IMF* WP/23/14. https://www.imf.org/en/Publications/WP/Issues/2023/01/27/Gold-as-International-Reserves-A-Barbarous-Relic-No-More-528089.

[32] Xing Yuqing. 2019. How the iPhone Widens the US Trade Deficit with China: the Case of the iPhone X. *National Graduate Institute for Policy Stuthes (GRIPS) Discussion Paper.* pp. 19–21.

[33] Amiti Mary, Redding Stephen and Weinstein David. 2019. The Impact of the 2018 Tariffs on Prices and Welfare. *Journal of Economic Perspectives*, 33(4), pp. 187–210.

[34] Bloomberg 2024. *Biden Surpasses Trumps Record for Blacklisting Chinese Entities.* Bloomberg. https://www.bloomberg.com/news/articles/2024-04-12/biden-surpasses-trump-s-record-for-blacklisting-chinese-entities?utm_source=substack&utm_medium=email&embedded-checkout=true.

[35] U.S. CBP 2024. *Trade Statistics.* U.S. Customs and Border Protection. https://www.cbp.gov/newsroom/stats/trade.

from $314bn in 2021 to $15bn in 2023 through the first three quarters of the year.[36]China's payment of Western banking fees has similarly collapsed.[37]

The February 2022 renewed outbreak of Russia-Ukraine war accelerated the shift away from the U.S. dollar as a proxy world currency and towards gold as an international reserve. After Russia's invasion of the Ukraine Western agencies froze Russian assets mainly held in European banks. Central bank assets are protected under a foundational principle of international law but like the international rules-based order, these rules given, they do not fall from the sky. The EU commission estimated around €260bn of Moscow's central bank assets were immobilised in G7 countries, the EU and Australia. Around €210bn in the EU, and around $5bn in the U.S.[38] Gold cannot be frozen so nations outside the core Western bloc are expanding their gold reserves. The U.S. Federal Reserve tabulated the 10 largest annual increases in the gold share of reserves since 1999, half of the countries had been sanctioned or increases followed "irregular political events, such as bomb blasts, coup attempts, and financial crises".[39] The U.S. dollar proportion of foreign exchange reserves fell from 72% in 2000 to 56% in 2024 when adjusted for exchange and interest rate changes.[40] In 2008 50% of marketable U.S. treasury securities outstanding were held by foreign investors, both official and private by the end of 2022 31% with the extent of the general decline obscured by an increase of Japanese and UK holdings. The U.S. issued about half

[36] Lardy Nicholas R. 2024. *Foreign direct investment is exiting China, new data show*. Peterson Institute for International Economics (PIIE). https://www.piie.com/blogs/realtime-economics/foreign-direct-investment-exiting-china-new-data-show.

[37] Lockett Hudson 2024. *Wall Street is contorting to replace China trade*. Reuters. https://www.reuters.com/breakingviews/wall-street-is-contorting-replace-china-trade-2024-06-06/.

[38] Dubois Laura and Fleming Sam 2023. *The legal case for seizing Russia's assets*. Financial Times. https://www.ft.com/content/adb09fd6-e5f7-4099-9994-806814b4c9b4.

[39] Bertaut Carol, Beschwitz Bastian von, and Curcuru Stephanie 2023. *The International Role of the U.S. Dollar Post-COVID Edition*. Board of Governors of the Federal Reserve System. https://www.federalreserve.gov/econres/notes/feds-notes/the-international-role-of-the-us-dollar-post-covid-edition-20230623.html.

[40] Arslanalp Serkan, Eichengreen Barry and Simpson-Bell Chima 2024. *Dollar Dominance in the International Reserve System: An Update*. IMF Blog. https://www.imf.org/en/Blogs/Articles/2024/06/11/dollar-dominance-in-the-international-reserve-system-an-update.

of sovereign debt and China about a third. China owned 49% of the top 50 global banks by tier 1 capital up from 15% in 2007, including 5 of the top 10.[41] The U.S. dollar share of global trade invoices over the period 1999–2019 was estimated at 96% in the Americas, 74% in the Asia-Pacific region and 79% in the rest of the world. In Europe the Euro dominated with 66%,[42] but this is a backward-looking measure, the direction of travel will accelerate away from the U.S. in the coming years. In July 2024 53% of China's inbound and outbound transactions used the Chinese currency up from about 40% in 2021.[43] In 1995 China produced 3% of world manufacturing exports and by 2020 it was 20%, nonetheless the significance of these exports for its domestic economy has fallen, China's exports to GDP rose from 1995, 11%, peaked at 2004, 18%, before falling to 13% in 2020.[44]In 1990 OECD nations owned 94% of the world Foreign Direct Investment (FDI) stock by 2021 their share had fallen to 76% as China increased its share from 0.2% in 1990 to 7.4% in 2021.[45] Even this overstates the significance of Western FDI in China, much apparent FDI is so-called "round tripping" Chinese investment dressed up as FDI to take advantage of "benefits awarded to foreign investors in China"[46] accounting for "perhaps up to 50%" of FDI in China.[47]

[41] Official Monetary and Financial Institutions Forum, (OMFIF) 2024 *Competitiveness of European financial services.* London, Luxembourg for Finance. https://cloudpdf.io/view/7jLIxhGcw.

[42] Bertaut Carol, Beschwitz Bastian von, and Curcuru Stephanie 2023. *The International Role of the U.S. Dollar Post-COVID Edition.* Board of Governors of the Federal Reserve System. https://www.federalreserve.gov/econres/notes/feds-notes/the-international-role-of-the-us-dollar-post-covid-edition-20230623.html.

[43] Sandlund William 2024. *China's international use of renminbi surges to record highs.* Financial Times. https://www.ft.com/content/ae08b6ed-d323-4a95-a687-0172a98857f4.

[44] Baldwin Richard 2024. *China is the world's sole manufacturing superpower: A line sketch of the rise.* VOXEU. https://cepr.org/voxeu/columns/china-worlds-sole-manufacturing-superpower-line-sketch-rise 1/11.

[45] UNCTAD 2023. *Foreign direct investment: Inward and outward flows and stock, annual.* https://unctadstat.unctad.org/datacentre/dataviewer/US.FdiFlowsStock.

[46] Grimes, Seamus and Yutao Sun. 2014. Implications of China's on-going dependence on foreign technology. *Geoforum,* pp. 59–69, 54.

[47] Johannesen, Niels. *2020 Niels Johannesen FDI database.* University of Copenhagen (Department of Economics), Niels Johannesen, 2016, https://www.nielsjohannesen.net/FDIdatabase/. Accessed 07/09/2020.

Unequal exchange[48] is the difference between what Western corporations pay for foreign goods and the amount the sell them for in the domestic market. Through restricting market access Western governments retain this surplus which is credited to their GDP even while the products that create it are produced abroad.[49] Circulation redistributes profits from relatively dependent nations to relatively powerful ones. A gain for one through circulation, is a loss for the other, to the same amount but in the opposite direction. Marx observed in the *Theories of Surplus Value* that in foreign trade that "profit can also be made by cheating, one person gaining what the other loses. Loss and gain within a *single* country cancel each other out. But not so with trade between different countries...Here the law of value undergoes essential modification... In this case, the richer country exploits the poorer one, even where the latter gains by the exchange".[50] Cheating through non-equivalent exchange enables nations to exploit other nations.[51]

Modern Western politics divides the management of society amongst ostensibly different, but practically identical, political parties albeit with particular designated roles. The absence of class conflict during the period of globalisation has facilitated this division of labour amongst the managers of the contemporary state. The European Trade Union Institute (ETUI) surveyed strike levels across the UK, Sweden, U.S., Germany and France. Strike rates had collapsed everywhere except France, which went from the nation with lowest level of strikes before 1990, to the highest level of strike rates simply by remaining the same.[52] Party politics reflects this relative class peace and is reduced to variations of the same neo-liberal consensus, based on slightly different constituencies of state or aspirant state employees. In the U.S. the election is similarly contested by two fundamentally identical parties. Both their candidates represent

[48] Finger, Barry. 2020. Unequal Exchange: Key Issues for the Labor Theory of Value. Critique, 48 (2–3), pp. 169–187.

[49] Smith, John. 2016. Imperialism in the Twenty-First Century: Globalization, Super-Exploitation, and Capitalism's Final Crisis. New York: Monthly Review Press.

[50] Marx Karl 1972 [1863]. *Theories of Surplus Value Part 3*. Moscow, Progress. p. 105.

[51] Ricci Andrea 2021. *Value and Unequal Exchange in International Trade*. London, Routledge. p. 143 (Ricci claimed Marx did not explain the mechanism for national exploitation but Ricci did not include Marx's reference to cheating).

[52] ETIU 2023. *Rich World Economies See Decades of Ebbing Industrial Action*. ETIU. chart.png (1320 × 800) (reuters.com).

the neo-liberal consensus albeit the Republicans have more reactionary rhetoric domestically but slightly less warmongering internationally while the Democrats are slightly less reactionary domestically but slightly more warmongering internationally, but both are reactionary and warmongering. In 2024 the U.S. jailed 1.9 mn people while 4.9 mn have been incarcerated, 79 mn have a criminal record and 42% of those are black.[53] The system of violent racist oppression is their common currency.

Margaret Thatcher considered Tony Blair her greatest achievement and the respect was mutual. Blair commented "I always thought my job was to build on some of the things she had done rather than reverse them".[54]The UK 2024 election illustrated this well. The five electoral parties effectively presented the same economic and social programme albeit with marginally different emphases based on their membership and the constituency they sought to represent; the Conservative Party big business neo-liberals, the Labour Party state administrative neo-liberals, the Liberal Party nominally reluctant neo-liberals, the Green Party environmental neo-liberals and the Reform Party racist neo-liberals. The range of opinions even between the designated extremes the most liberal Green Party and the most reactionary Reform Party are fundamentally presentational and diminish further when in office. The Labour Party as the administrative party of UK neo-liberalism is particularly susceptible to being bought and sold by big business lobbyists, with ministers, advisers and pressure groups rotating to ensure they gobble their slice of the pie.[55] All are united against the threat of "populists" parties beholden to the popular masses of the right and left, outside of the neo-liberal consensus, and who are largely excluded from the electoral process.

As the wealth generated by globalisation increased the stratification of society, and overall wealth, particularly through the rise in house prices, the identification of millions of people with the system increased. Blair's

[53] Sawyer Wendy and Wagner Peter 2024. *Mass Incarceration: The Whole Pie 2024.* Prison Policy Initiative. https://www.prisonpolicy.org/reports/pie2024.html.

[54] BBC 2013. *Tony Blair: 'My job was to build on some Thatcher policies'.* https://www.bbc.co.uk/news/av/uk-politics-22073434.

[55] Geoghegan Peter 2024. *Labour and the Lobbyists.* London Review of Books, 46(16). https://www.lrb.co.uk/the-paper/v46/n16/peter-geoghegan/labour-and-the-lobbyists.

government like Clinton in the U.S. Blair implemented "progressive neo-liberalism"[56] an oxymoron described by Nancy Fraser, a U.S. philosophy professor as "an alliance of mainstream currents of new social movements (feminism, anti-racism, multiculturalism, and LGBTQ rights), on the one side, and high-end 'symbolic' and service-based business sectors (Wall Street, Silicon Valley, and Hollywood), on the other". Contemporary political discourse is framed within neo-liberal limits, albeit the necessity of exploiting the world tests its practical application and the hypocrisy which underpins it. Migrants must be demonised, the Chinese threat embroidered, the Russian's denounced and the Palestinians ignored and excluded. The necessity of demonstrating the practical use of violence requires vicious client state wars, the relentlessly genocidal bombing campaign against the Palestinians by the U.S. client state Israel, sends a message. To remind the world that the only nation to have dropped the nuclear bomb is the U.S. twice.

The rise of China poses a direct threat to the international rules-based order and so challenges the foundation of Western dominance in general and U.S. in particular. It is not a matter of bad intentions, China proclaims the need for a co-operative future of nations built on peace, harmony and mutual respect. This is incompatible with U.S. hegemony and is viewed by the U.S. political and military strategists as a direct threat to their world domination. They are right, it is such a challenge, and it will only grow. The U.S. challenge to the British Empire was resolved through two world wars by the U.S. allying with Britain to defeat its other more immediate and direct enemies. The price the British Empire paid for U.S. support was its dissolution. The is no comparison with China, which poses a similarly overwhelming challenge to U.S. world domination. It is possible that as the fractures and fissures in the world economy grow there could be a realignment within the Western bloc, but it is hard to see how the U.S. could reconcile themselves with a newly subordinate position to China. Therefore conflicts, economic, political and military will inevitably intensify in the next years.

[56] Fraser Nancy 2017. *The End of Progressive Neoliberalism*. https://www.dissentmagazine.org/online_articles/progressive-neoliberalism-reactionary-populism-nancy-fraser/.

CHAPTER 10

The End of Globalisation and the New Period of Crisis

"When the war came in 1914, I was very soon impressed with two points. ... I saw that you could not separate the idea of commerce from the idea of war and peace. ... [and] that wars were often largely caused by economic rivalry conducted unfairly. ... But toward 1916 I embraced the philosophy that I carried throughout my twelve years as Secretary of State. ... From then on, to me, unhampered trade dovetailed with peace; high tariffs, trade barriers, and unfair economic competition, with war". Cordell Hull U.S. Secretary of State 1948.[1]

"The tariff rate on certain steel and aluminium products under Sect. 301 will increase from 0–7.5% to 25% in 2024. The tariff rate on semiconductors will increase from 25 to 50% by 2025. The tariff rate on electric vehicles under Sect. 301 will increase from 25 to 100% in 2024. The tariff rate on lithium-ion EV batteries will increase from 7.5% to 25% in 2024, while the tariff rate on lithium-ion non-EV batteries will increase from 7.5% to 25% in 2026. The tariff rate on battery parts will increase from 7.5% to 25% in 2024. The tariff rate on solar cells (whether or not assembled into modules) will increase from 25 to 50% in 2024. The tariff rate on ship-to-shore cranes will increase from 0 to 25% in 2024. The tariff

[1] Hull Cordell 1948. The Memoirs of Cordell Hull. New York, Macmillan. pp. 81, 84.

W. Jefferies, *War and the World Economy*, Palgrave Insights into Apocalypse Economics,
https://doi.org/10.1007/978-3-031-85236-7_10

rates on syringes and needles will increase from 0 to 50% in 2024". Joe Biden 2024.[2]
Tariff is "the most beautiful word in the dictionary".[3] Donald Trump 2024

In 2021 the People's Republic of China (PRC) was the "pacing challenge and a Taiwan contingency the pacing scenario"[4] for the U.S. Department of Defense (DoD). Niall Ferguson the Scottish historian and empire nostalgist observed that "losing or not even fighting for Taiwan would be seen all over Asia as the end of American predominance in the region. It would surely cause a run on the dollar and US treasuries. It would be an American Suez",[5] the end of empire equivalent to the 1956 British-French-Israeli debacle. Public wargames of a Chinese invasion of Taiwan in 2023 concluded the island may be defended but that the "defense came at high cost. The United States and its allies lost dozens of ships, hundreds of aircraft, and tens of thousands of service members. Taiwan saw its economy devastated. Further, the high losses damaged the U.S. global position for many years…Victory is therefore not enough. The United States needs to strengthen deterrence immediately".[6] In most game iterations the U.S. Navy lost two carriers and more than a dozen surface ships as well as four submarines. This victory was only possible on the assumption that China exhausted its missile inventory in a month, only landed 30,000 troops and that Taiwan would fight faced with such overwhelming force. Classified wargames produced even worse results, the U.S. were defeated, unable to defend the island.

[2] Biden Joe 2024. *FACT SHEET: President Biden Takes Action to Protect American Workers and Businesses from China's Unfair Trade Practices*. The White House. https://www.whitehouse.gov/briefing-room/statements-releases/2024/05/14/fact-sheet-president-biden-takes-action-to-protect-american-workers-and-businesses-from-chinas-unfair-trade-practices/.

[3] FT 2024. From cars to planes: global manufacturers brace for Trump's tariffs. Financial Times. https://www.ft.com/content/716b7c10-1bfd-4927-8789-c65bf70afe69.

[4] Ratner Dr. Ely 2021. *Statement to Committee on Foreign Relations*. United States Senate. https://www.foreign.senate.gov/imo/media/doc/120821_Ratner_Testimony.pdf.

[5] Ferguson Niall and Robinson Peter 2023. *Cold War II: Niall Ferguson On The Emerging Conflict With China*. Hoover Institution. https://www.hoover.org/research/cold-war-ii-niall-ferguson-emerging-conflict-china.

[6] Cancian Mark F., Cancian Matthew and Heginbotham Eric 2023. *The First Battle of the Next War Wargaming a Chinese Invasion of Taiwan*. Washington D.C. Center for Strategic & International Studies (CSIS).

Ferguson reflected "right now, if there were a showdown between the US and China over Taiwan, I would not put money on the US winning that showdown... Don't do this. Let's not have a showdown over Taiwan. You're not in the kind of position you were in back in the 1990s, the last time there was a Taiwan Strait crisis".[7]Ferguson's swing from fight to flight was no mere anomaly. The Chinese had reassured the U.S. that they need not be concerned about nuclear escalation over Taiwan as "they were absolutely convinced that they are able to prevail in a conventional fight over Taiwan without using nuclear weapons".[8] Presidential candidate Donald Trump endorsed the potential policy shift commenting that Taiwan had taken the U.S. chip industry, should pay for its own defence and that anyway Taiwan was "the apple of President Xi's eye" and it "is 9,500 miles away" from the U.S., while only "68 miles away from China".[9] If the U.S. cede Taiwan to China they will lose control of the South China Sea, cease to be a regional power there and so the world power. On the other hand, if they do fight for Taiwan, they will lose to China, lose control of the South China Sea, cease to be a regional power there and so the world power. The choice is over how to lose not whether to.

Military conflict aims to break the will of the enemy, to bring peace by surrender, to resolve political conflict through violent means. For the U.S. Joint Chiefs of Staff military strategy is the "art and science of employing the armed forces of a nation to secure the objectives of national policy by the application of force or the threat of force".[10] According to the U.S. DoD "China's foreign policy promotes changes to the international system on Beijing's terms and according to ideas and principles it views as essential to its concept of a 'community with a shared future for mankind'". The notion of a community with a shared future for

[7] Ferguson Niall 2024. *China most likely to win war against US over Taiwan: Niall Ferguson*. Business Today. https://www.businesstoday.in/wef-2024/story/china-most-likely-to-win-war-against-us-over-taiwan-niall-ferguson-at-wef2024-413626-2024-01-16.

[8] Torode Greg, Doyle Gerry and Chen Laurie 2024. *U.S. and China hold first informal nuclear talks in five years*. Reuters. https://www.reuters.com/world/us-china-hold-first-informal-nuclear-talks-5-years-eyeing-taiwan-2024-06-21/.

[9] Sabur Rozina 2024. *Donald Trump signals he would not defend Taiwan from Chinese invasion*. Daily Telegraph. https://www.telegraph.co.uk/us/politics/2024/07/17/donald-trump-defend-taiwan-china/.

[10] Joint Chiefs of Staff (JCS) 1987. Publication 1. *Department of Defense Dictionary of Military and Associated Terms*. Washington DC, US Government Printing Office, p. 232.

mankind conflicts with a community dominated by U.S. interests and so China's pursuit of equality constitutes its "Coercive Approach" which at present uses "tactics short of armed conflict to pursue China's objectives. China calibrates its coercive activities to fall below the threshold of provoking armed conflict with the United States, its allies and partners, or others in the Indo-Pacific region... China also employs non-military tools coercively, including economic tools during periods of political tensions with countries that China accuses of harming its national interests".[11] The transition from peaceful to violent coercion occurs as there is no juridical mechanism in a capitalist system to know the relative power of a rival state without military proof. Military power reflects economic and social power, while subjective determination, the desire for war, the will to defeat your rival by killing them, reflects the irreconcilable nature of social conflict. Franz Mehring,[12] the German socialist and close comrade of Rosa Luxemburg, observed at the outset of the First World War that,

> War is an explosion (Entladung) of historical contradictions which have sharpened to the point where no other means are available for their solution since there are no judges in a class society who can decide by juridical or moral means those conflicts which will be solved by weapons in war. War is therefore a political phenomenon, and not a juridical, moral or even a penal one. War is not conducted in order to punish an enemy for supposed or real sins, but in order to break his resistance to the pursuit of one's own interests. War is not a thing in itself, possessing its own goal: it is an organic part of a policy to whose presuppositions it remains attached and to whose needs it has to adapt its own successes.[13]

Military coercion is a development of peaceful coercion. Global hegemony cannot be shared. As inevitable as economic conflict is in a capitalist system built on economic conflict, rivalry and competition, so are political conflicts and their violent expression in war.

[11] DoD 2020. *Annual Report to Congress: Military and Security Developments Involving the People's Republic of China 2020.* Washington DC, Office of the Secretary of Defense.

[12] Mandel Ernest 1986. *The Meaning of the Second World War*. London, Verso. (Elements of this section take inspiration from Mandel's study).

[13] Mehring Franz 1976 [1914]. Vom Wesen des Krieges. *Die Neue Zeit.* 33 (I), Gesammelte Werke, Band 8, Berlin. pp. 291–92.

The objectives of U.S. national policy are not an internationally shared community but a rules-based order determined by U.S. national self-interest. Self-interest arising from economic competition, driven by, and subject to, *the law of value*, the necessity of maximising profits by minimising costs. This *law of value* requires that capitalists maximise the productivity of labour, such that the difference between the sale price and the cost price, the profit, is as large as possible such that the price of goods tends to fall. The individual capitalist "endeavours to reduce the *individual value* of his commodity *below* its socially determined value in order to break through this law, or to *cheat* it to gain an advantage for himself"[14] so that paradoxically the law of value operates through the attempts of the capitalists to supersede it. Efficiency requires that the scale of production expands to the maximum, that capital is centralised and concentrated and that technological innovation is relentless and unlimited. Efficiency requires that the small-scale capitalist is wiped out, their costs are higher than are socially necessary. They go bust and their assets are transferred to more efficient rivals. Efficiency requires that the increase in the scale of production is matched by the expansion of the market too, *production for production's sake* becomes the guiding principle of production. The *law of value* is the defining principle of the capitalist mode of production and determines both the functioning of the national economy and the struggle of nations for absolute and comparative advantage, within the international capitalist system.

In 1910 Ruldoph Hilferding, an Austrian Marxist, defined a new imperialist period of capitalist development or *Finance Capital*.[15] Capitalist cartels combining banks and industry had overcome the former separation of industrial, banking and commercial capital to produce the "enormous, concentrated power of finance capital, in which all the partial forms of capital are brought together into a totality". Money capital with the circuit, money to more money (M-M'), dominated the circuit of production, profits appeared as interest from nowhere without equivalent, capital formed one integrated social organism.

[14] Marx, Karl. 1976 [1867]. *Capital a Critique of Political Economy Volume I*. London: Penguin.

[15] Hilferding Rudolph 1983 [1910]. *Finance Capital*. Translated by Tom Bottomore. London, RKP.

> Thus the specific character of capital is obliterated in finance capital. Capital now appears as a unitary power which exercises sovereign sway over the life process of society; a power which arises directly from ownership of the means of production, of natural resources, and of the whole accumulated labour of the past, and from command over living labour as a direct consequence of property relations. At the same time property, concentrated and centralised in the hands of a few giant capitalist groups, manifests itself in direct opposition to the mass of those who possess no capital.

The scale of this financial capital was so enormous as to determine state policy; colonies provided markets for goods, supplies of raw materials and access to practically unlimited quantities of oppressed labour. The division of the world between the imperialist powers followed inevitably, such that in the era of imperialism Mandel observed "even a quest for regional zones of influence presupposes a readiness to fight on a world scale".[16] During the Belle Époque the golden period of capitalist expansion that ended with the First World War, Britain and France, as the original dominant colonial imperialist powers were challenged by upstart rivals, Germany, Japan, Russia and the U.S. The constrictions of the world market imposed by the rules of the international colonial system meant there was little room for their expansion. The potential for the universal application of new technologies, the chemical industry, Bessemer steel process, aeroplanes, automobiles and lorries, was constricted by the limits on the world market.

In 1889 the British Empire adopted the Two-Power Standard, British Naval strength must exceed the next two strongest continental naval powers—Russia and France.[17] Britain was a naval power with a small professional army adapted to fighting unarmed colonial rebellions, sadistic but unsophisticated. The naval arms race up to the 1914 Great War was "closely rooted in the tenor of the time- Social Darwinism, imperialism, and militarism". Naval expansion followed the industrial revolution, the needs of empire and the balance of power. Alfred von Tirpitz Germany's Minister of Marine explained Germany's 1900 Fleet Law, which saw the huge expansion of its own navy, was necessary so as to "protect Germany's sea-trade and colonies, in the existing circumstances there is only one

[16] Mandel Ernest 1986. *The Meaning of the Second World War*. London, Verso.

[17] St. John Ronald B. 1971. *European Naval Expansion and Mahan, 1889–1906. Naval War College Review*, 23(7), pp. 74–83.

means: Germany must have a battle-fleet so strong that, even for the adversary with the greatest sea-power, a war against it would involve such dangers as to imperil his position in the world". Lenin's *Imperialism, the Highest Stage of Capitalism* explained how the growth of monopolies and export of finance capital, determined inter-imperialist rivalry. In 1916 the colonial possessions of the U.S., Japan and Germany were a fraction of those of Britain and France.[18]Lenin observed five key features that defined this highest stage of monopoly capitalism: the concentration of production and monopolies, the new roles of banks, financial capital and oligarchy, the export of capital and the division of the world between colonialists and colonies. Lenin considered that semi-colonial powers, formally independent but nonetheless dominated by imperialism, were transitional to colonial status. History proved that the transition was the other way around, from colonialism to semi-colonialism.

The contradiction between the industrial and financial power of these upstart rivals exploded in the First World War. Germany's fleet played little part in the conflict, although the mutiny of the Kiel naval base in November 1918 signalled its end. Britain's two power standard was downgraded to a one power standard, naval equality with, not Germany, but the U.S. In 1921 the British Vice Admiral Sir Osmond Brock, the deputy chief of the Royal Naval staff, reflected that Germany's defeat had not ended naval rivalry as "the ultimate cause of all our wars - even though these causes may apparently be covered by dynastic or territorial reasons, or balance of power - has been commercial rivalry. In the Dutch wars, the Spanish, the French, and the last War certainly, the ultimate cause was commercial rivalry, and if the United States perseveres in her aims, we shall inevitably, not necessarily go to war with her, but we shall come into conflict with her in various parts of the world".[19] Naval equality with the U.S. exposed Britain's diminished post-war status,[20] and set the pattern for the eventual dissolution of the Empire itself. U.S. assistance

[18] Lenin, Vladimir. 1974 [1917]. *Imperialism, the Highest Stage of Capitalism A Popular Outline*. Moscow, Progress Publishers.

[19] Bell Christopher M. 1997. Thinking the Unthinkable: British and American Naval Strategies for an Anglo-American War, 1918–1931. *The International History Review*, 19(4), pp. 789–808.

[20] Bell Christopher M. 2000. *The Royal Navy, Seapower and Strategy between the Wars*. London, Palgrave Macmillan.

in Britain's wars with Germany was paid for by the abolition of British colonial rivalry to it.

The failure of the First World War to resolve the first contradiction of the colonial system was exacerbated by, an additional, even more fundamental, second contradiction, the 1917 overthrow of capitalism in Soviet Russia. The crisis years of the 1920s and 1930s reflected the depth of these mutually reinforcing crises of the capitalist system itself. The Great Depression which followed the 1929 Wall Street Crash, accession of the Nazis in 1933, and the defeat of many socialist uprisings, meant that the Second World War was a logical and inevitable outcome of First World War. Mandel noted, "once again the stake was the international hegemony of one imperialist power, to be won and maintained by an active combination of military conquest or pressure and economic domination or plunder - the exact mix depending on the relative strength or weakness of the individual contestants".[21]

After the Spanish-American War of 1898 the U.S. largely "practiced imperialism without colonialism" with a system of "client" only "nominally independent" states.[22] In 1942 Cordell Hull, the US Secretary of State, observed that the "leadership towards a new system of international relationships in trade and other economic affairs will devolve largely upon the United States because of our great economic strength. We should assume this leadership, and the responsibility that goes with it, primarily for reasons of pure national self-interest". General Patton, who, with the Allied Commander in Chief General Eisenhower, planned the D-Day landings, was rebuked when he declared 25 April 1944 that it was "the destiny of the United States and Britain to rule the world". There can be no shared hegemony. The U.S. would rule a nominally at least post-imperial world without formal colonies, under the guise of an international alliance. Such was the dominance of U.S. capitalism that only the world was an adequate colony for it, although its constitutional predisposition towards the respect of private property meant that Britain retained its foreign property. Much as during the post-civil war Reconstruction, slave owners were allowed to keep their plantations, the fruit of slavery, ensuring their racist legacy poisoned the U.S. body politic, so Perfidious

[21] Mandel Ernest 1986. *The Meaning of the Second World War*. London, Verso.

[22] Duara, Prasenjit. 2019. The Chinese World Order in Historical Perspective: The Imperialism of Nation-states or Soft Power. *China and the World: Ancient and Modern Silk Road*, 2(4), pp. 1–33.

Albion was allowed to keep the fruits of the colonial system, if not the colonies from which they had been extracted. Britain would play the role of the U.S.' vicious poodle in world affairs and provide the U.S. with a toolkit for violent post-colonial domination.[23]

The Second World War resolved the first contradiction of the imperial system, at least temporarily, U.S. hegemony at the war's end dismantled the colonial system. The 1950s to 1960s Long Boom, the upward expansive wave that resulted from this post-war settlement continued until the early 1970s. The second unresolved contradiction was, if anything, even more fundamental. The end of the Second World War saw the USSR expand into Central and Eastern Europe (CEE) shortly after to be joined by Mao's China and North Korea, and later Cuba and Vietnam. American power was at its apogee after World War II, with the establishment of the Bretton Woods framework currency framework in 1944, nonetheless, the General Agreement on Tariffs and Trade (GATT) recognised the limitations this imposed. Unlike the World Trade Organisation (WTO) founded in 1995, GATT could not inspect the internal functioning of a domestic economy for competitive purposes. The now U.S. dominated world market was ruled through a set of international institutions that formed the new rules-based order, the United Nations, World Bank, International Monetary Fund alongside an enlarged bloc of centrally planned economies. As part of its anti-Communist policy the U.S. provided Japan, South Korea, Israel and West Germany with Most Favoured Nation status which provided privileged access to the world market and oversaw and sponsored their industrial recovery.

U.S. dominance amongst capitalist powers was eroded during the long post-war boom by the rise of West Germany and Japan, reflected in the collapse of Bretton Woods currency peg in 1971, the oil shocks of the early 1970s and its 1975 defeat in Vietnam. 1979 revolutions in Nicaragua and Iran and a deep recession in 1981 and 1983 meant a period of crisis enveloped U.S. leadership of the world and capitalist economy, only to be resolved by the fall of the Berlin Wall in 1989 followed shortly by the collapse of the USSR in 1991. The re-establishment of U.S. as a sole hegemonic world power, brought in a new institutional framework signalled by the founding of the World Trade Organisation (WTO) in 1995. The terms of China's accession in 2001 designed to open China to

[23] Elkins Caroline 2022. *Legacy of Violence: A History of the British Empire*. London, Bodley Head.

U.S. competition, with the expectation that China would collapse faced with the power of U.S. industry.[24] The extension of Most Favoured Nation status to the whole world through the systematic dismantling of tariffs, dissolved Germany and Japan's industrial challenge. The truly global market defined the new period of globalisation, it had solved the outstanding contradictions of the capitalist system and was as Francis Fukuyama observed the End of History. At least until it wasn't.

Now Western financiers took the logical development of money capital to its ultimate limit. The specific character of capital was obliterated, as Factoryless Goods Producers (FGPs) Western capitalists divested themselves of their capitalist base, to the newly capitalist economies of Central and Eastern Europe and China. In the search for efficiency Western capitalists outsourced capitalist production, profits arose from nowhere without equivalent, they were the natural product of private property, ownership itself created wealth, do nothing, sit back and wait for the cash to roll in. The new offshored firms took advantage of the cheap low waged workforce inherited from the centrally planned economies; relatively healthy, with good education and skills, and amenable to exploitation, defeated by the transition to the market or the process of urbanisation, the move from the countryside into factory work as migrants or immigrants, these workforces were concentrated and centralised in enormous plants, with integrated production systems forming a dense system of mutually reliant firms, and in China, with new, modern more, effective and efficient, infrastructure.

Western financial exploitation rested on three pillars: the ownership and control of finance, key technologies and market access. While the West retained their control their more productive and efficient suppliers had little option but to suck up the lower profit rates the international rules-based order imposed.[25] Sellers of key inputs like Intel, AMD, Samsung, Apple, etc., controlled the key technologies necessary to produce the output and so received a disproportionately large share of value added at the beginning of the supply chain and at the end through the control of final sales. The small manufacturers who assembled the inputs received

[24] Jefferies, William, 2021. China's Accession to the WTO and the Collapse That Never Was. *Review of Radical Political Economics*, 53(2), pp. 300–319.

[25] Ye Ming, Bo Meng and Shang-jin Wei. 2020. Measuring Smile Curves in Global Value Chains. *Oxford Bulletin of Economics and Statistics,* 82(5), pp. 988–1016.

the cost of production and a disproportionately low profit rate.[26] This unequal exchange could only be remedied through state action. All money is equal in the market and so is equally entitled to an aliquot share of profits. The West may have owned and controlled these export producing firms or their subsidiaries, but they had failed to control the states, and particularly the Chinese state, within which they were situated. They were not China's colonial masters, or even its semi-colonial ones. Quite the opposite. China vividly remembered the oppression of the British and Japanese empires. Western Foreign Direct Investment (FDI) was limited to the export producing Southern coastal Chinese Special Economic Zones (SEZ).

Once the pro-market reforms there were generalised across China by the late 1990s, China's domestic capitalists began catch-up. China never ceded control of its financial institutions. Foreign lending within China was a mere fragment of total domestic investment which remained in the hands of the state. As the Chinese economy grew the state concentrated national savings and invested them into infrastructure, research and development and Chinese national champions that were to, and now do, form the alternatives to Western multinationals. Expressed in initiatives like Made in China 2025,[27] these are the opposite of outsourced FGPs but vertically and horizontally integrated conglomerates that directly own all aspects of the production process. The savings in costs, the profits of the outsourced suppliers used by the Western FGPs, and the unproductive legal paraphernalia necessary to protect property rights in this outsourced system, provide China with an insurmountable competitive advantage. The output of their factories is cheaper and better than their Western counterparts.

The laws which define capitalist production are predicated on the equality implicit in the trade of equivalents, and are modified by inequalities between nations in capital compositions, wage levels, rates of absolute and relative surplus value extraction, monopoly pricing and rents. Absolute rent is a minimum yielded by the owner of scarce land, a benefit from the existence of capitalist property itself, relative rents occur when a surplus above the price of production is appropriated by a landlord,

[26] Cope Zac. 2019. The Wealth of (Some) Nations Imperialism and the Mechanics of Value Transfer. London: Pluto.

[27] US CoC. 2017. *Made in China 2025: Global Ambitions Built on Local Protections*. Washington, United States Chamber of Commerce (US CoC).

monopolist or financial aristocrat. All commodity exchange is a transfer of property so any objective factor, barrier or advantage, that prevents the equalisation of profit rates could be the source of excess profits or rents. Typically and most classically this is a natural barrier, like land that cannot be easily reproduced, or a natural advantage, like a source of water power; but it may also be a social barrier, like cultural norms of living standards, or a social advantage, like improved infrastructure; or non-reproducible technological barrier like control of microchip design or an advance like free renewable electricity; or a military barrier, like pay us or we will bomb your hospitals and kill your children or a military advantage like ally with us to share in the pillage the earth.

These, not strictly, economic mechanisms explain how the profits of one nation may increase at the expense of the other, they modify but do not abolish the law of value, that capitalists will seek to reduce their costs below the socially necessary average to maximise profit rates The increase in China's capital intensity will enable it to offset this fall through increasing the proportion of monopoly profits it captures, as its more efficient production displaces that of its foreign competitors, and as it reduces its reliance on Western property related business services. Trade restrictions imposed by Western powers to defend their sources of financial profits and as preparation for rearmament in the run up to war, increase the proportion of constant capital advanced to living labour, as research and development and other fixed costs will be defrayed across a smaller amount of output, while increased tariffs will slow the turnover of capital and reduce the scale of the market, in their turn impacting profit rates. The combination of these factors will eventually cause the rate of profit to fall. The exhaustion of China's labour reserves will cause labour costs to rise and the increase in the technical and organic composition of capital through investment in productivity raising capital like robots, will increase the proportion of constant capital advanced to living labour, the ultimate source of all profit, exacerbated by the decline of Western financial services and de-dollarisation.

Western social scientists deny the science of society or that the laws that determine social life exist or can be understood. John Roberts, a philosophy professor, joked that the "regularity" of the misnamed law of supply and demand "holds, unless for some reason it does not, and we cannot specify all of the possible conditions under which it will not".[28] This is hardly original, in 1924, Frank Fetter, a Princeton economist, wrote the "most noteworthy 'economic laws'" including "supply and demand" are "hardly more than general descriptive phrases",[29] but the vehemence of the opposition of social scientists to the notion of a social science is a paradoxical social phenomenon of contemporary academe. Social laws are no mere regularities, their obedience is a condition of life. Aristotle explained several millennia ago that commodity exchange, the buying and selling of useful things had a universal "twofold aspect – *use-value and exchange-value*".[30] Every purchase of a useful object is an exchange of property without exception. A law so powerful and universal, that philosophy professors obey it every time they go shopping. The more ubiquitous the social law the less the philosophers of social law acknowledge its existence.

The law of value asserts itself through the attempts of individual firms to supersede it. The most efficient firm, the firm with the cheapest goods, will triumph in market competition. What remains of the conditions for Western domination rests, to the extent that it does at all, on the ownership of certain technologies and access to markets. The Chinese domestic market is not large enough to satisfy the international ambitions of Chinese conglomerates but it can provide a testing ground for technological development to ready them for international domination. Whether it be in Huawei's HarmonyOS, the domestic airliner Comac C919, BYD electric cars or CATL batteries.

In August 1914 Leon Trotsky described the objective forces that lead to the first Great War. Capitalism during its period of imperial expansion from roughly 1890 to 1914, had connected the whole world into one economic workshop. This period included the so-called Scramble for Africa, or colonisation fever dominated by the established imperial powers UK and France. The war signalled the breakdown of the national basis of that system. The revolt of the productive relations against the confines of national states. The governments of the world sought to resolve these problems, not through cooperation and peaceful mutual development,

[28] Roberts J.T. 2004. There are no laws of the social sciences. *Contemporary debates in philosophy of science*. Edited by Christopher Hitchcock pp. 151–167. Malden, Blackwell.

[29] Fetter Frank A. 1924. The Economic Law of Market Areas. The Quarterly Journal of Economics, 38(3), pp. 520–529.

[30] Marx Karl 1977. *A Contribution to the Critique of Political Economy*, Moscow, Progress Publishers.

but imperialism "through the exploitation of the world's economic system by the capitalist class of the victorious country". The question to be answered by the World War One was "which country is by this War to be transformed from a Great Power into the World Power".[31] Today the U.S. is the world power, and it too seeks to resolve the problems of the present national system, not through cooperation but national self-interest. The question posed by the emerging conflict is, will it remain so?

The fall in profit rates will be felt outside China first of all and as the size of the cake decreases, competition between multinational corporations and the nations will increase, this will in turn exacerbate trade tensions, tariffs and de-dollarisation. A vicious circle will ensue, as economic tensions mount, this will in turn result in increased political conflict and ultimately a violent political conflict or war, the continuation of politics by other violent means. It is the discontinuity between China's actual power and its place in the world, inherited from the U.S.'s prior monopolar dominance after the collapse of the USSR, which is a source of tension not the overaccumulation of capital. The West retains only a narrow lead in certain technological areas, particularly the most cutting-edge chips designs, hence its current focus on reviving these sectors. It wants to restrict access to its domestic market through tariffs. But production for production's sake, not consumption, is the motto of capitalist accumulation, who can produce the cheapest will triumph in market competition, not who can buy the most. The ability to buy, income, depends on the ability to sell, revenue. Once again transformative technologies, this time based on carbon-free energy, batteries and electrical vehicles, and Artificial Intelligence find their application hindered by the constraints of the existing international rules-based order. External barriers may halt, hinder or delay the transition from the old order to the new one but they cannot stop it. The inevitable economic rivalry between China and the West arises from market competition. Political rivalry expresses those interests, naturally and inevitably, as does military conflict, its violent enactment. The West wants to turn back the clock of history, but the clock of history cannot be turned back.

[31] Trotsky Leon 1996 [1914]. *The War and the International* (The Bolsheviks and World Peace).
https://www.marxists.org/archive/trotsky/1914/war/index.htm.

For most of history the masses are passive bystanders that are shaped by but do not shape events. History is something done to them by great leaders. Globalisation has been such a period. The collapse of the centrally planned economies removed the subjective alternative to capitalism, while the boom that followed removed the objective alternative. It consolidated the defeat by enriching whole layers of the middle class and providing the neo-liberal masters of society with the resources to buy social peace for an entire historical period. Regular financial crises occurred, and of astonishing ferocity and depth, most notably the 2008 Great Crash, but not beyond the ability of the system to cope. These were crises for capitalism, but not of it. They did not threaten the existence of these systems as a whole, they were resolved at least to the extent necessary to ensure extended reproduction. The end of the long wave of globalisation is different. The multiple crises for capitalism, trade wars and wars, climate change, migration, environmental degradation, may be transformed into a crisis of capitalism. The only real crisis for capitalism, a social threat to the continuation of the system itself. Leon Trotsky, the leader of the Russian revolution and founder of the Red Army, observed in his *History of the Russian Revolution* that,

> "in ordinary times the state, be it monarchical or democratic, elevates itself above the nation, and history is made by specialists in that line of business - kings, ministers, bureaucrats, parliamentarians, journalists" but when the old order becomes unendurable the masses "break over the barriers excluding them from the political arena, sweep aside their traditional representatives" so that "the history of a revolution is for us first of all a history of the forcible entrance of the masses into the realm of rulership over their own destiny".[32]

[32] Trotsky Leon 1930. *The History of the Russian Revolution Volume one*. Translated by Marx Eastman. https://www.marxists.org/archive/trotsky/works/download/hrr-vol1.pdf.

Index

W. Jefferies, *War and the World Economy*, Palgrave Insights into Apocalypse Economics, https://doi.org/10.1007/978-3-031-85236-7

The manufacturer's authorised representative in the EU is Springer Nature Customer Service Centre GmbH, Europaplatz 3, 69115 Heidelberg, Germany. If you have any concerns regarding our products, please contact ProductSafety@springernature.com

Printed and bound by CPI Group (UK) Ltd, Croydon, CR0 4YY
01/10/2026
02225953-0002